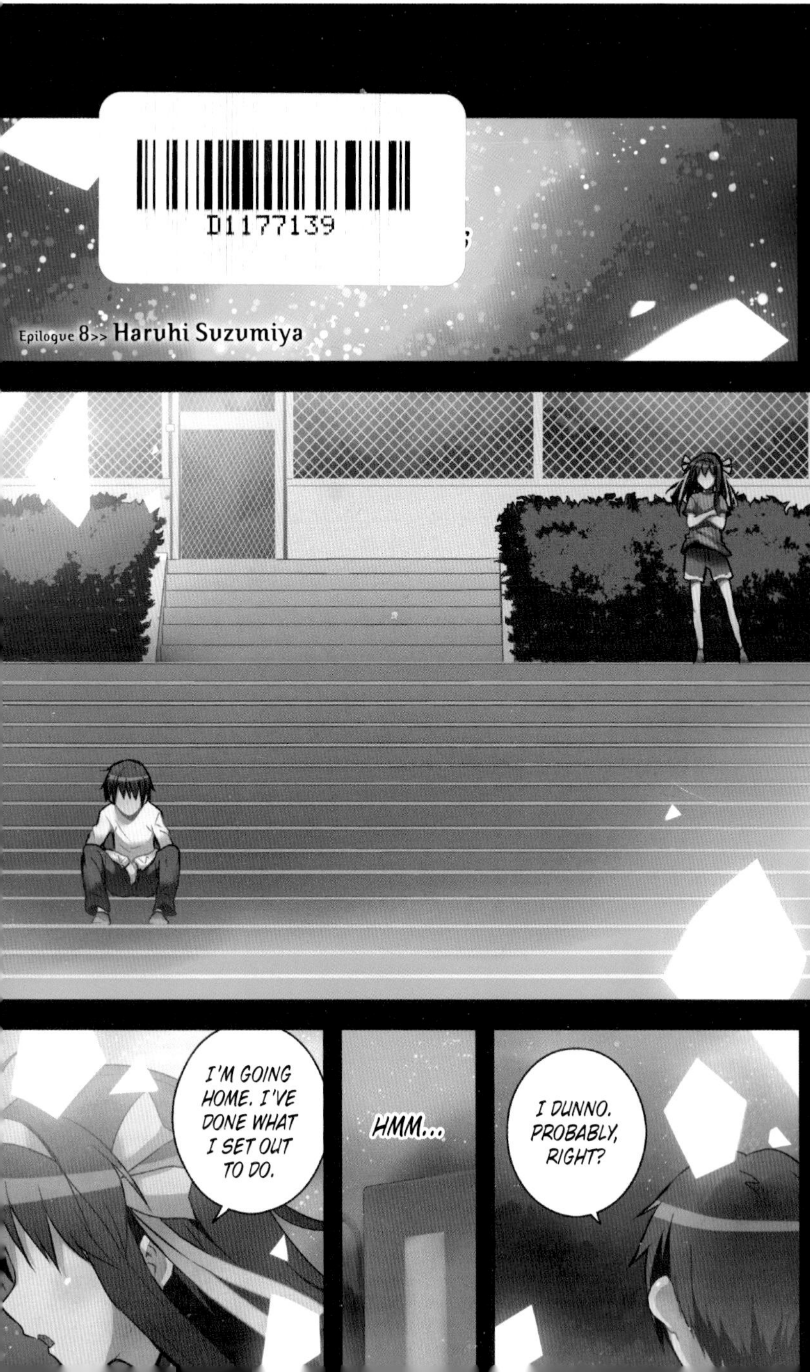
Epilogue 8>> Haruhi Suzumiya
I DUNNO. PROBABLY, RIGHT?
HMM...
I'M GOING HOME. I'VE DONE WHAT I SET OUT TO DO.

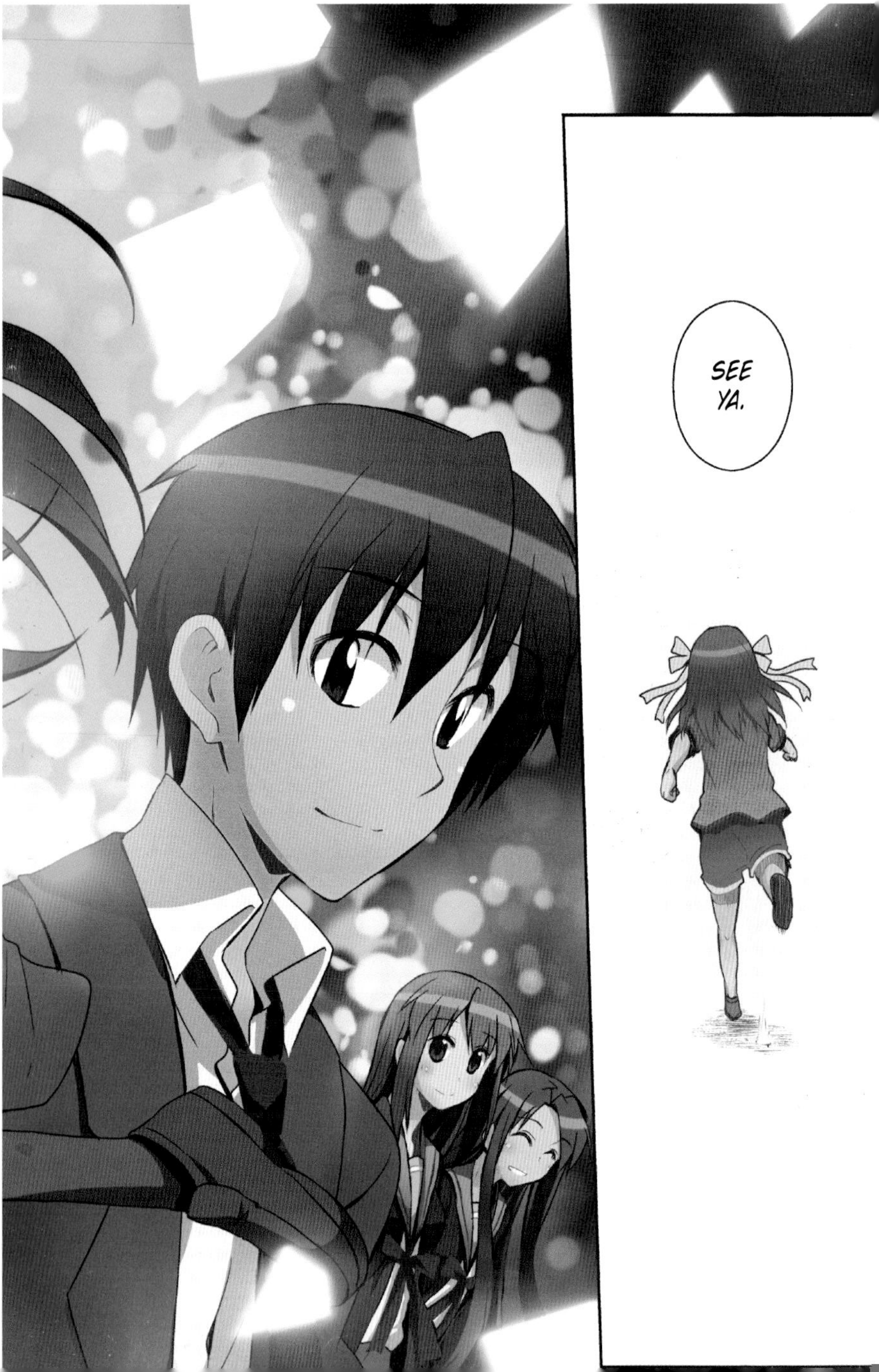
SEE YA.

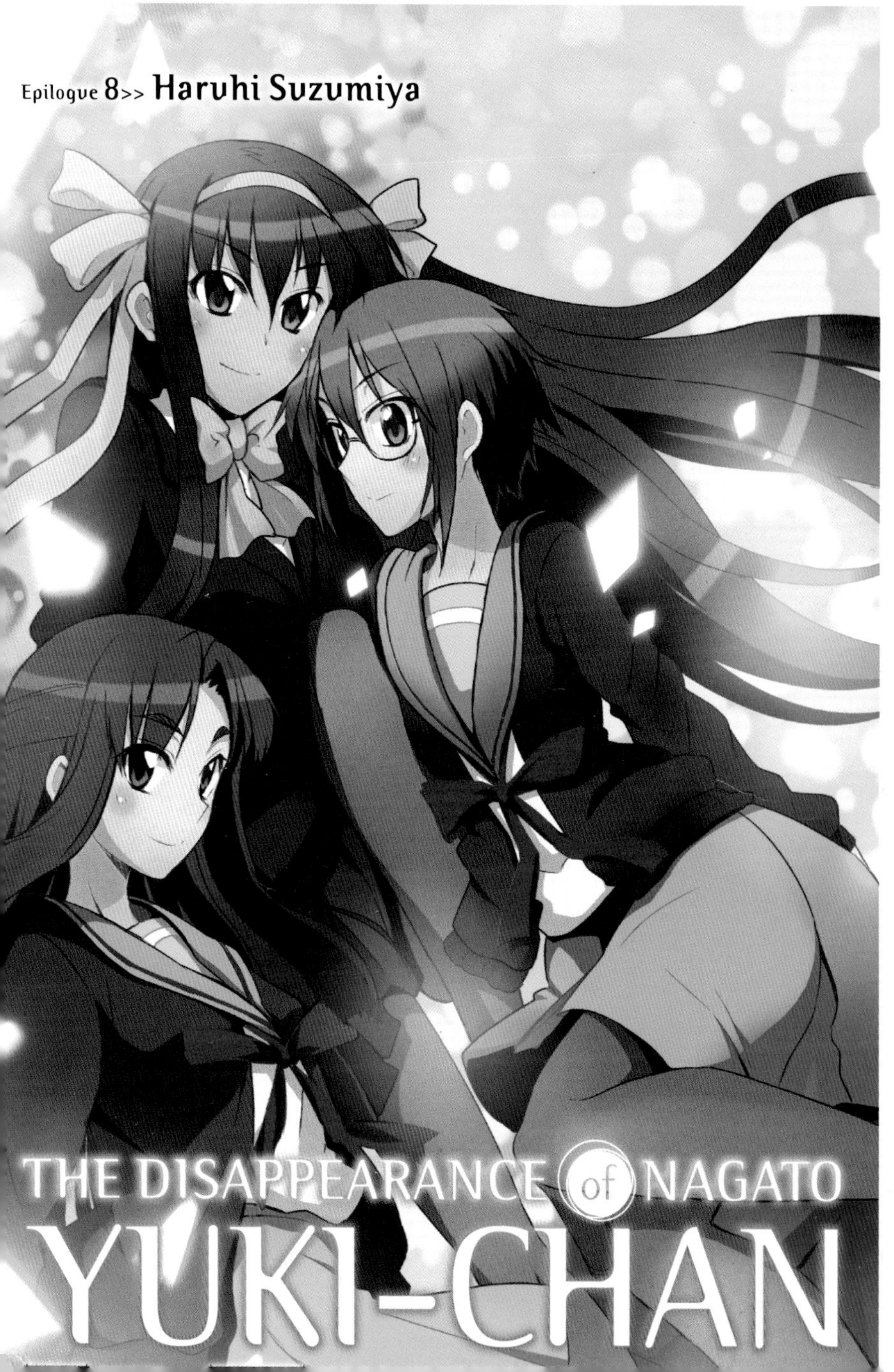
Epilogue 8>> Haruhi Suzumiya
THE DISAPPEARANCE of NAGATO
YUKI-CHAN

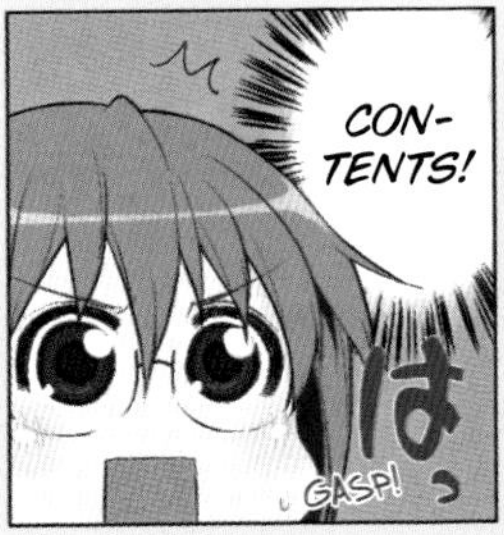
CON-
TENTS!
はっ
GASP!

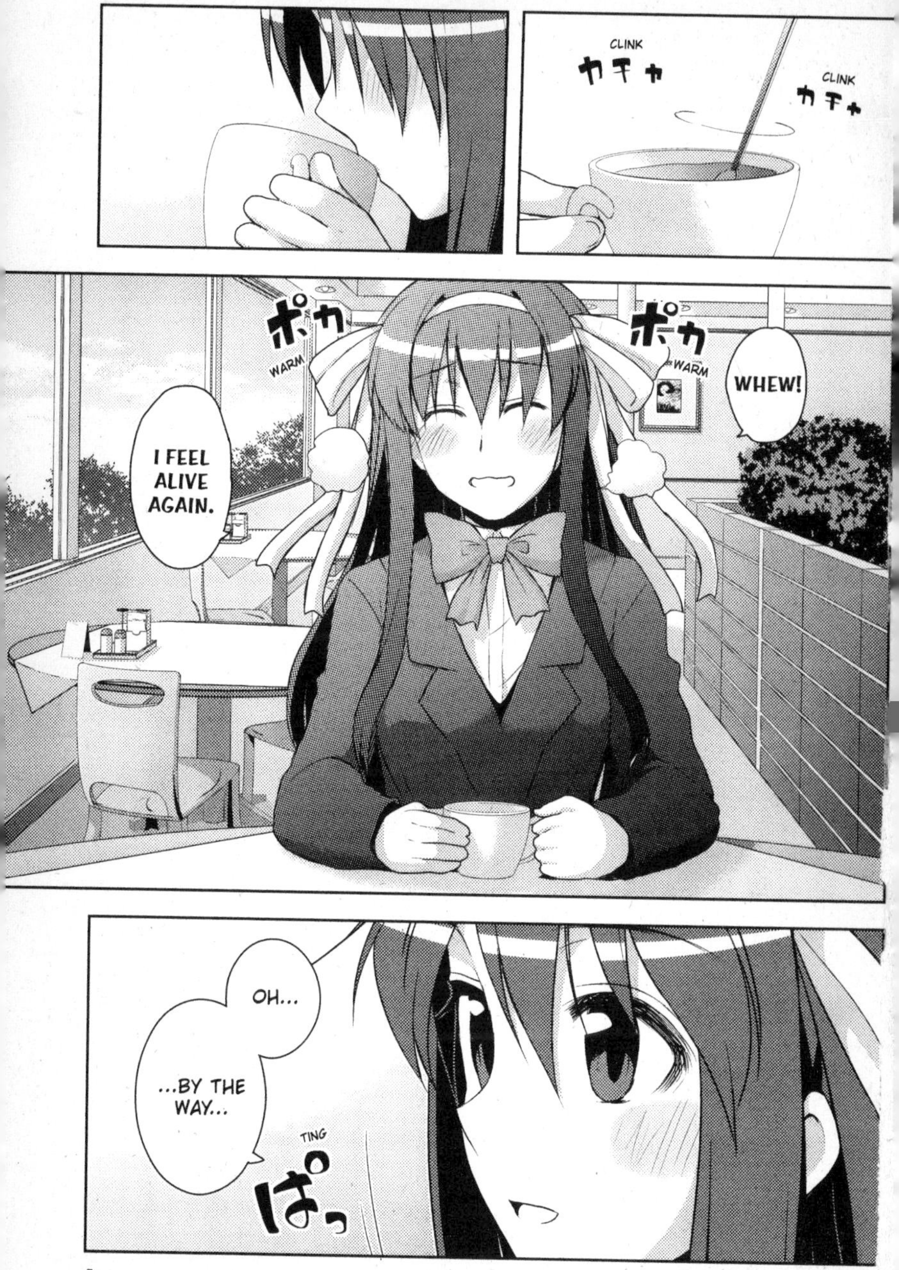
CLINK
カチャ
CLINK
カチャ
ポカ
WARM
WHEW!
ポカ
WARM
I FEEL ALIVE AGAIN.
OH...
...BY THE WAY...
TING
ぱっ

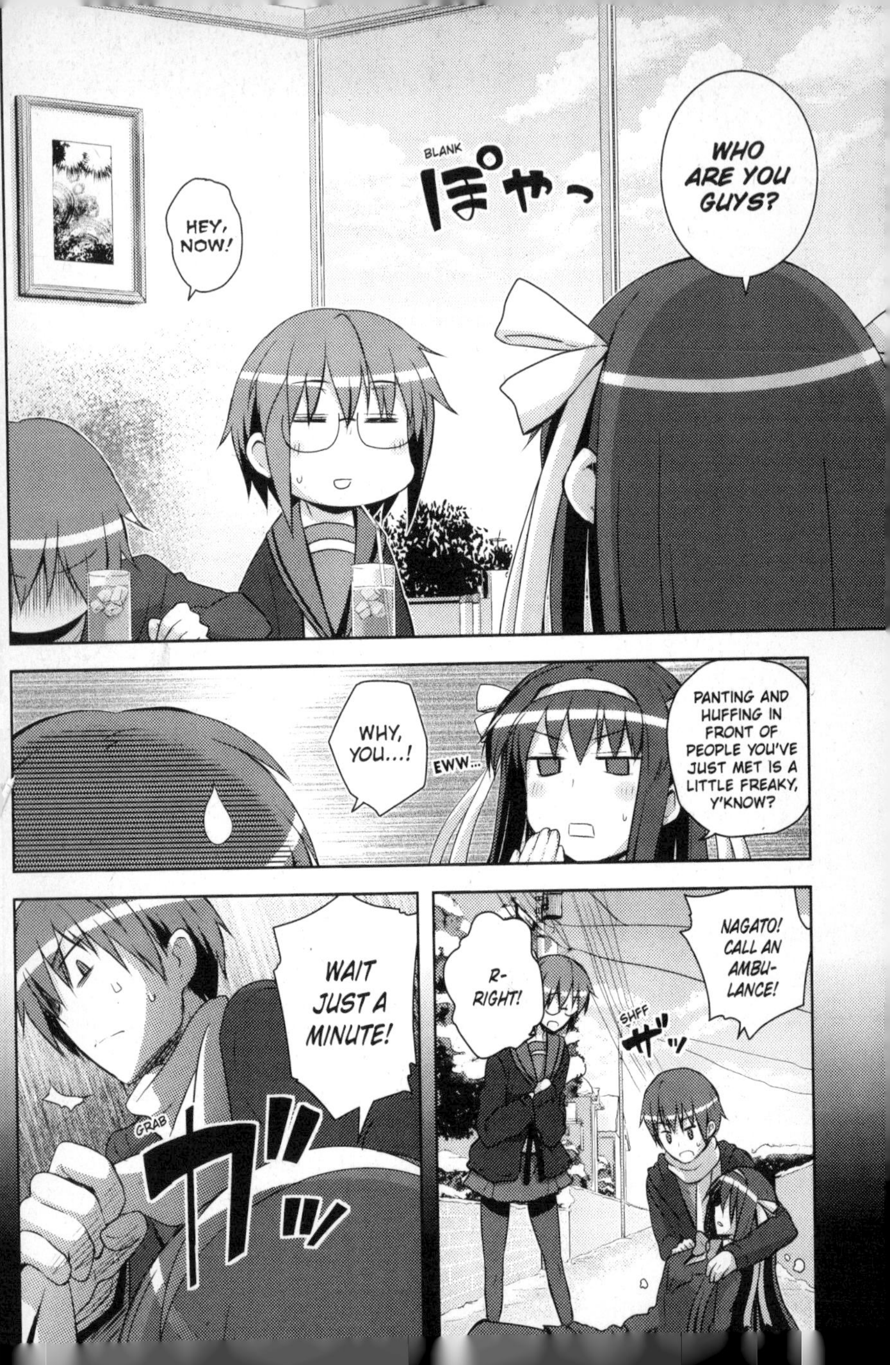
WHO ARE YOU GUYS?
BLANK
ぽやっ
HEY, NOW!
PANTING AND HUFFING IN FRONT OF PEOPLE YOU'VE JUST MET IS A LITTLE FREAKY, Y'KNOW?
EWW...
WHY, YOU...!
NAGATO! CALL AN AMBU-LANCE!
SHFF
ザッ
R-RIGHT!
WAIT JUST A MINUTE!
GRAB
ガッ

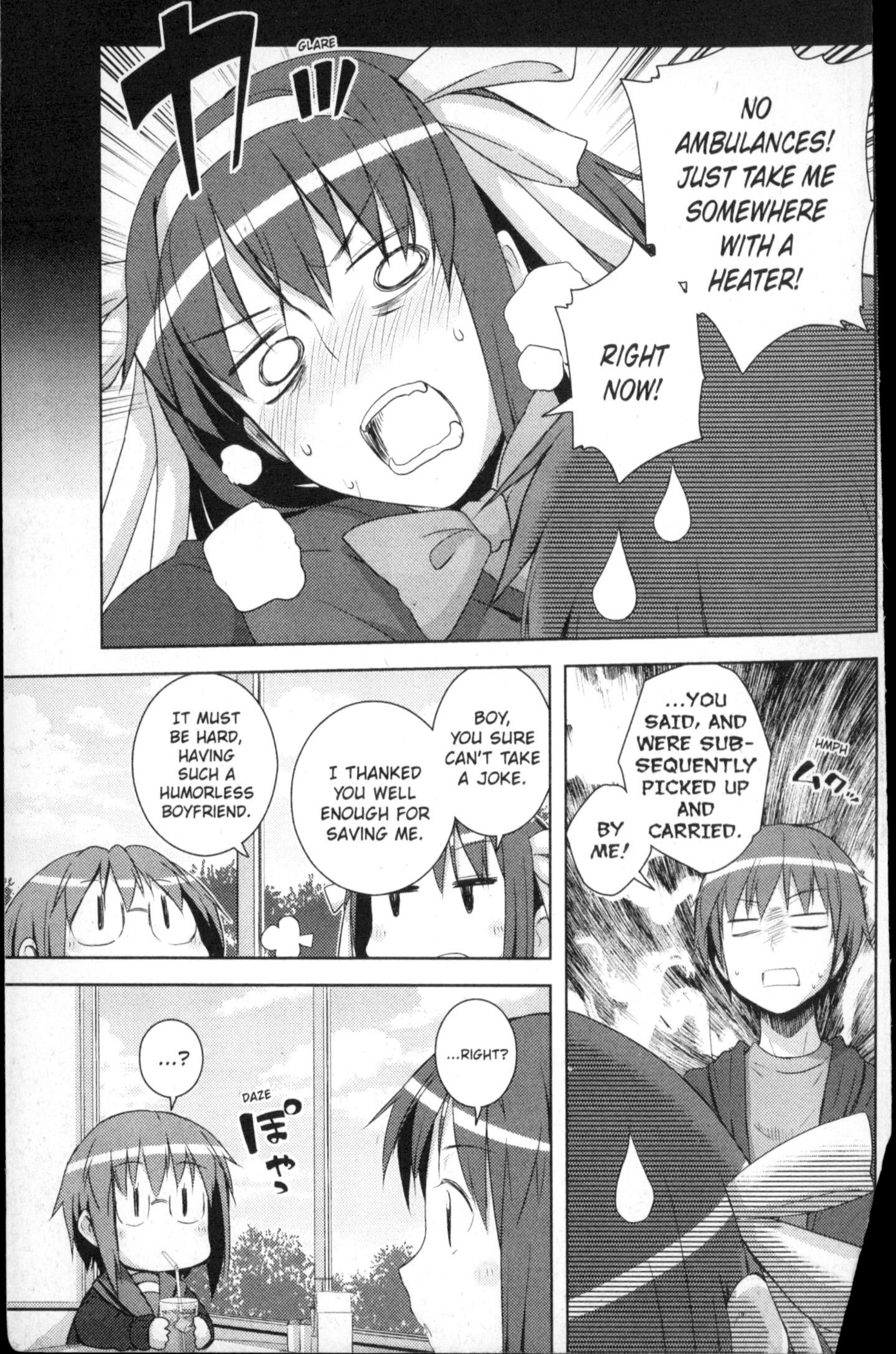
GLARE
NO AMBULANCES! JUST TAKE ME SOMEWHERE WITH A HEATER!
RIGHT NOW!
...YOU SAID, AND WERE SUB-SEQUENTLY PICKED UP AND CARRIED.
BY ME!
HMPH
ムク
BOY, YOU SURE CAN'T TAKE A JOKE.
I THANKED YOU WELL ENOUGH FOR SAVING ME.
IT MUST BE HARD, HAVING SUCH A HUMORLESS BOYFRIEND.
...RIGHT?
DAZE
ぽやっ
...?

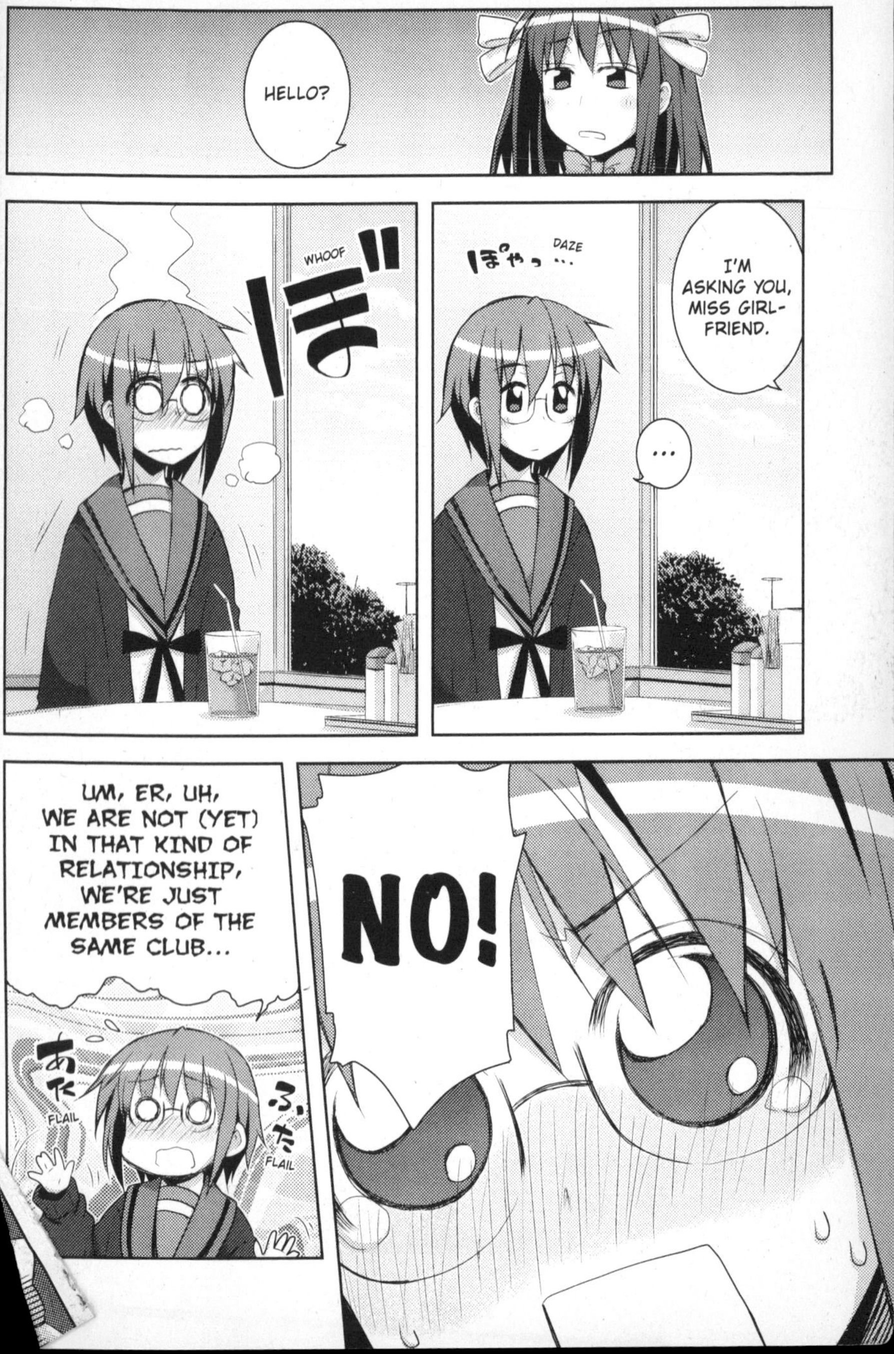
HELLO?
I'M ASKING YOU, MISS GIRL-FRIEND.
ぽやっ…
DAZE
...
ぼ
WHOOF
NO!
UM, ER, UH, WE ARE NOT (YET) IN THAT KIND OF RELATIONSHIP, WE'RE JUST MEMBERS OF THE SAME CLUB...
あた
FLAIL
ふた
FLAIL

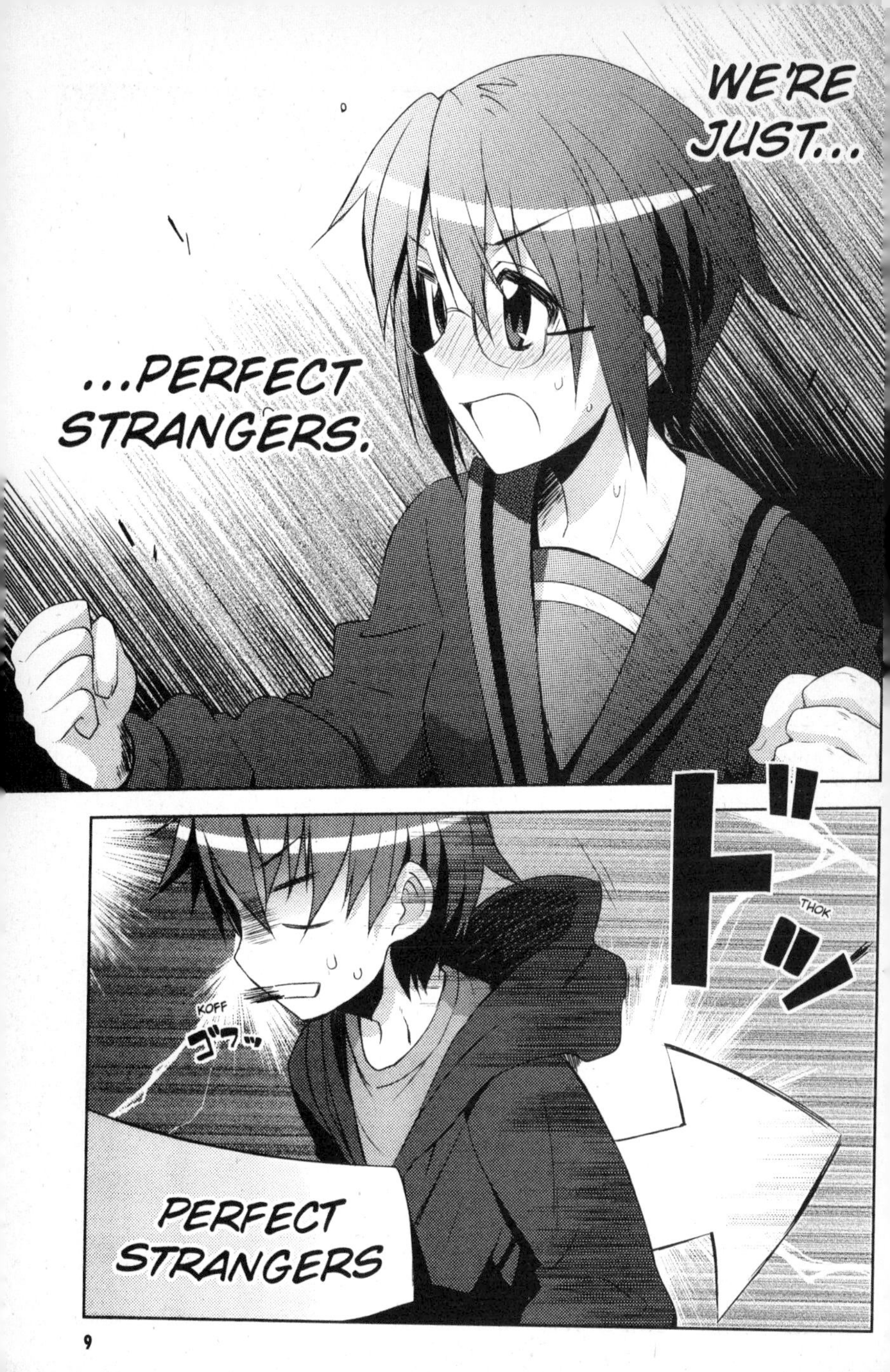

WE'RE JUST...
...PERFECT STRANGERS.
THOK
ドッ
KOFF
ゴフッ
PERFECT STRANGERS

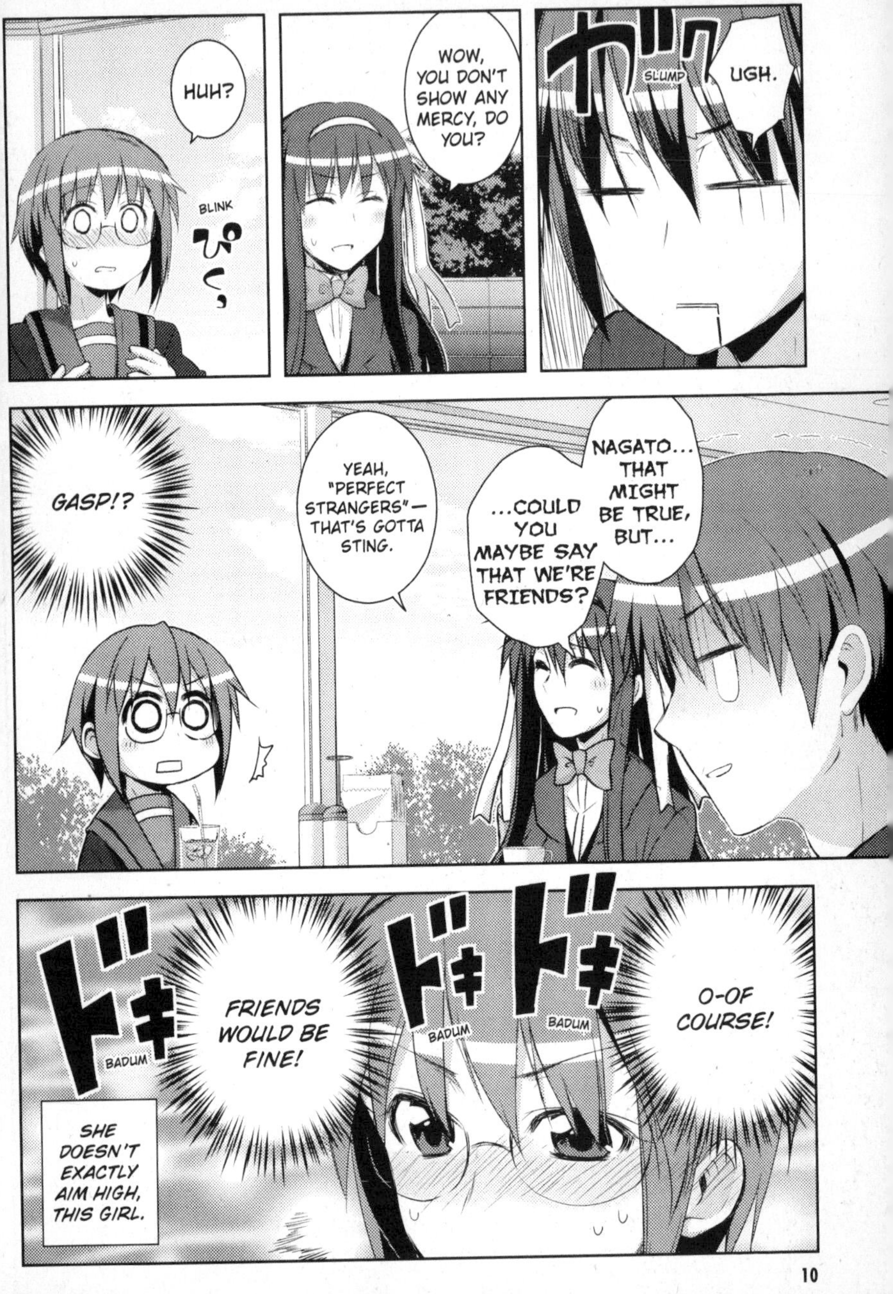
SLUMP
UGH.
WOW, YOU DON'T SHOW ANY MERCY, DO YOU?
HUH?
BLINK
ぴく
NAGATO... THAT MIGHT BE TRUE, BUT...
...COULD YOU MAYBE SAY THAT WE'RE FRIENDS?
YEAH, "PERFECT STRANGERS"—THAT'S GOTTA STING.
GASP!?
O-OF COURSE!
ドキ
BADUM
ドキ
BADUM
FRIENDS WOULD BE FINE!
ドキ
BADUM
SHE DOESN'T EXACTLY AIM HIGH, THIS GIRL.

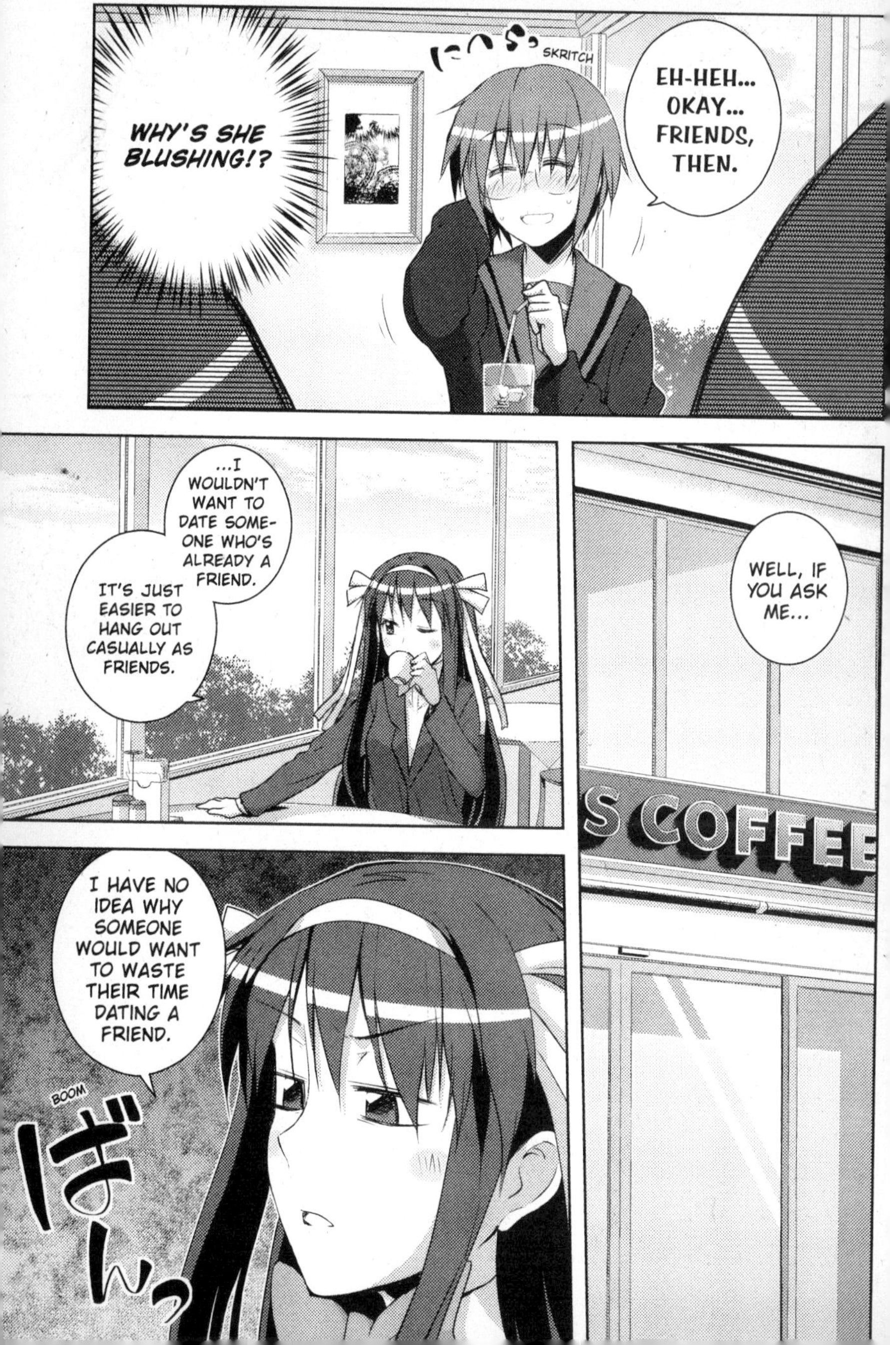
EH-HEH... OKAY... FRIENDS, THEN.
にへらっ
SKRITCH
WHY'S SHE BLUSHING!?
WELL, IF YOU ASK ME...
...I WOULDN'T WANT TO DATE SOME-ONE WHO'S ALREADY A FRIEND.
IT'S JUST EASIER TO HANG OUT CASUALLY AS FRIENDS.
S COFFEE
I HAVE NO IDEA WHY SOMEONE WOULD WANT TO WASTE THEIR TIME DATING A FRIEND.
BOOM
ばんっ

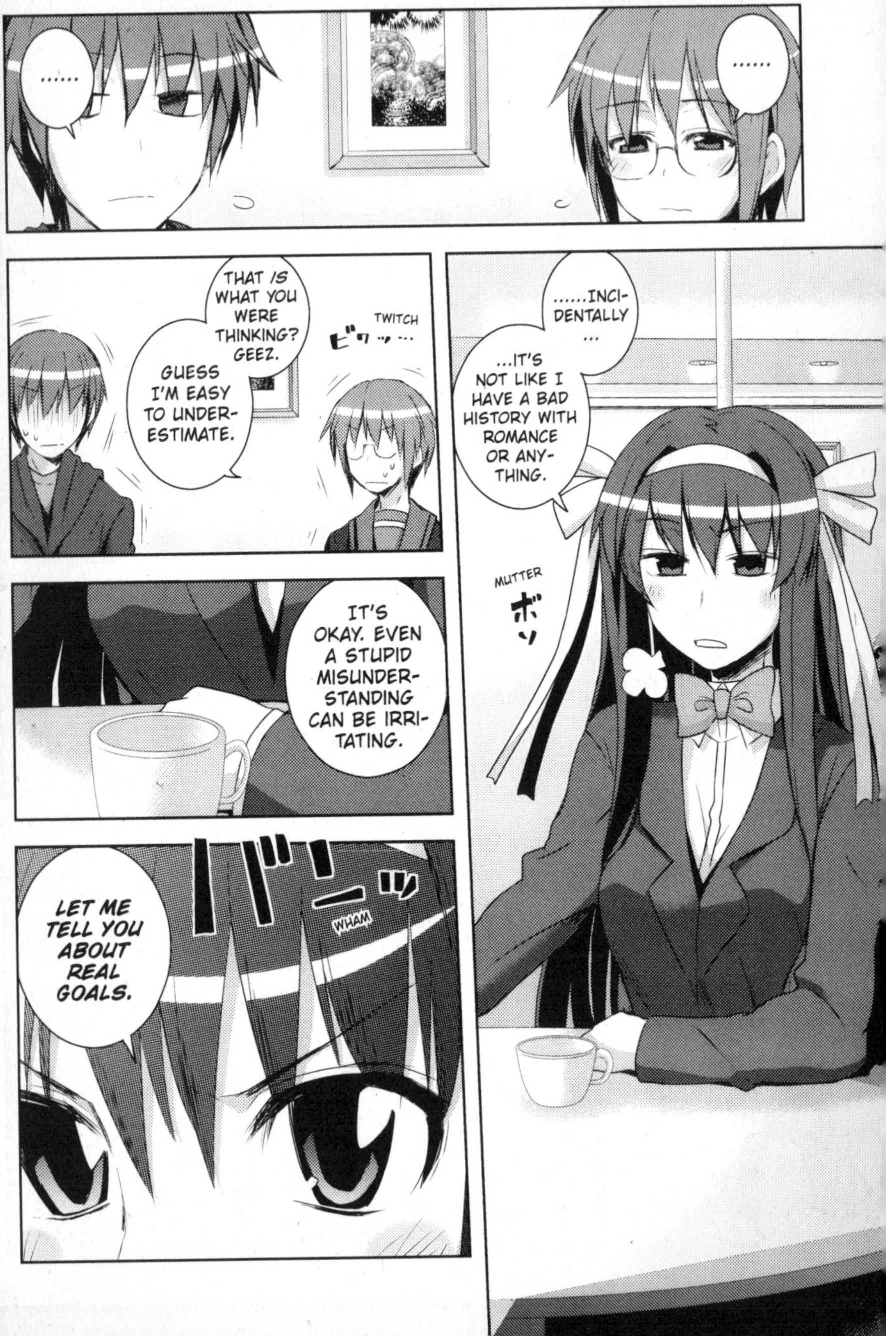
......
......
......INCI-DENTALLY...
...IT'S NOT LIKE I HAVE A BAD HISTORY WITH ROMANCE OR ANYTHING.
MUTTER
ボソ
TWITCH
ビクッ…
THAT IS WHAT YOU WERE THINKING? GEEZ.
GUESS I'M EASY TO UNDER-ESTIMATE.
IT'S OKAY. EVEN A STUPID MISUNDER-STANDING CAN BE IRRI-TATING.
WHAM
LET ME TELL YOU ABOUT REAL GOALS.

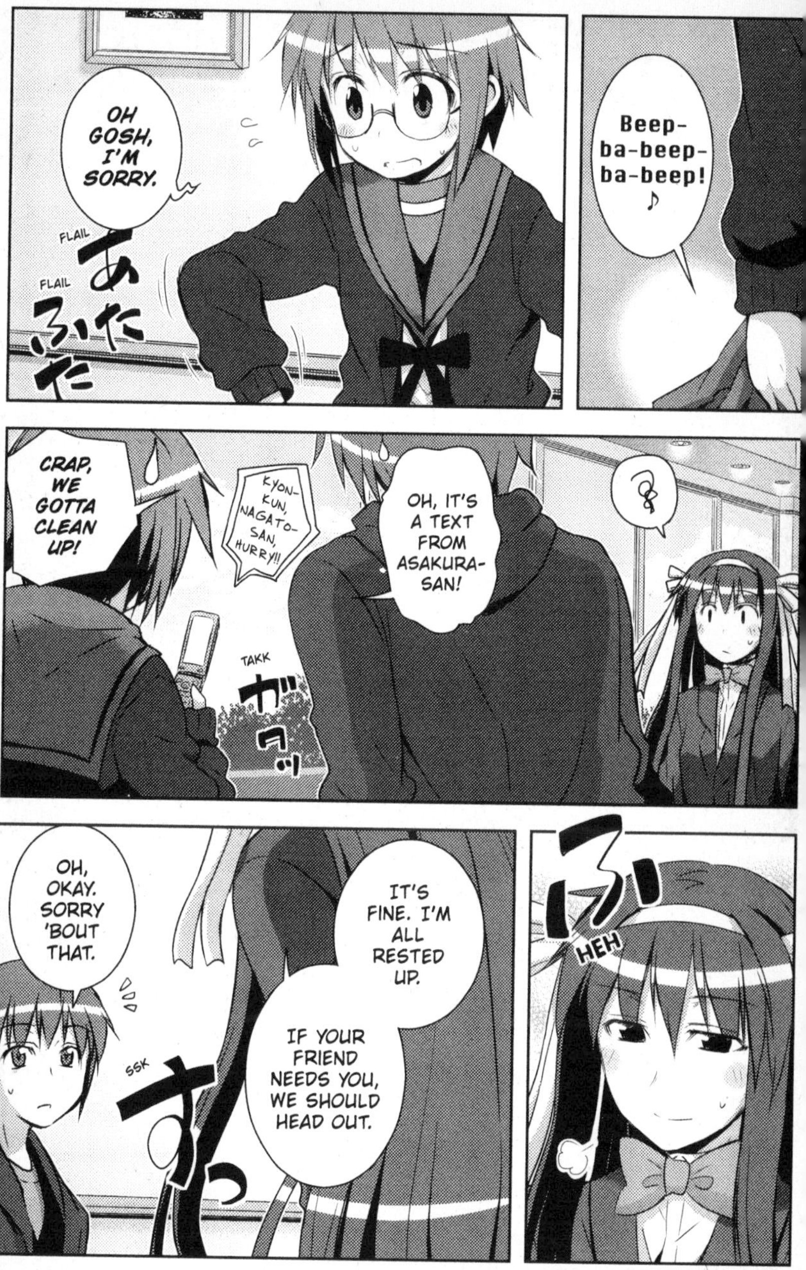
Beep-ba-beep-ba-beep! ♪
OH GOSH, I'M SORRY.
FLAIL
FLAIL
OH, IT'S A TEXT FROM ASAKURA-SAN!
KYON-KUN, NAGATO-SAN, HURRY!!
CRAP, WE GOTTA CLEAN UP!
TAKK
HEH
IT'S FINE. I'M ALL RESTED UP.
IF YOUR FRIEND NEEDS YOU, WE SHOULD HEAD OUT.
OH, OKAY. SORRY 'BOUT THAT.
SSK

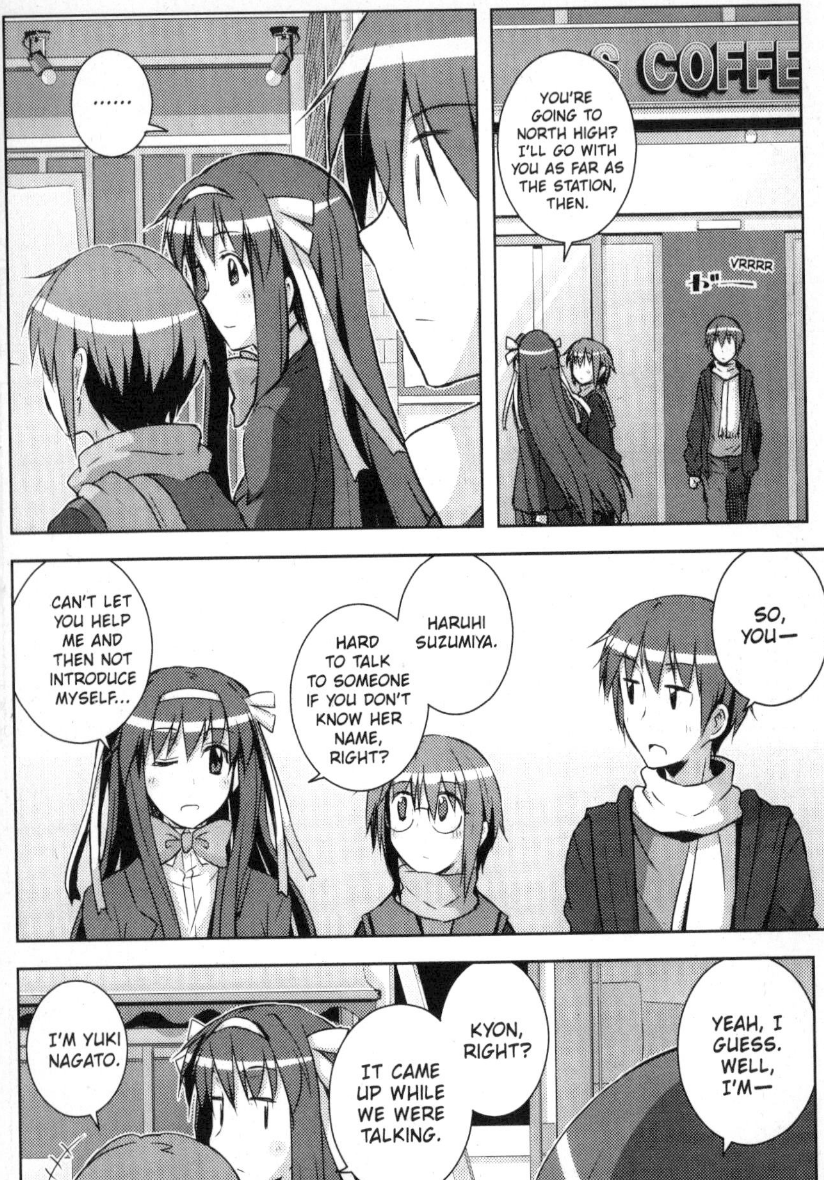
S COFFE
YOU'RE GOING TO NORTH HIGH? I'LL GO WITH YOU AS FAR AS THE STATION, THEN.
VRRRR
......
SO, YOU—
HARUHI SUZUMIYA.
HARD TO TALK TO SOMEONE IF YOU DON'T KNOW HER NAME, RIGHT?
CAN'T LET YOU HELP ME AND THEN NOT INTRODUCE MYSELF...
YEAH, I GUESS. WELL, I'M—
KYON, RIGHT?
IT CAME UP WHILE WE WERE TALKING.
I'M YUKI NAGATO.

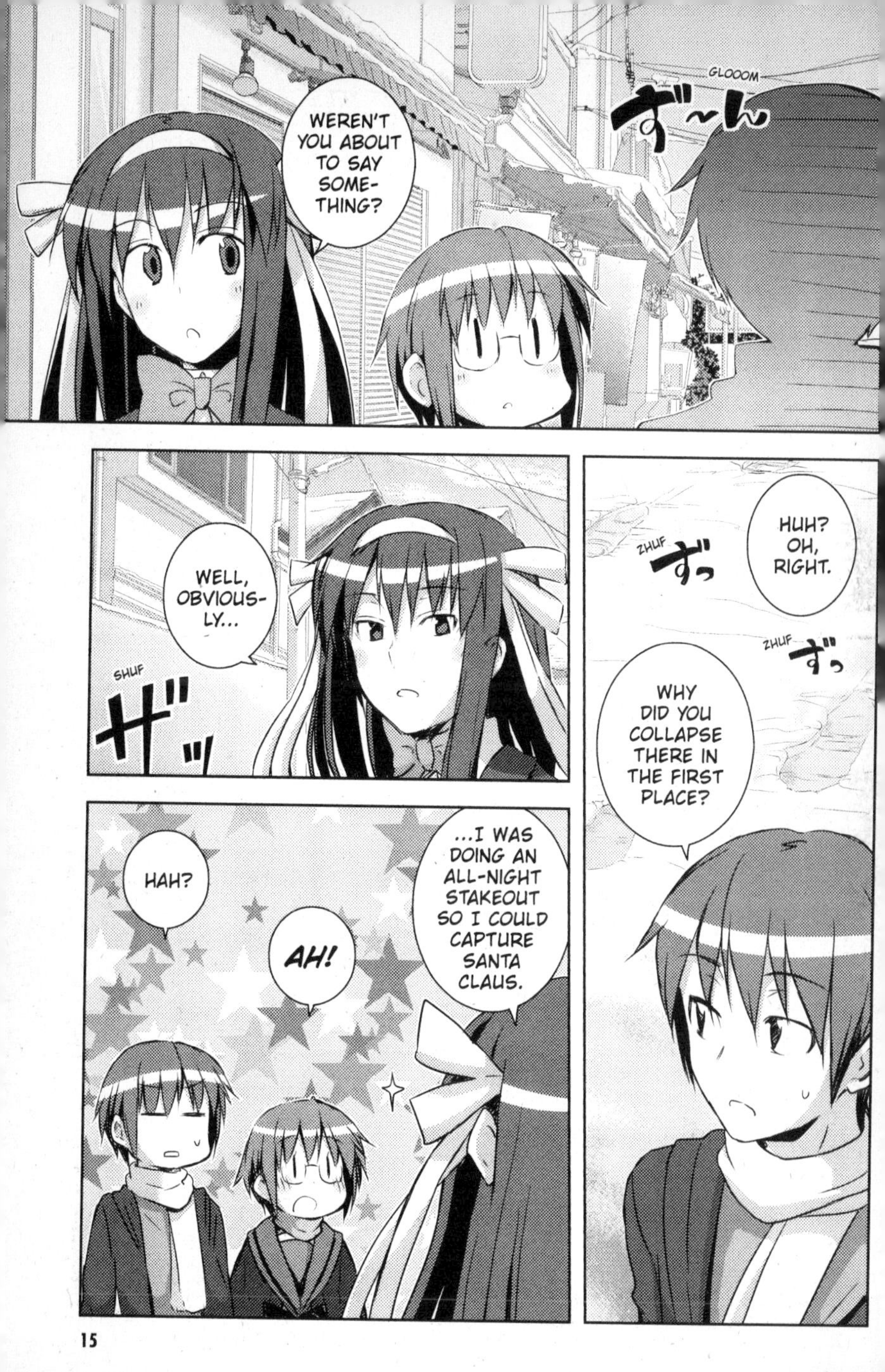
GLOOOM
ず〜ん
WEREN'T YOU ABOUT TO SAY SOME-THING?
ZHUF
ずっ
HUH? OH, RIGHT.
ZHUF
ずっ
WHY DID YOU COLLAPSE THERE IN THE FIRST PLACE?
WELL, OBVIOUS-LY...
SHUF
ザッ
...I WAS DOING AN ALL-NIGHT STAKEOUT SO I COULD CAPTURE SANTA CLAUS.
AH!
HAH?

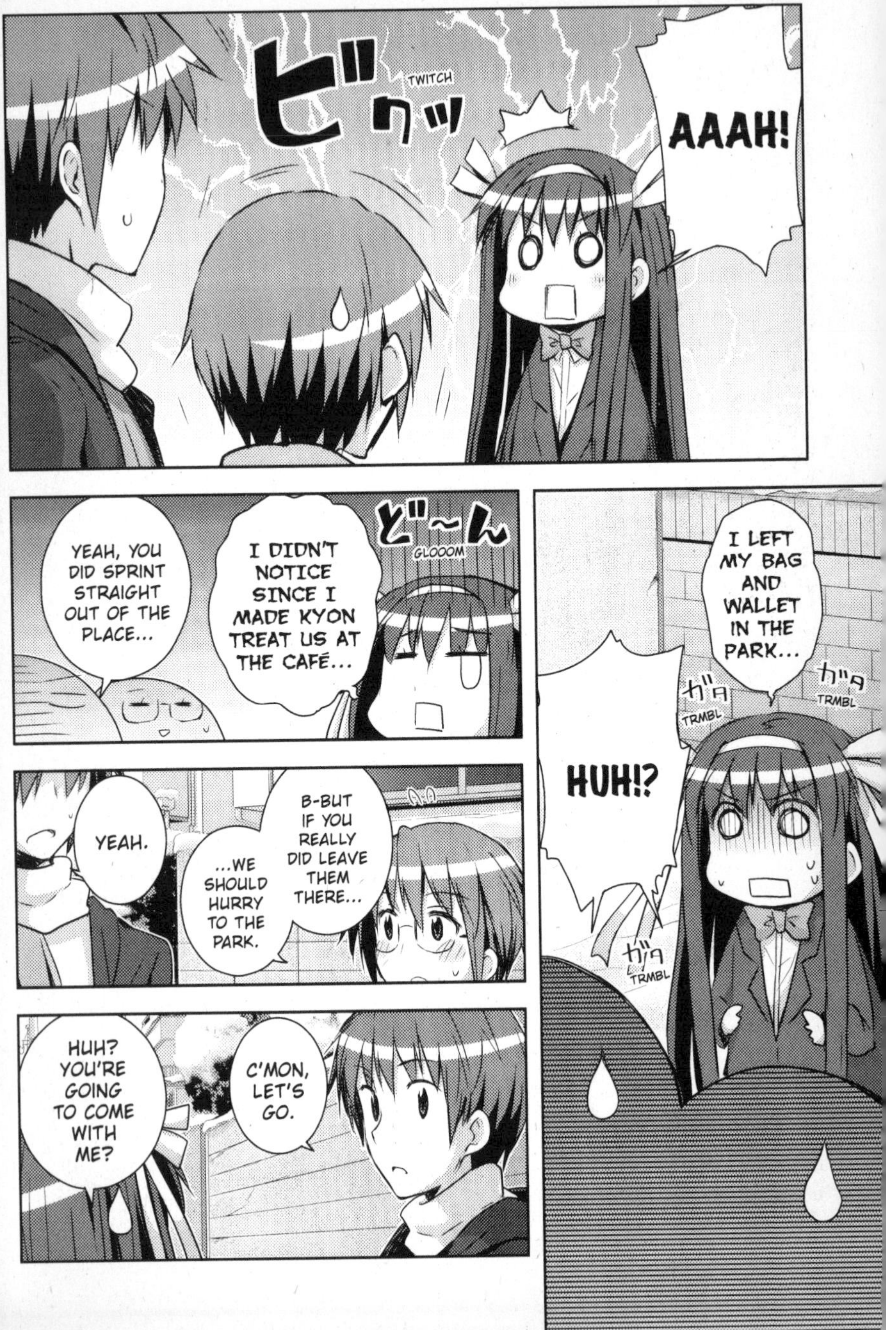
ビクッ
TWITCH
AAAH!
I LEFT MY BAG AND WALLET IN THE PARK...
ガタ
TRMBL
ガタ
TRMBL
HUH!?
ガタ
TRMBL
どーん
GLOOOM
I DIDN'T NOTICE SINCE I MADE KYON TREAT US AT THE CAFÉ...
YEAH, YOU DID SPRINT STRAIGHT OUT OF THE PLACE...
B-BUT IF YOU REALLY DID LEAVE THEM THERE...
...WE SHOULD HURRY TO THE PARK.
YEAH.
C'MON, LET'S GO.
HUH? YOU'RE GOING TO COME WITH ME?

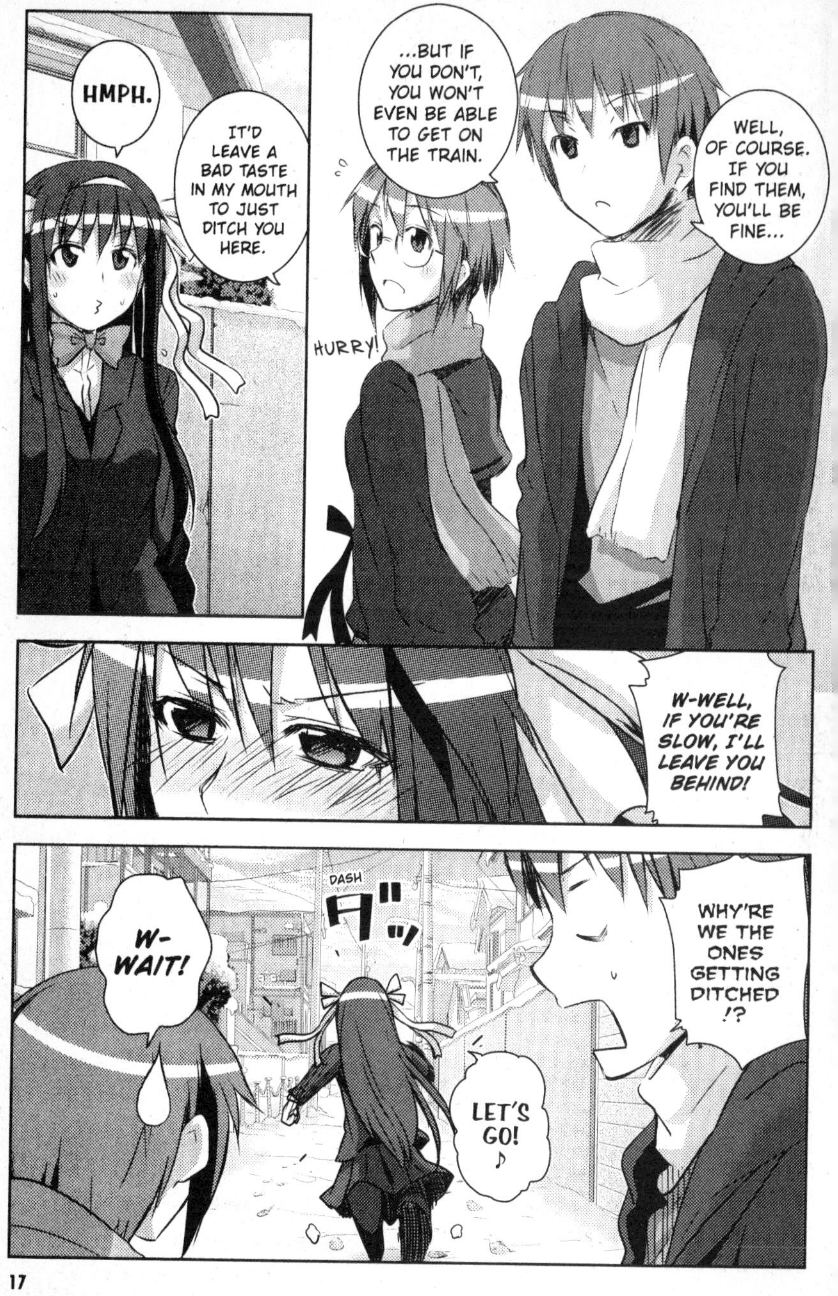
WELL, OF COURSE. IF YOU FIND THEM, YOU'LL BE FINE...
...BUT IF YOU DON'T, YOU WON'T EVEN BE ABLE TO GET ON THE TRAIN.
HURRY!
HMPH.
IT'D LEAVE A BAD TASTE IN MY MOUTH TO JUST DITCH YOU HERE.
W-WELL, IF YOU'RE SLOW, I'LL LEAVE YOU BEHIND!
WHY'RE WE THE ONES GETTING DITCHED !?
DASH
LET'S GO! ♪
W-WAIT!

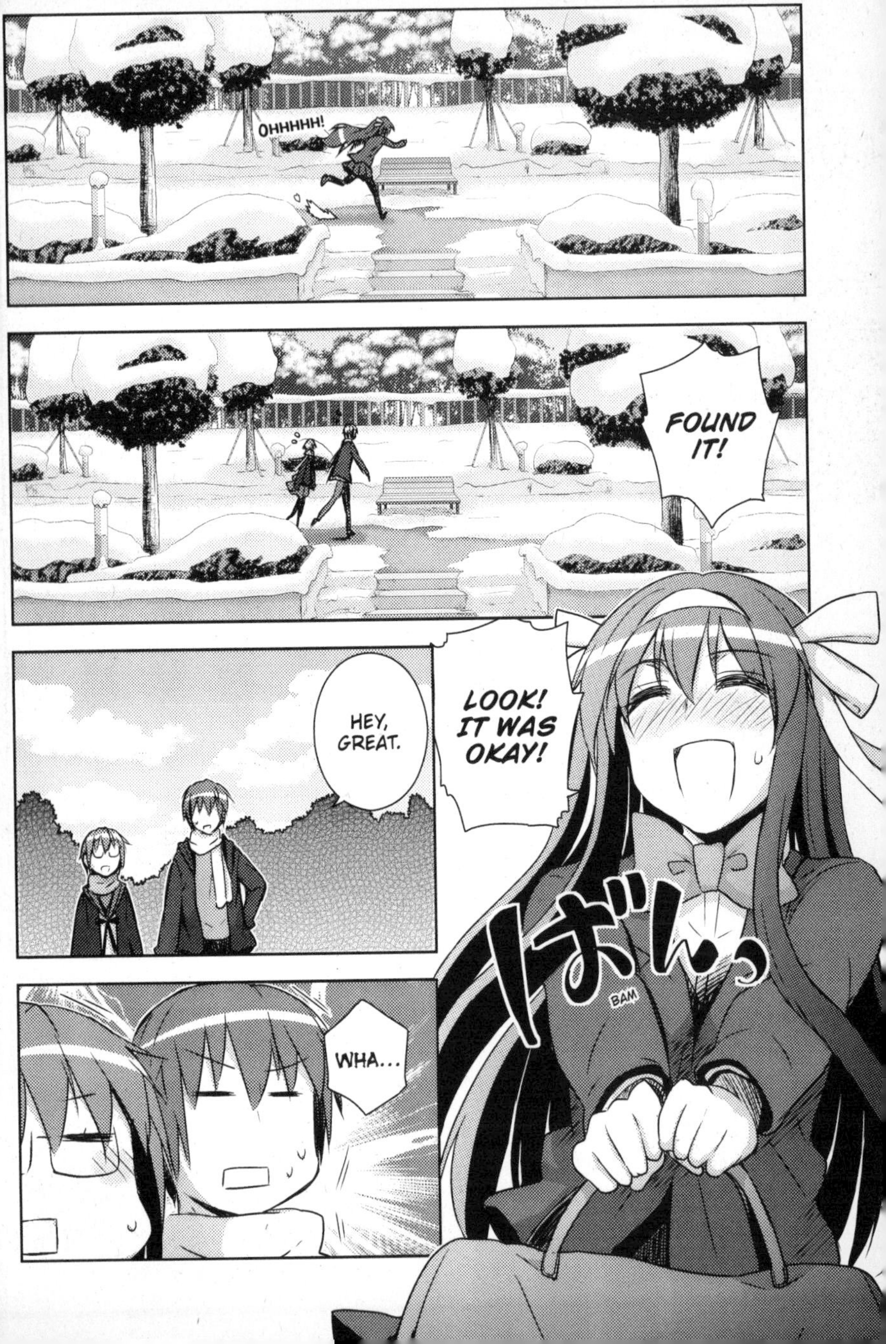
OHHHHH!
FOUND IT!
LOOK! IT WAS OKAY!
ばんっ
BAM
HEY, GREAT.
WHA...

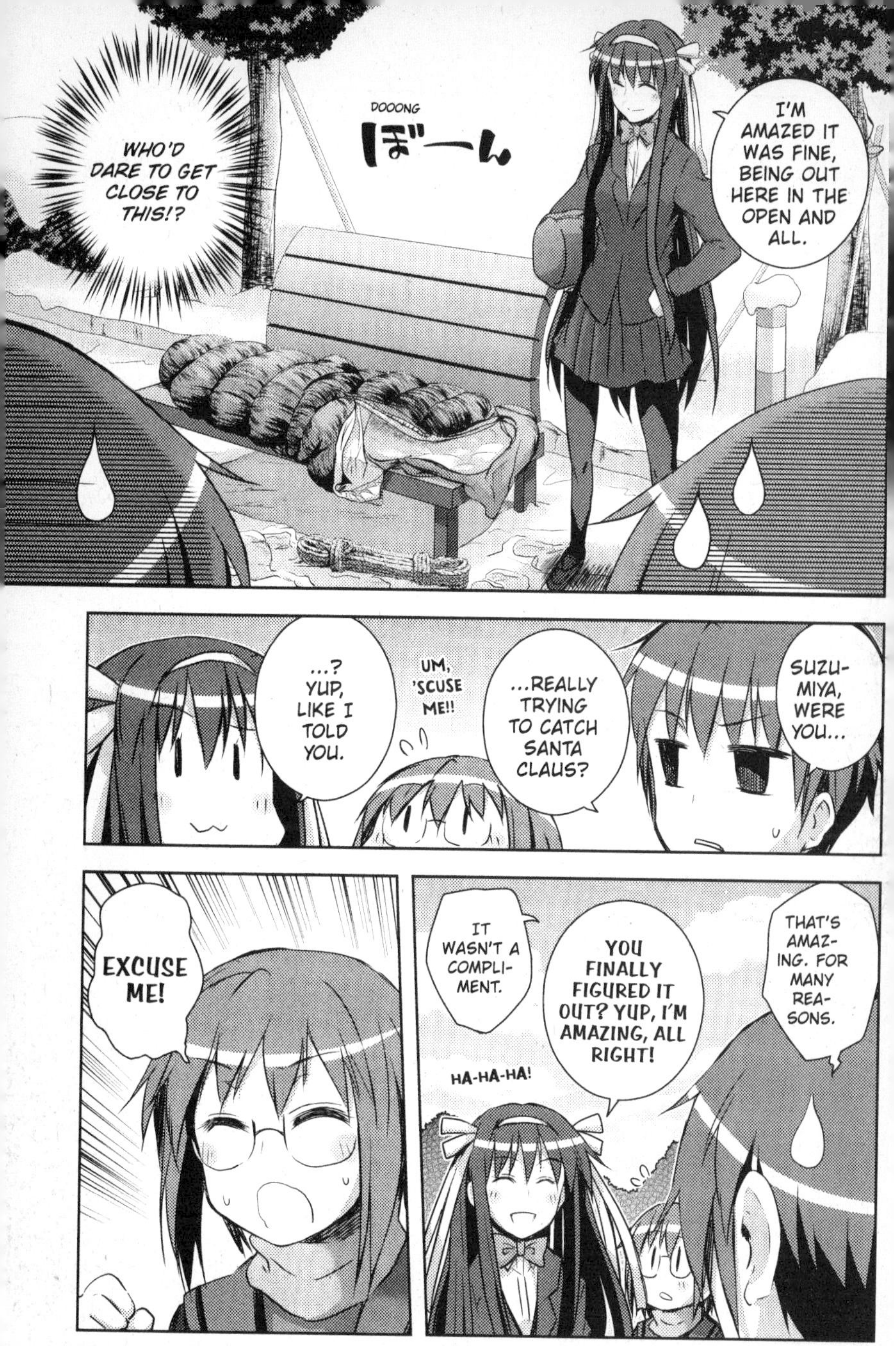
I'M AMAZED IT WAS FINE, BEING OUT HERE IN THE OPEN AND ALL.
DOOONG
ぼーん
WHO'D DARE TO GET CLOSE TO THIS!?
SUZU-MIYA, WERE YOU...
...REALLY TRYING TO CATCH SANTA CLAUS?
UM, 'SCUSE ME!!
...? YUP, LIKE I TOLD YOU.
THAT'S AMAZ-ING. FOR MANY REA-SONS.
YOU FINALLY FIGURED IT OUT? YUP, I'M AMAZING, ALL RIGHT!
IT WASN'T A COMPLI-MENT.
HA-HA-HA!
EXCUSE ME!

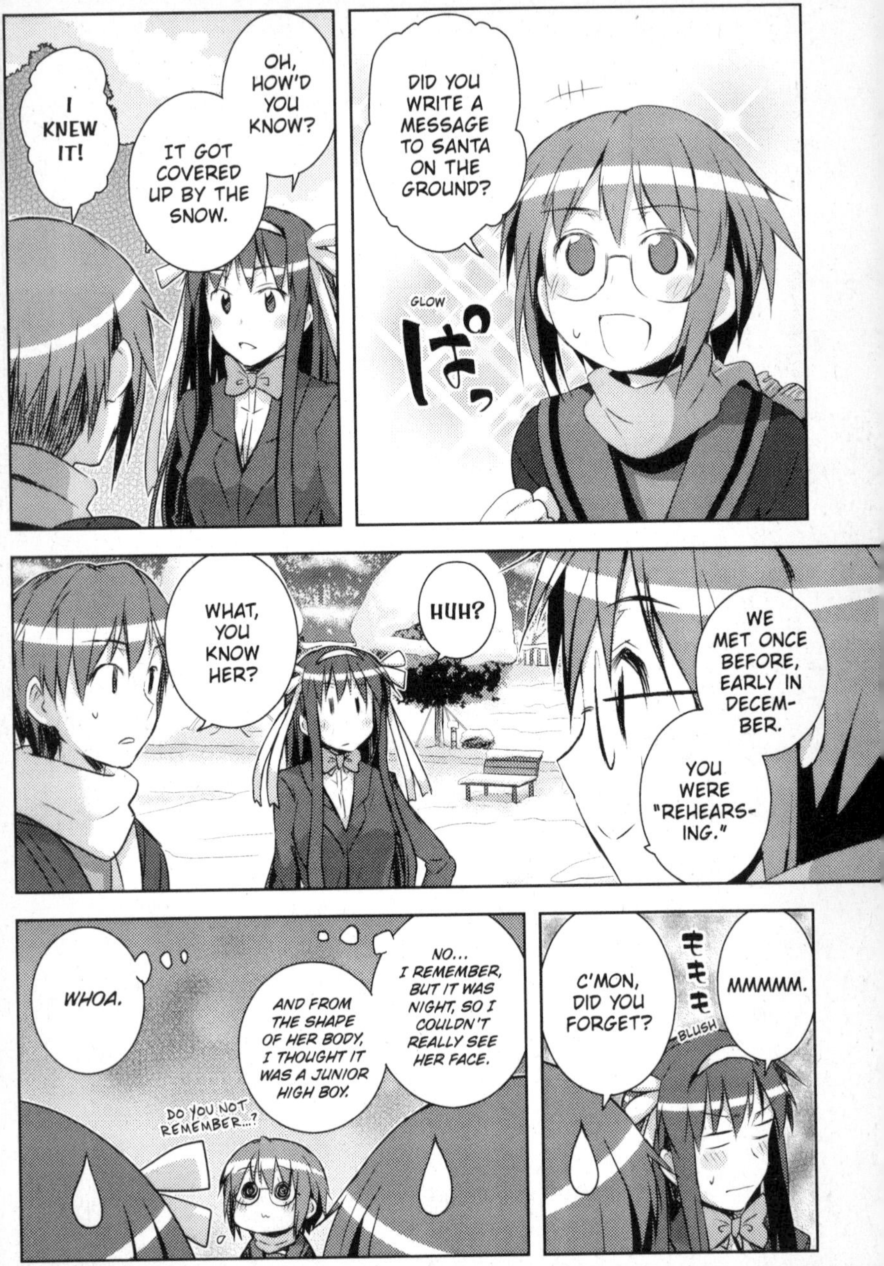
DID YOU WRITE A MESSAGE TO SANTA ON THE GROUND?
GLOW
ぱっ
OH, HOW'D YOU KNOW?
IT GOT COVERED UP BY THE SNOW.
I KNEW IT!
WE MET ONCE BEFORE, EARLY IN DECEMBER.
YOU WERE "REHEARSING."
HUH?
WHAT, YOU KNOW HER?
MMMMM.
BLUSH
C'MON, DID YOU FORGET?
NO... I REMEMBER, BUT IT WAS NIGHT, SO I COULDN'T REALLY SEE HER FACE.
AND FROM THE SHAPE OF HER BODY, I THOUGHT IT WAS A JUNIOR HIGH BOY.
WHOA.
DO YOU NOT REMEMBER...?

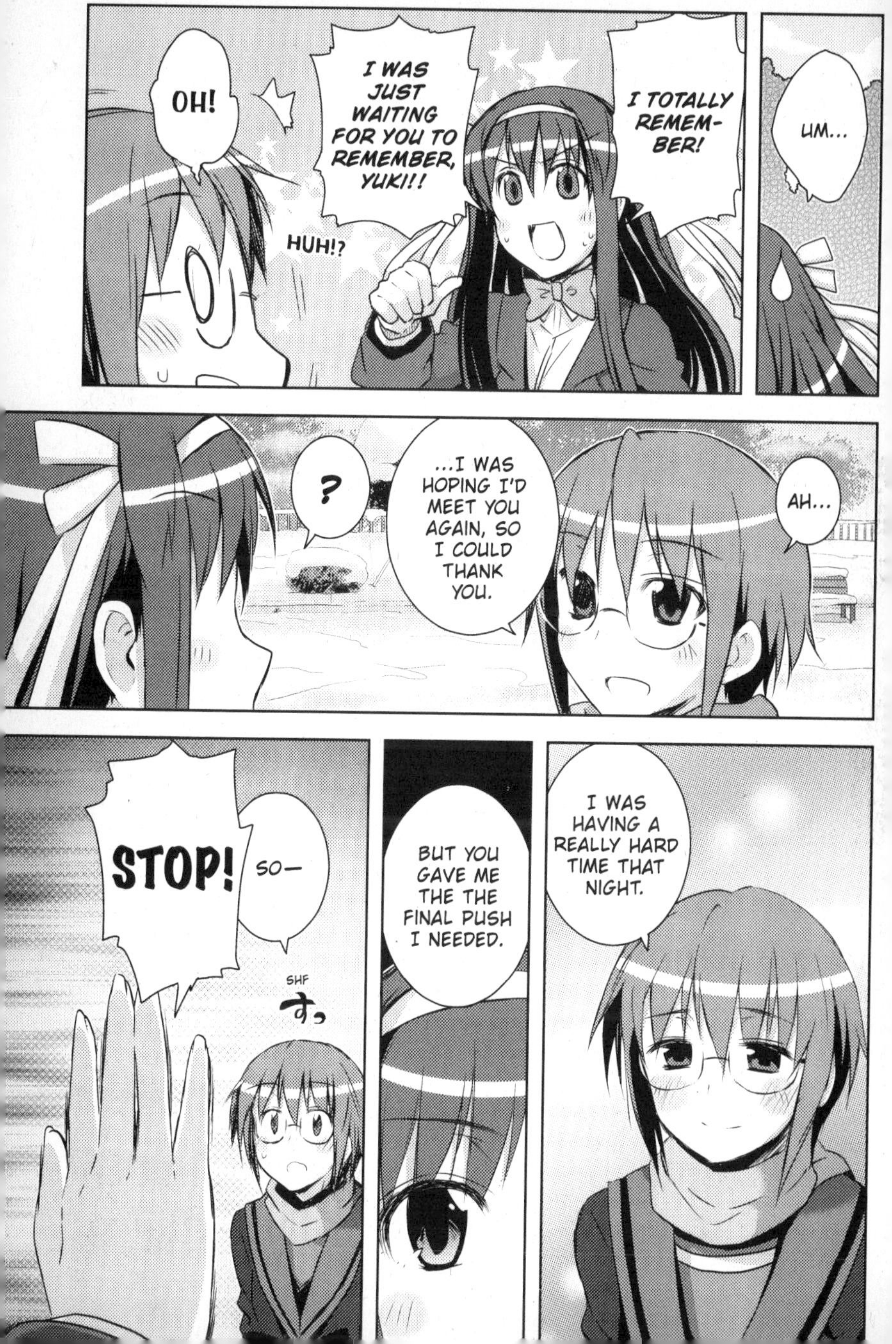
UM...
I TOTALLY REMEMBER!
I WAS JUST WAITING FOR YOU TO REMEMBER, YUKI!!
OH!
HUH!?
AH...
...I WAS HOPING I'D MEET YOU AGAIN, SO I COULD THANK YOU.
?
I WAS HAVING A REALLY HARD TIME THAT NIGHT.
BUT YOU GAVE ME THE THE FINAL PUSH I NEEDED.
SO—
STOP!
SHF
すっ

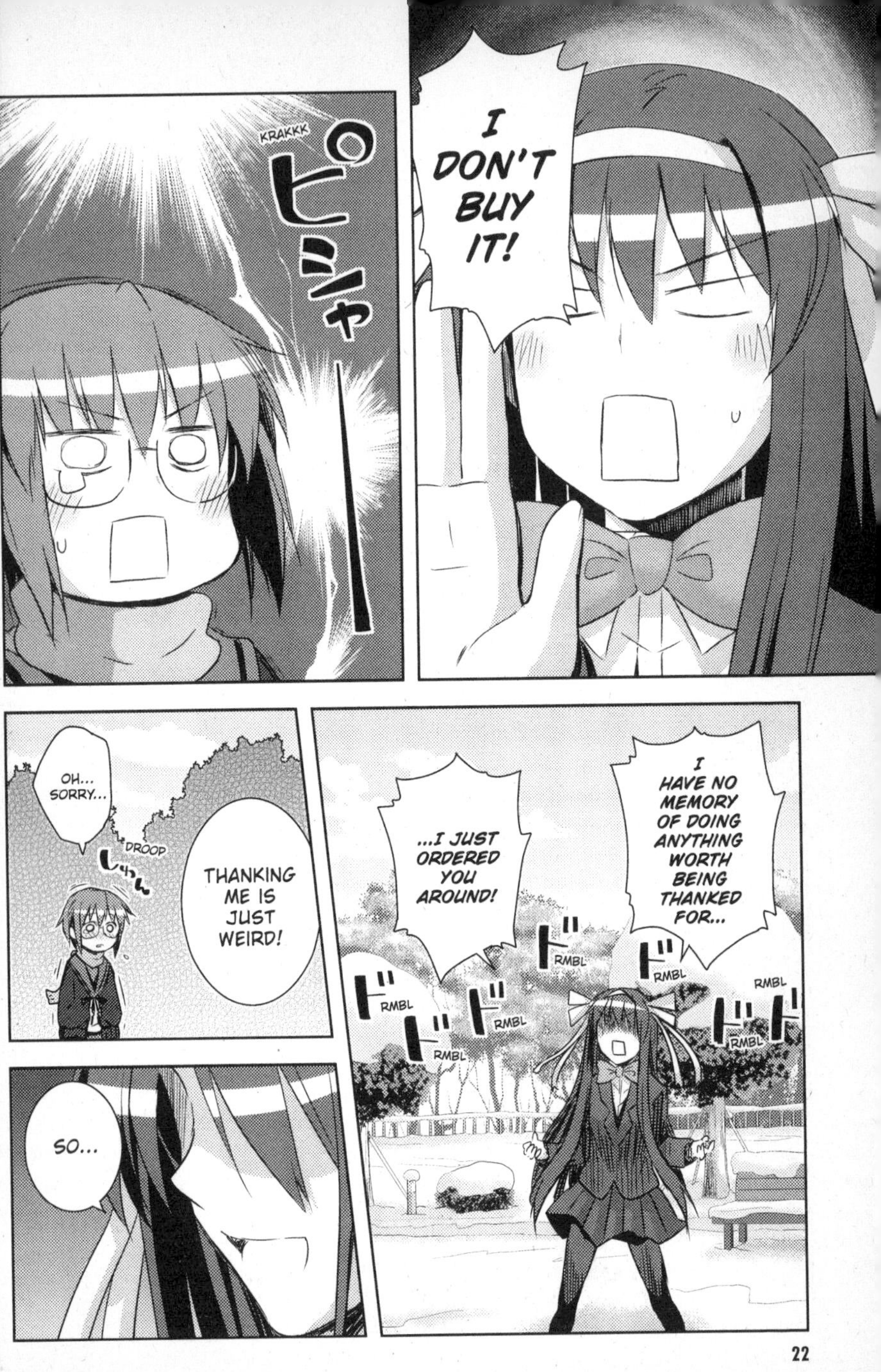
I DON'T BUY IT!
KRAKKK
ピシャー
I HAVE NO MEMORY OF DOING ANYTHING WORTH BEING THANKED FOR...
...I JUST ORDERED YOU AROUND!
ド RMBL
ド RMBL
ド RMBL
ド RMBL
ド RMBL
ド RMBL
ド RMBL
OH... SORRY...
THANKING ME IS JUST WEIRD!
DROOP
しゅん
SO...

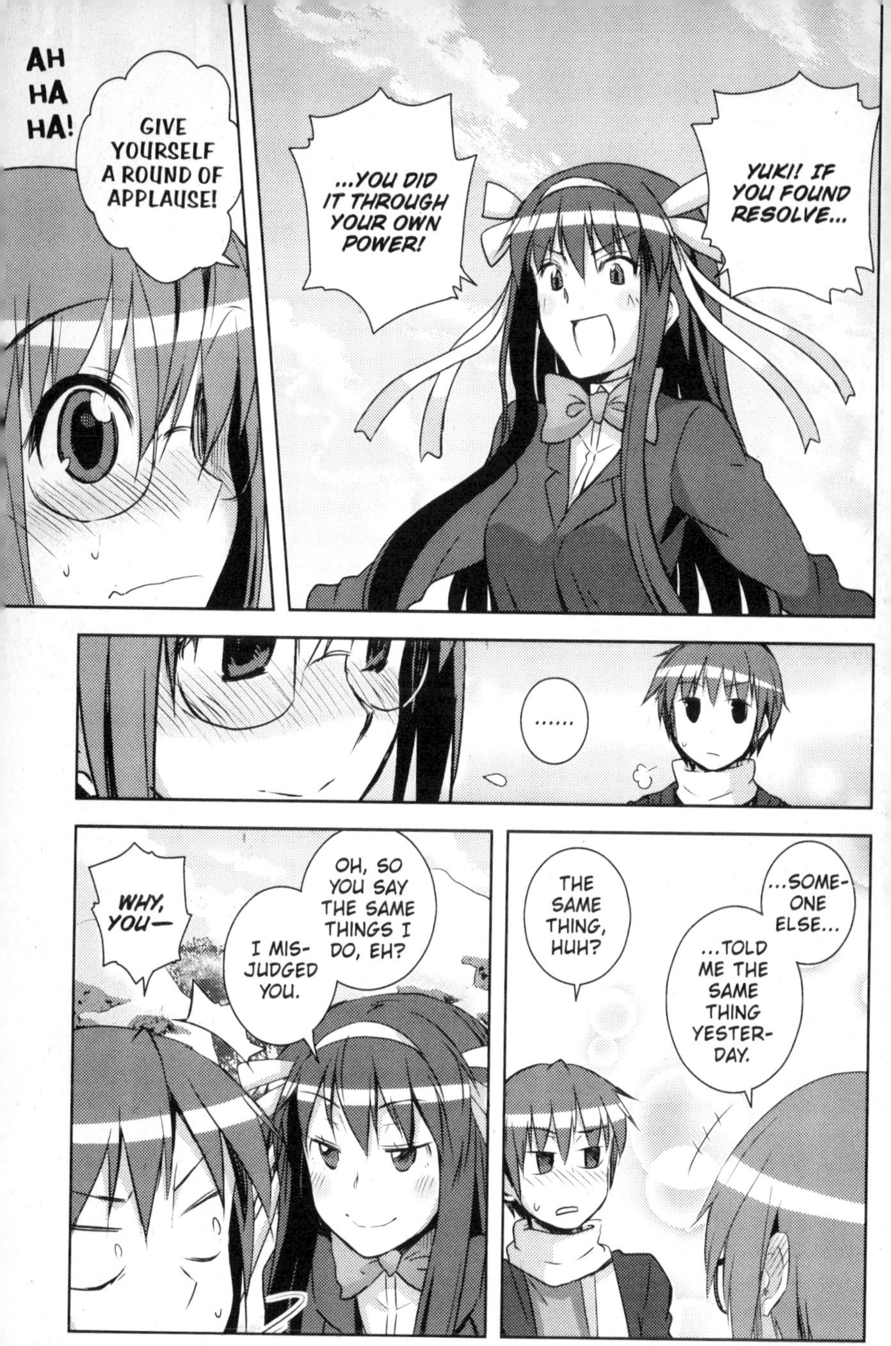
YUKI! IF YOU FOUND RESOLVE...
...YOU DID IT THROUGH YOUR OWN POWER!
GIVE YOURSELF A ROUND OF APPLAUSE!
AH HA HA!
......
...SOME-ONE ELSE...
...TOLD ME THE SAME THING YESTER-DAY.
THE SAME THING, HUH?
OH, SO YOU SAY THE SAME THINGS I DO, EH?
I MIS-JUDGED YOU.
WHY, YOU—

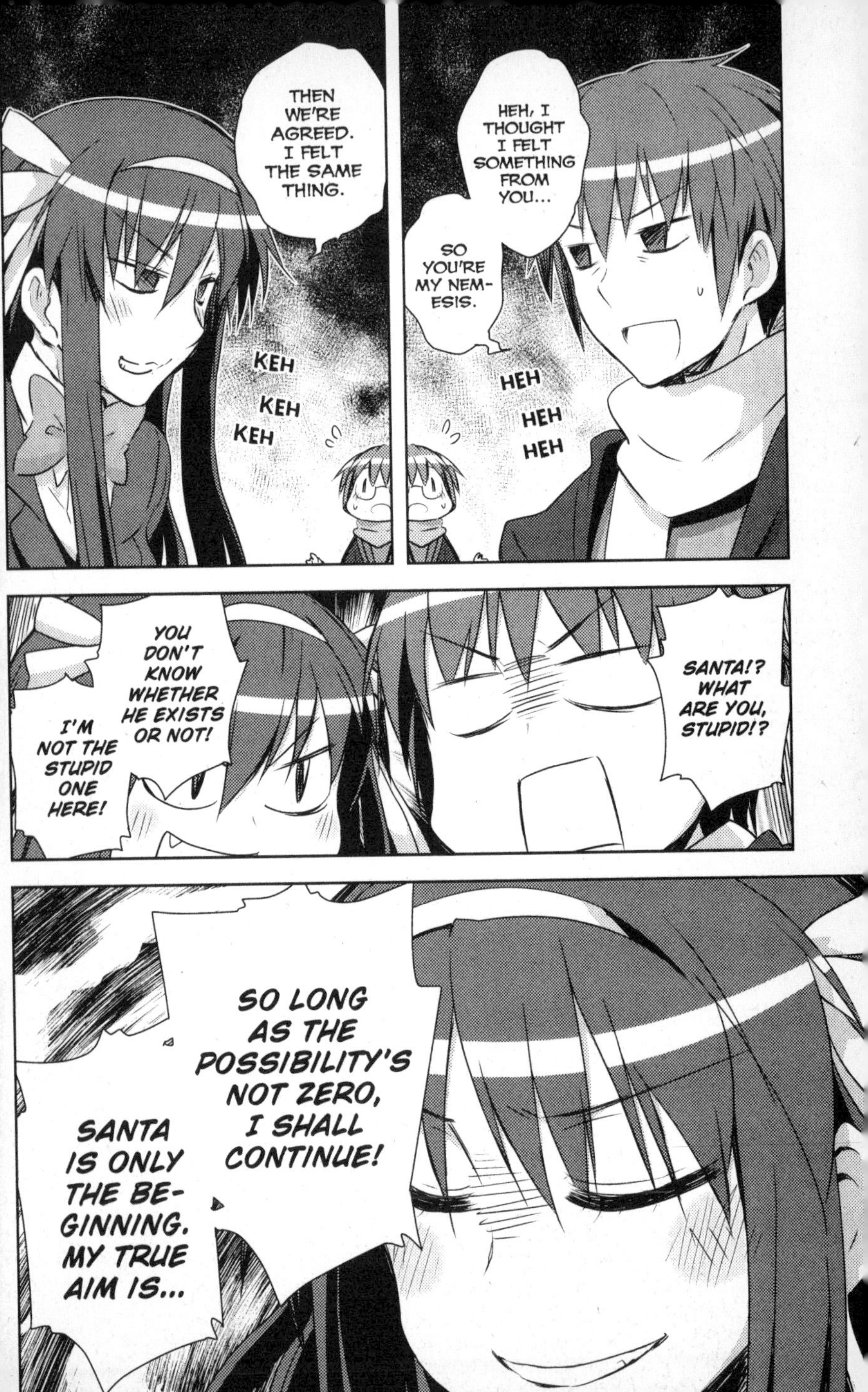
HEH, I THOUGHT I FELT SOMETHING FROM YOU...
SO YOU'RE MY NEM-ESIS.
HEH HEH HEH
THEN WE'RE AGREED. I FELT THE SAME THING.
KEH KEH KEH
SANTA!? WHAT ARE YOU, STUPID!?
YOU DON'T KNOW WHETHER HE EXISTS OR NOT!
I'M NOT THE STUPID ONE HERE!
SO LONG AS THE POSSIBILITY'S NOT ZERO, I SHALL CONTINUE!
SANTA IS ONLY THE BE-GINNING. MY TRUE AIM IS...

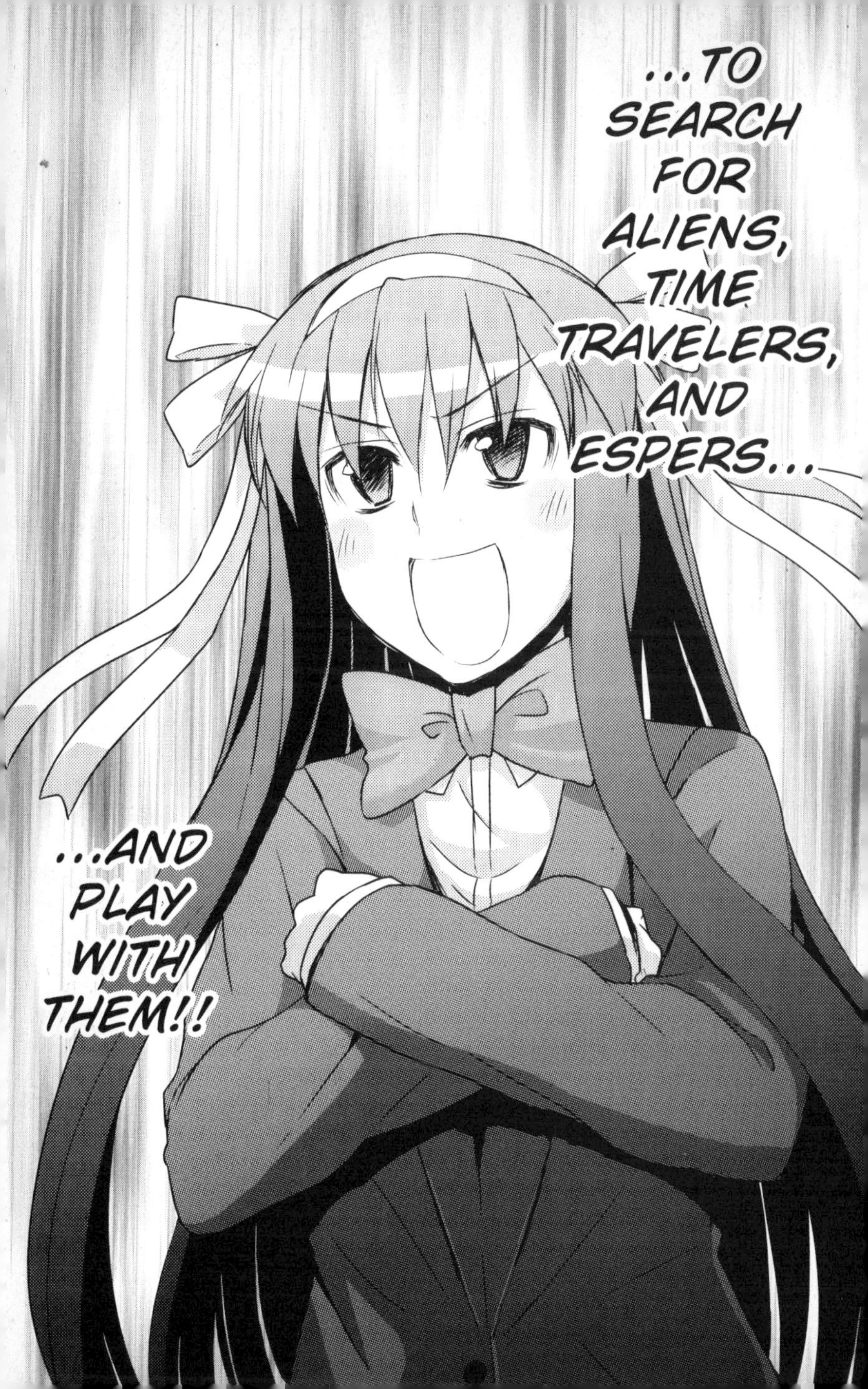
...TO SEARCH FOR ALIENS, TIME TRAVELERS, AND ESPERS...
...AND PLAY WITH THEM!!

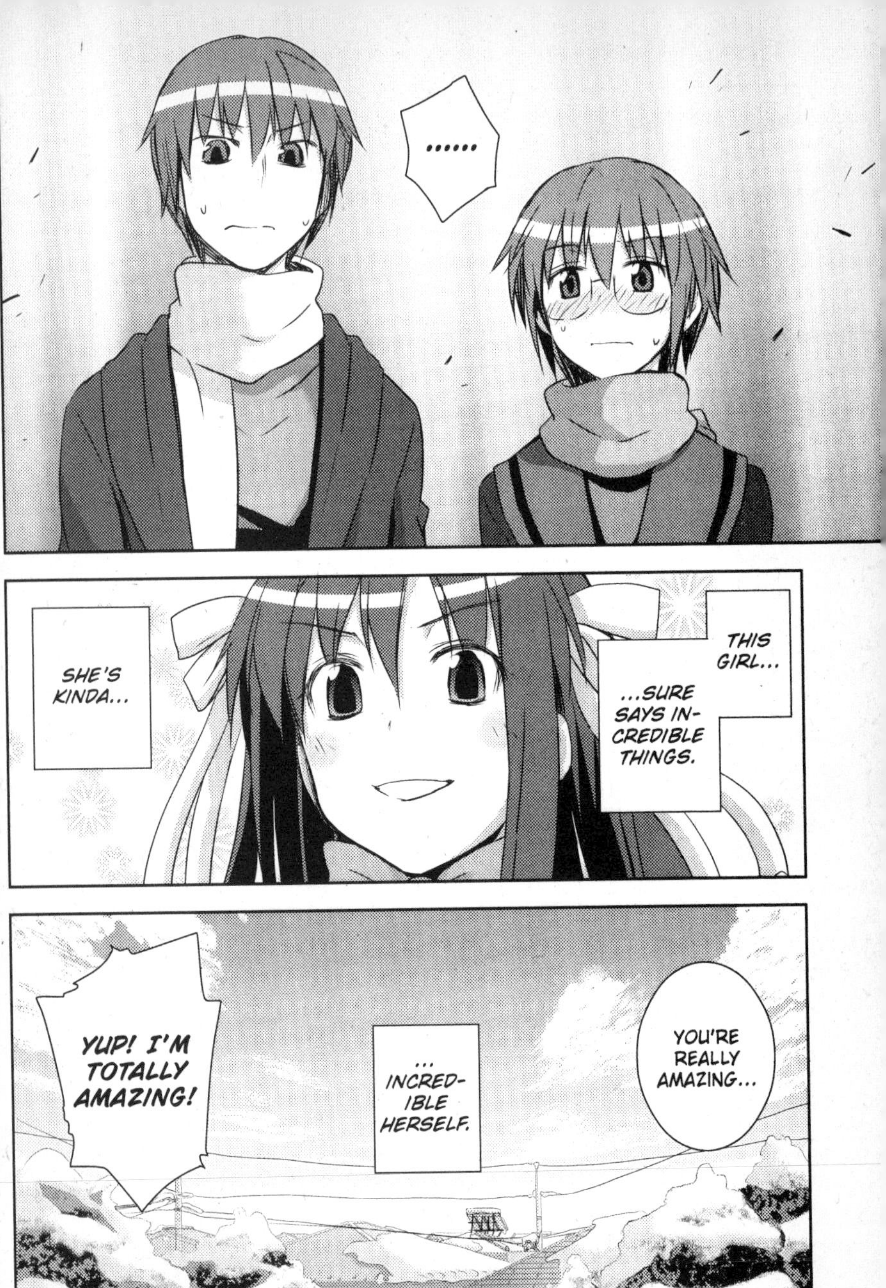
......
THIS GIRL...
...SURE SAYS IN-CREDIBLE THINGS.
SHE'S KINDA...
YOU'RE REALLY AMAZING...
...INCRED-IBLE HERSELF.
YUP! I'M TOTALLY AMAZING!

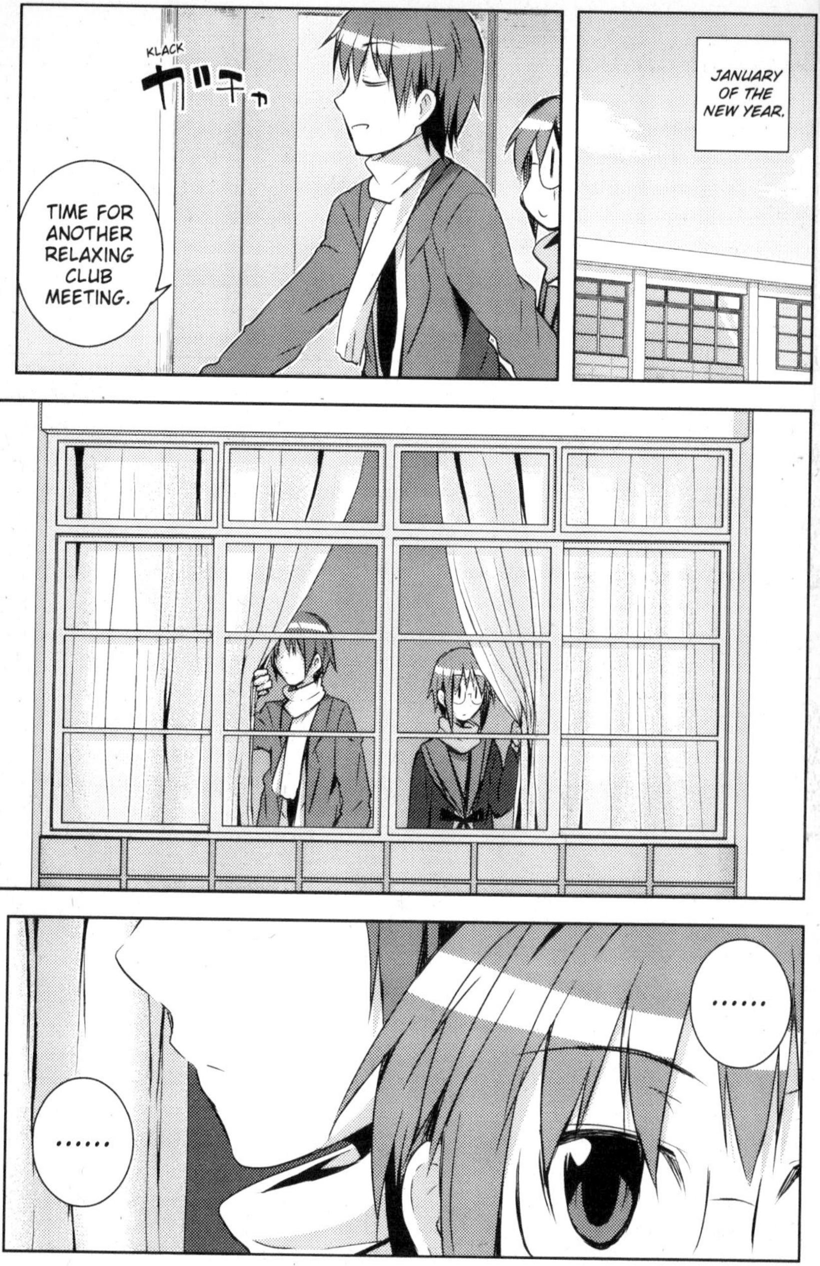
JANUARY OF THE NEW YEAR.
KLACK
ガチャ
TIME FOR ANOTHER RELAXING CLUB MEETING.
......
......

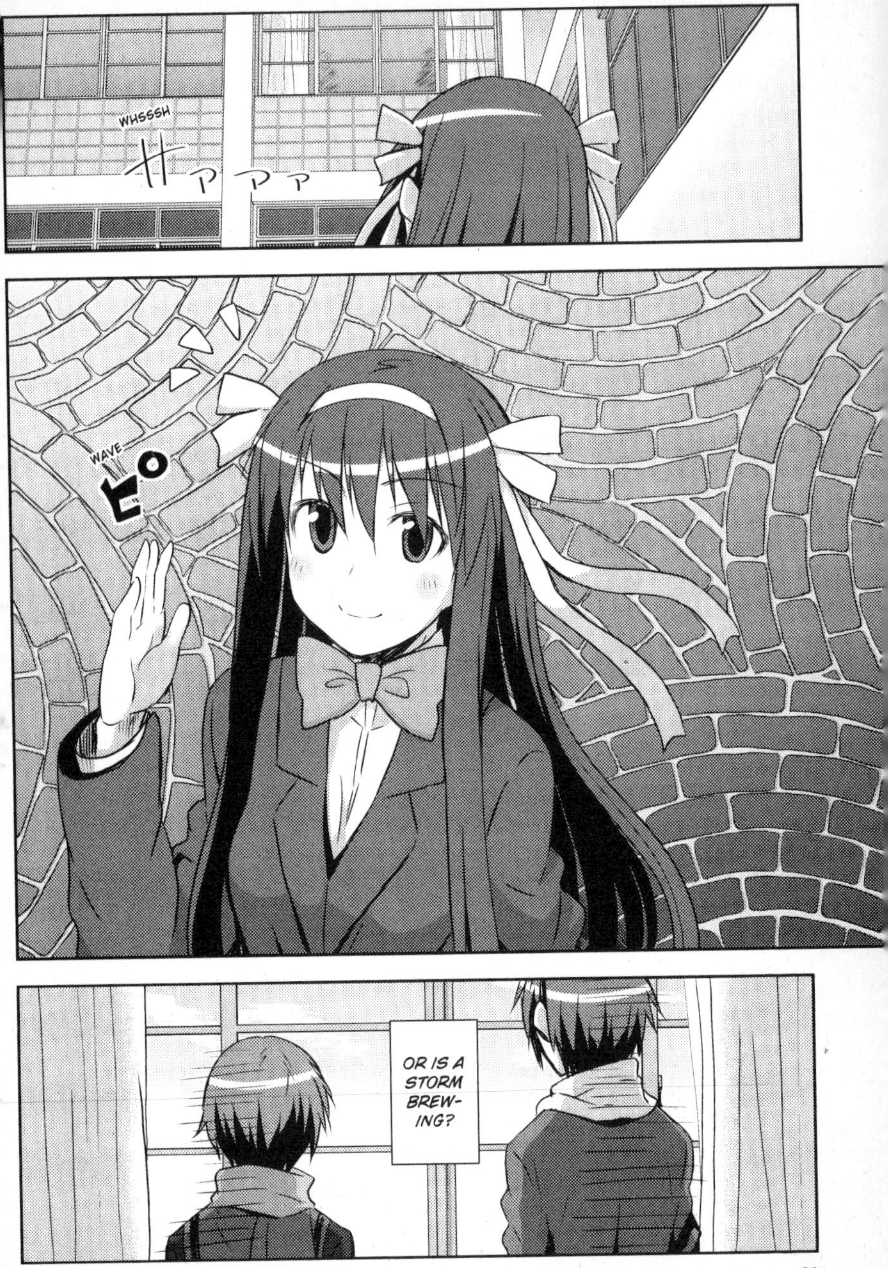
WHSSSH
ザァァァ
WAVE
ピッ
OR IS A STORM BREWING?

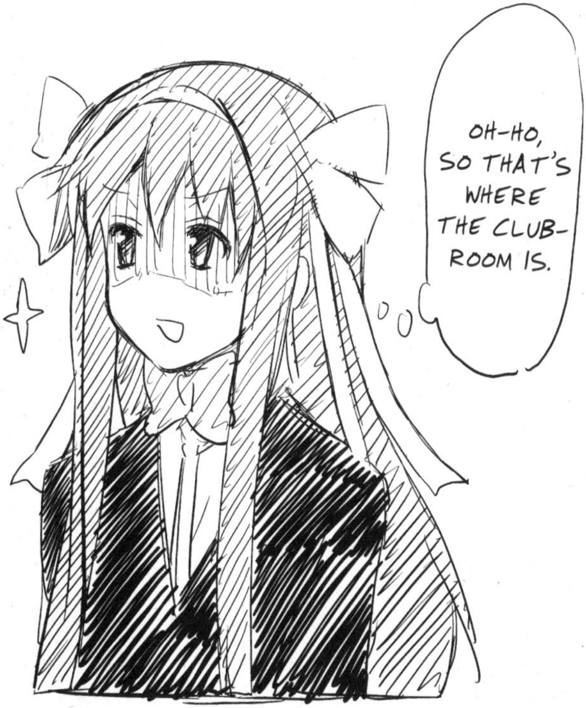
OH-HO, SO THAT'S WHERE THE CLUB-ROOM IS.

DASH

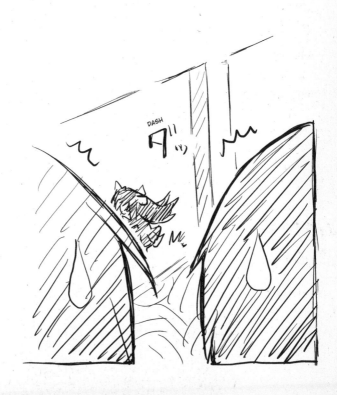

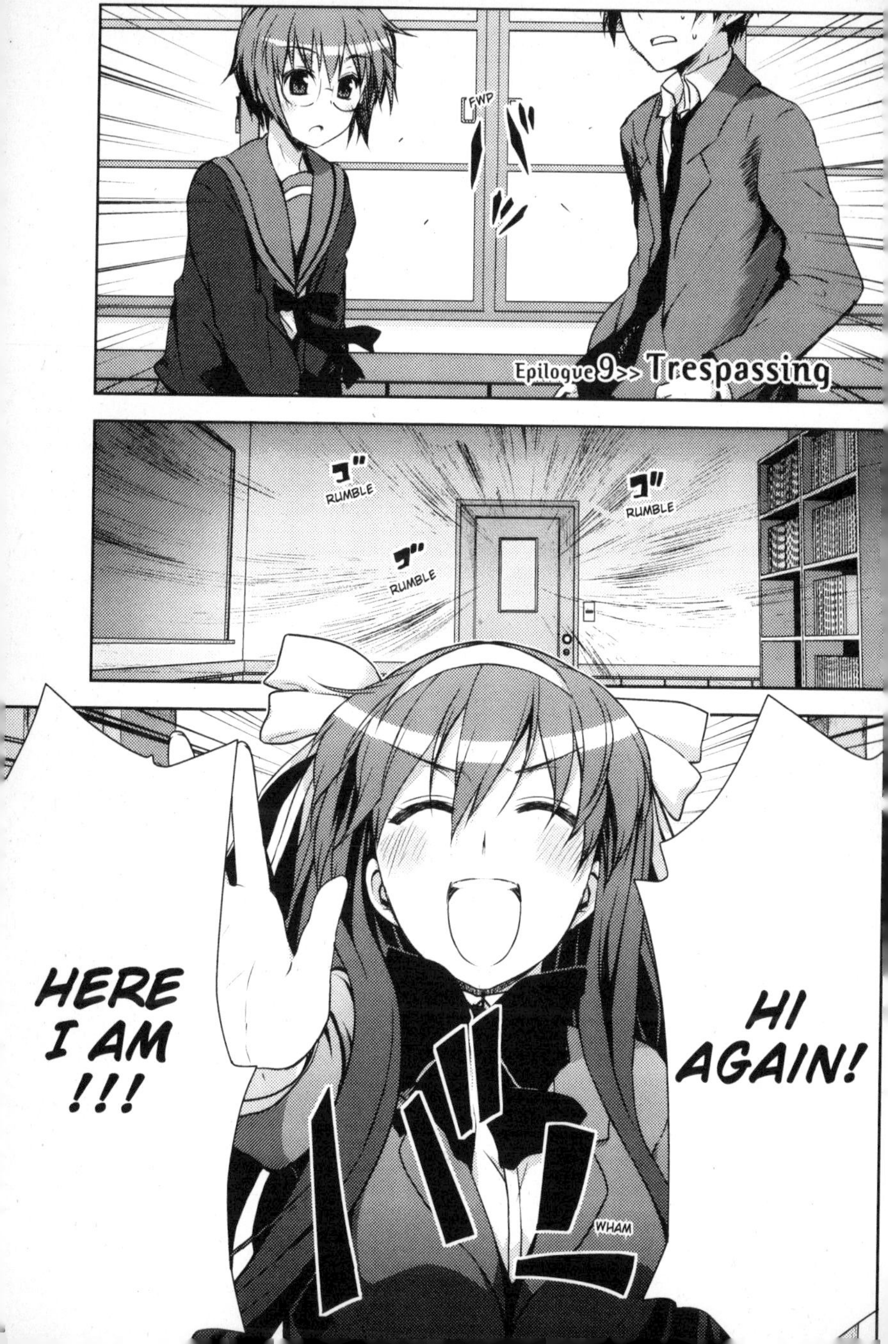
FWP
Epilogue 9>> Trespassing
RUMBLE
RUMBLE
RUMBLE
HI AGAIN!
HERE I AM !!!
WHAM

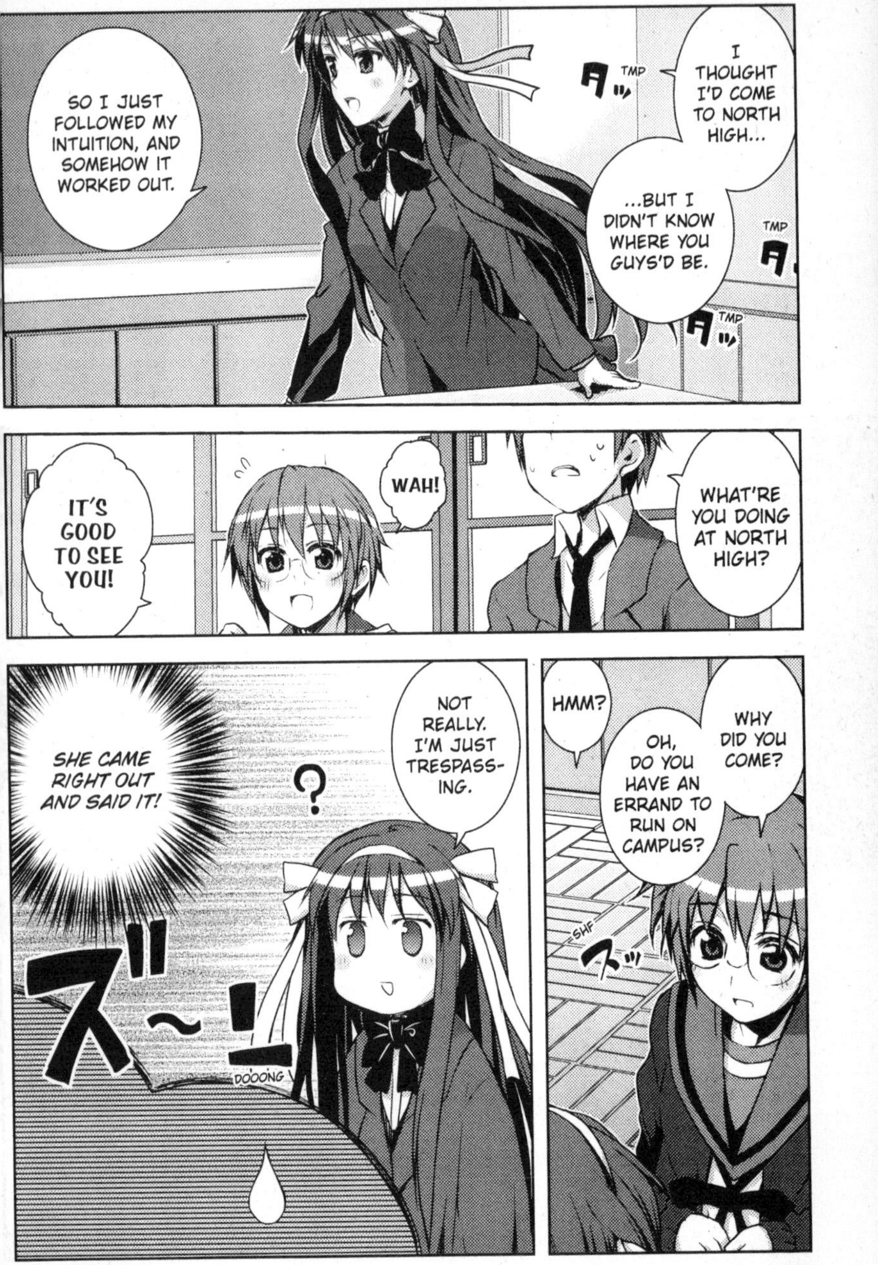

I THOUGHT I'D COME TO NORTH HIGH...
TMP
...BUT I DIDN'T KNOW WHERE YOU GUYS'D BE.
TMP
TMP
SO I JUST FOLLOWED MY INTUITION, AND SOMEHOW IT WORKED OUT.
WHAT'RE YOU DOING AT NORTH HIGH?
WAH!
IT'S GOOD TO SEE YOU!
WHY DID YOU COME?
OH, DO YOU HAVE AN ERRAND TO RUN ON CAMPUS?
HMM?
SHF
NOT REALLY. I'M JUST TRESPASSING.
SHE CAME RIGHT OUT AND SAID IT!
DOOONG

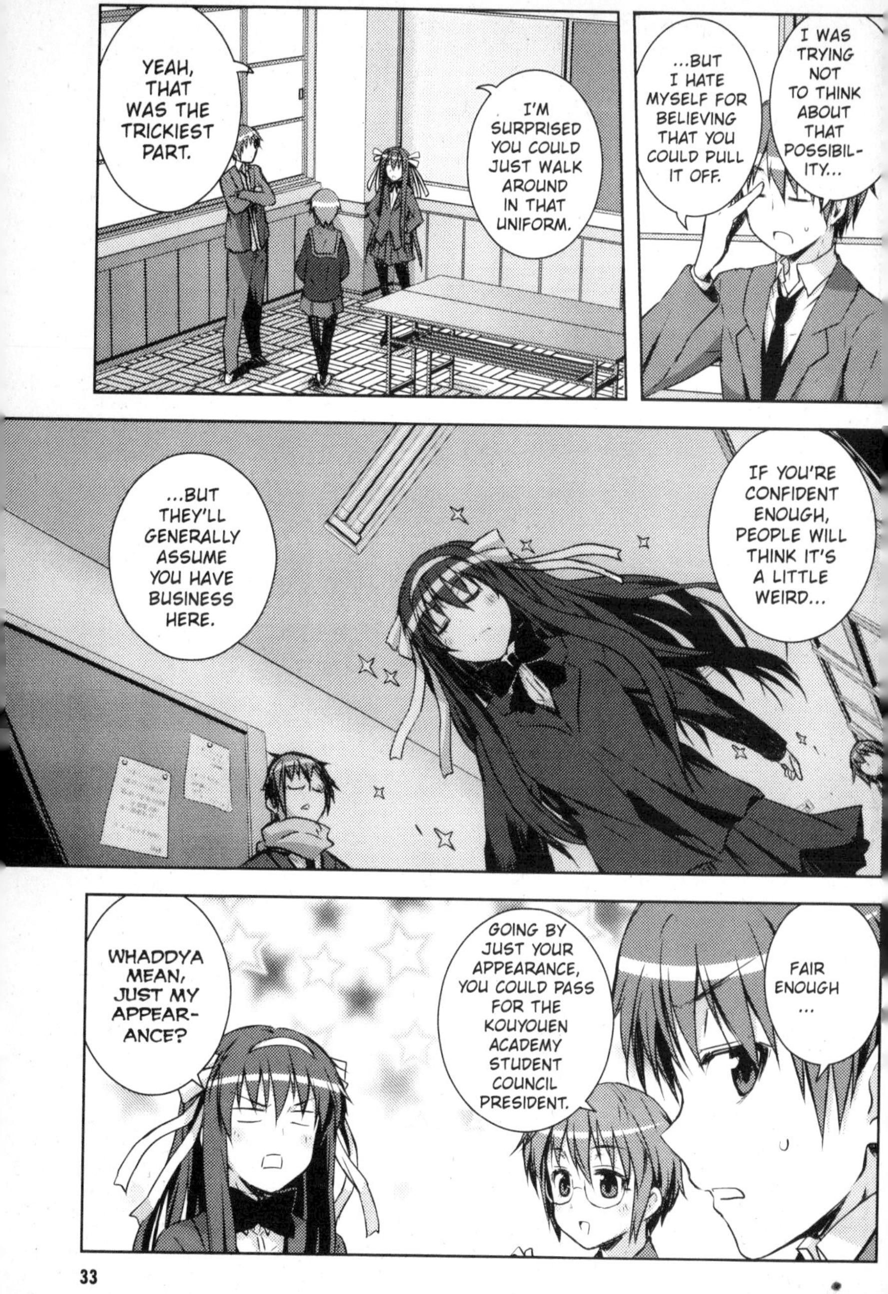
I WAS TRYING NOT TO THINK ABOUT THAT POSSIBIL-ITY...
...BUT I HATE MYSELF FOR BELIEVING THAT YOU COULD PULL IT OFF.
I'M SURPRISED YOU COULD JUST WALK AROUND IN THAT UNIFORM.
YEAH, THAT WAS THE TRICKIEST PART.
IF YOU'RE CONFIDENT ENOUGH, PEOPLE WILL THINK IT'S A LITTLE WEIRD...
...BUT THEY'LL GENERALLY ASSUME YOU HAVE BUSINESS HERE.
FAIR ENOUGH ...
GOING BY JUST YOUR APPEARANCE, YOU COULD PASS FOR THE KOUYOUEN ACADEMY STUDENT COUNCIL PRESIDENT.
WHADDYA MEAN, JUST MY APPEAR-ANCE?

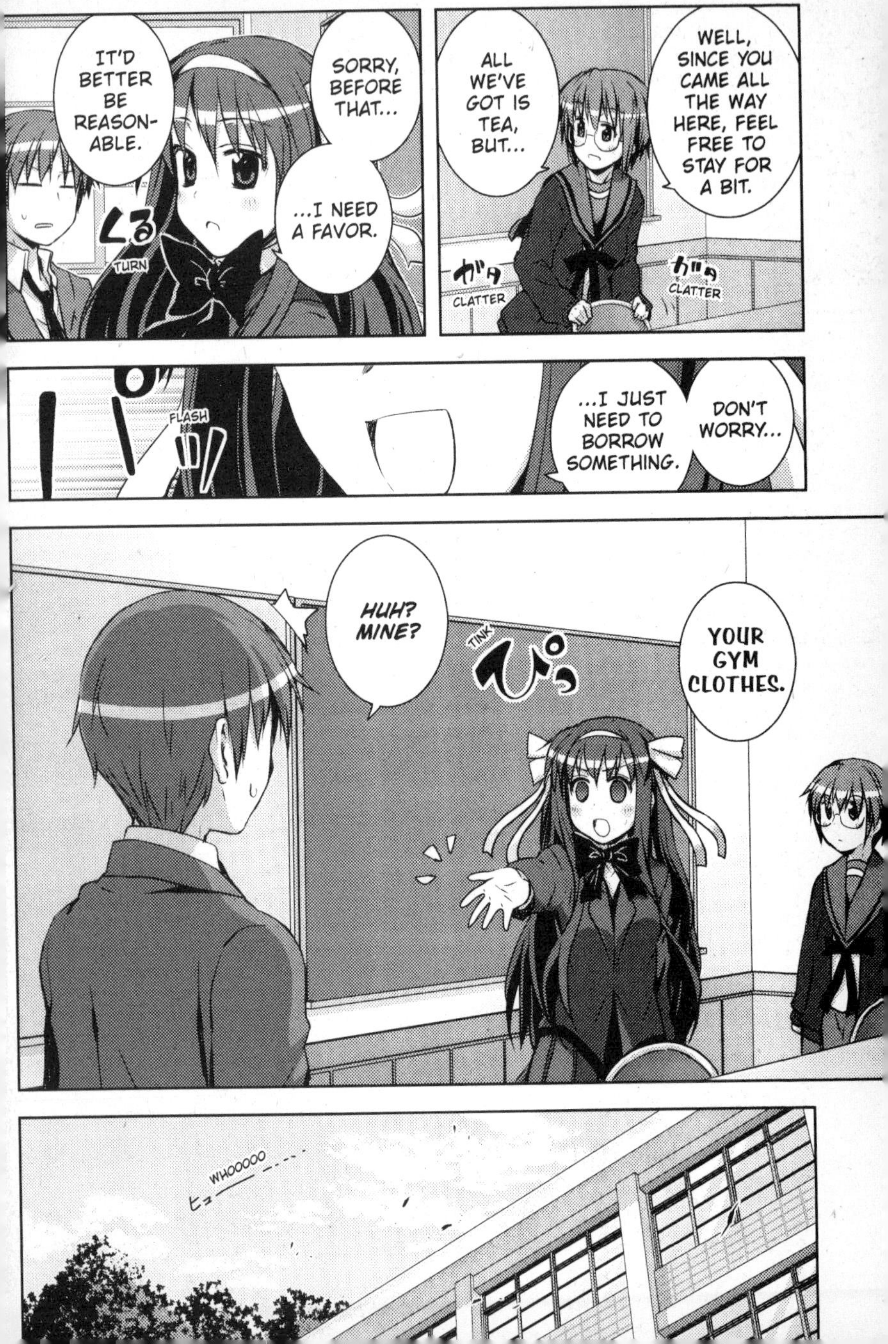
WELL, SINCE YOU CAME ALL THE WAY HERE, FEEL FREE TO STAY FOR A BIT.
ALL WE'VE GOT IS TEA, BUT...
ガタ
CLATTER
ガタ
CLATTER
SORRY, BEFORE THAT...
...I NEED A FAVOR.
IT'D BETTER BE REASONABLE.
くる
TURN
DON'T WORRY...
...I JUST NEED TO BORROW SOMETHING.
FLASH
YOUR GYM CLOTHES.
TINK
ぴっ
HUH? MINE?
WHOOOOO

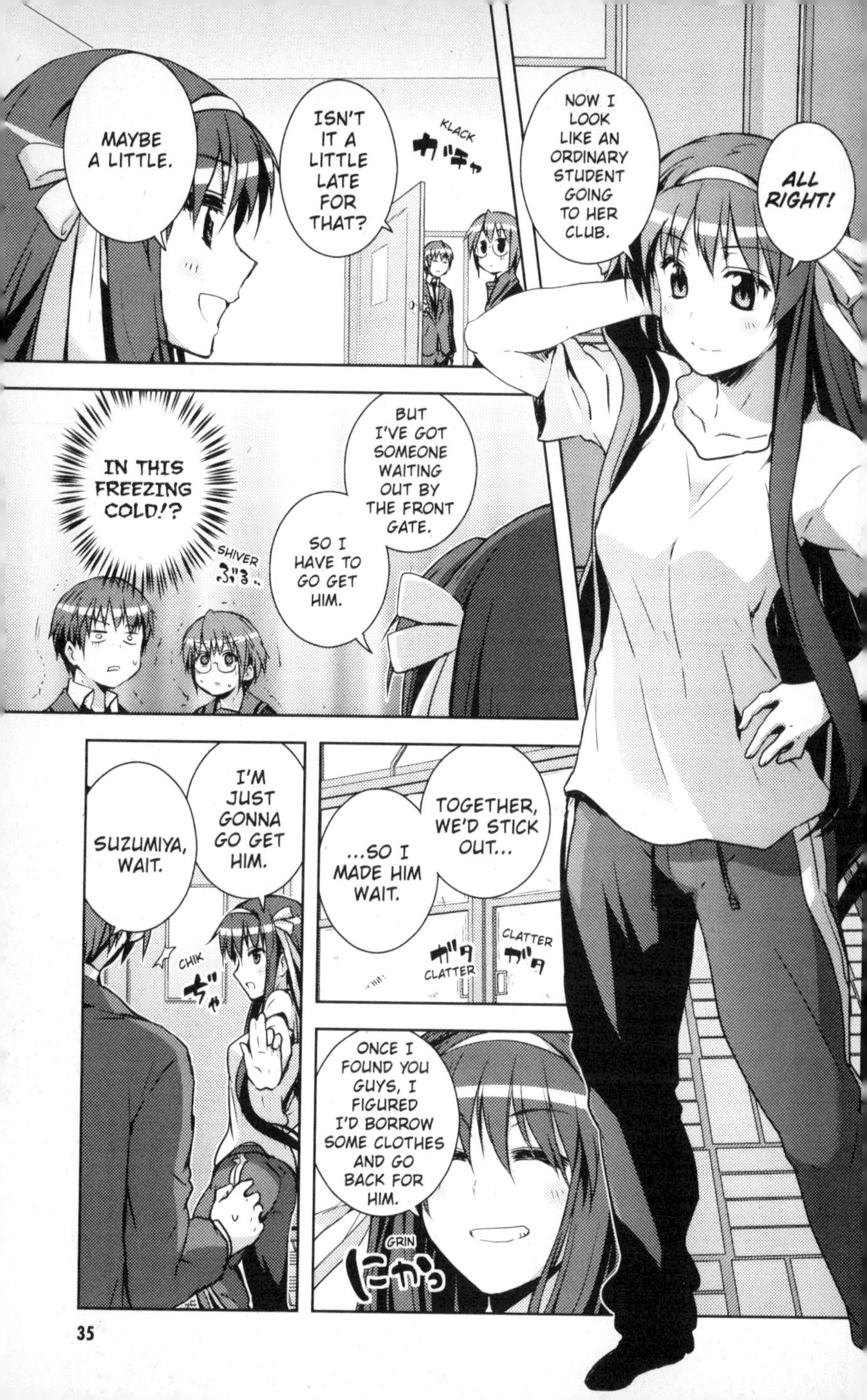
ALL RIGHT!
NOW I LOOK LIKE AN ORDINARY STUDENT GOING TO HER CLUB.
KLACK
ISN'T IT A LITTLE LATE FOR THAT?
MAYBE A LITTLE.
BUT I'VE GOT SOMEONE WAITING OUT BY THE FRONT GATE.
SO I HAVE TO GO GET HIM.
IN THIS FREEZING COLD!?
SHIVER
TOGETHER, WE'D STICK OUT...
...SO I MADE HIM WAIT.
CLATTER
CLATTER
ONCE I FOUND YOU GUYS, I FIGURED I'D BORROW SOME CLOTHES AND GO BACK FOR HIM.
GRIN
I'M JUST GONNA GO GET HIM.
SUZUMIYA, WAIT.
CHIK

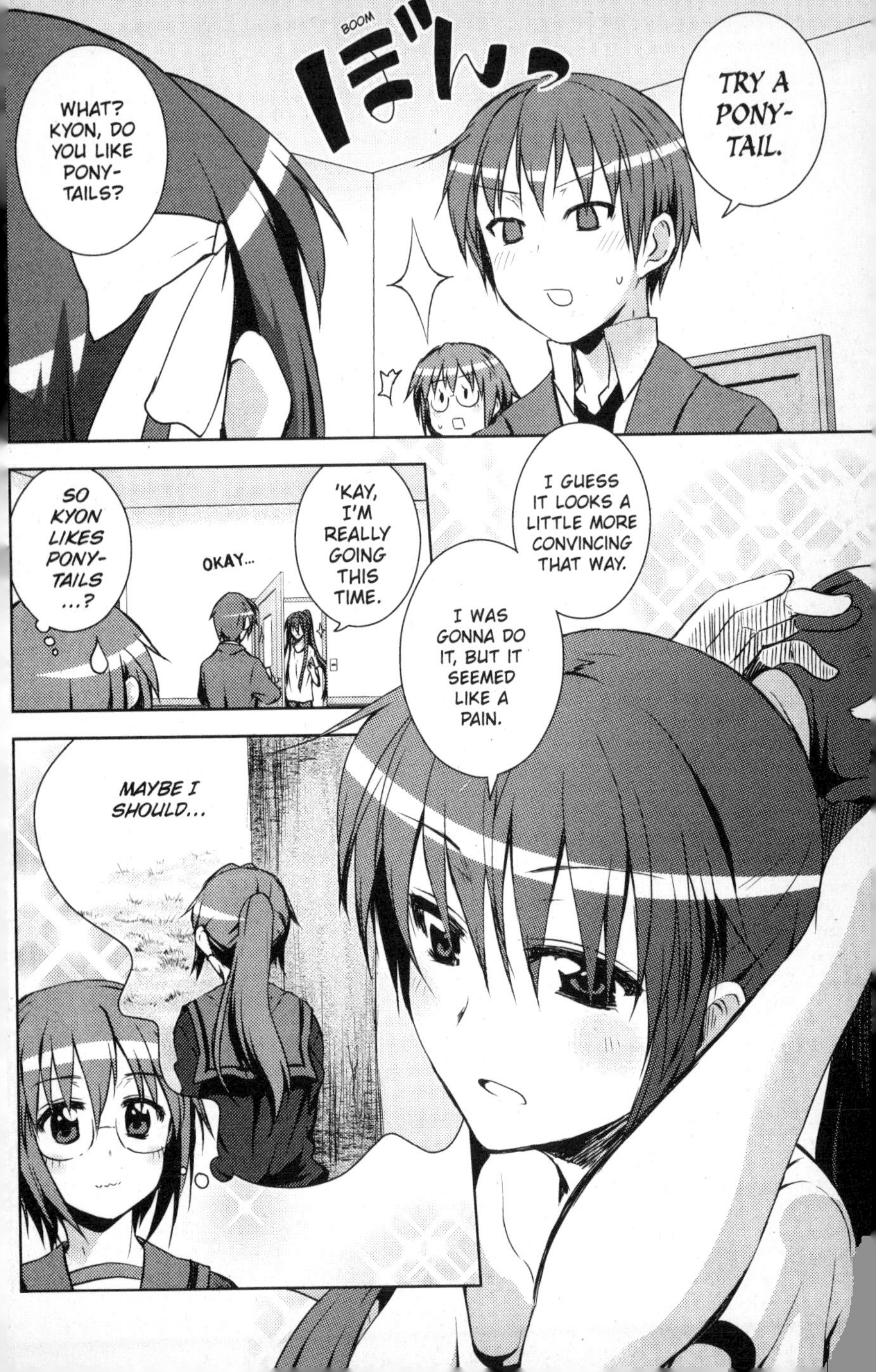
TRY A PONY-TAIL.
BOOM
ぼんっ
WHAT? KYON, DO YOU LIKE PONY-TAILS?
I GUESS IT LOOKS A LITTLE MORE CONVINCING THAT WAY.
I WAS GONNA DO IT, BUT IT SEEMED LIKE A PAIN.
'KAY, I'M REALLY GOING THIS TIME.
OKAY...
SO KYON LIKES PONY-TAILS ...?
MAYBE I SHOULD...

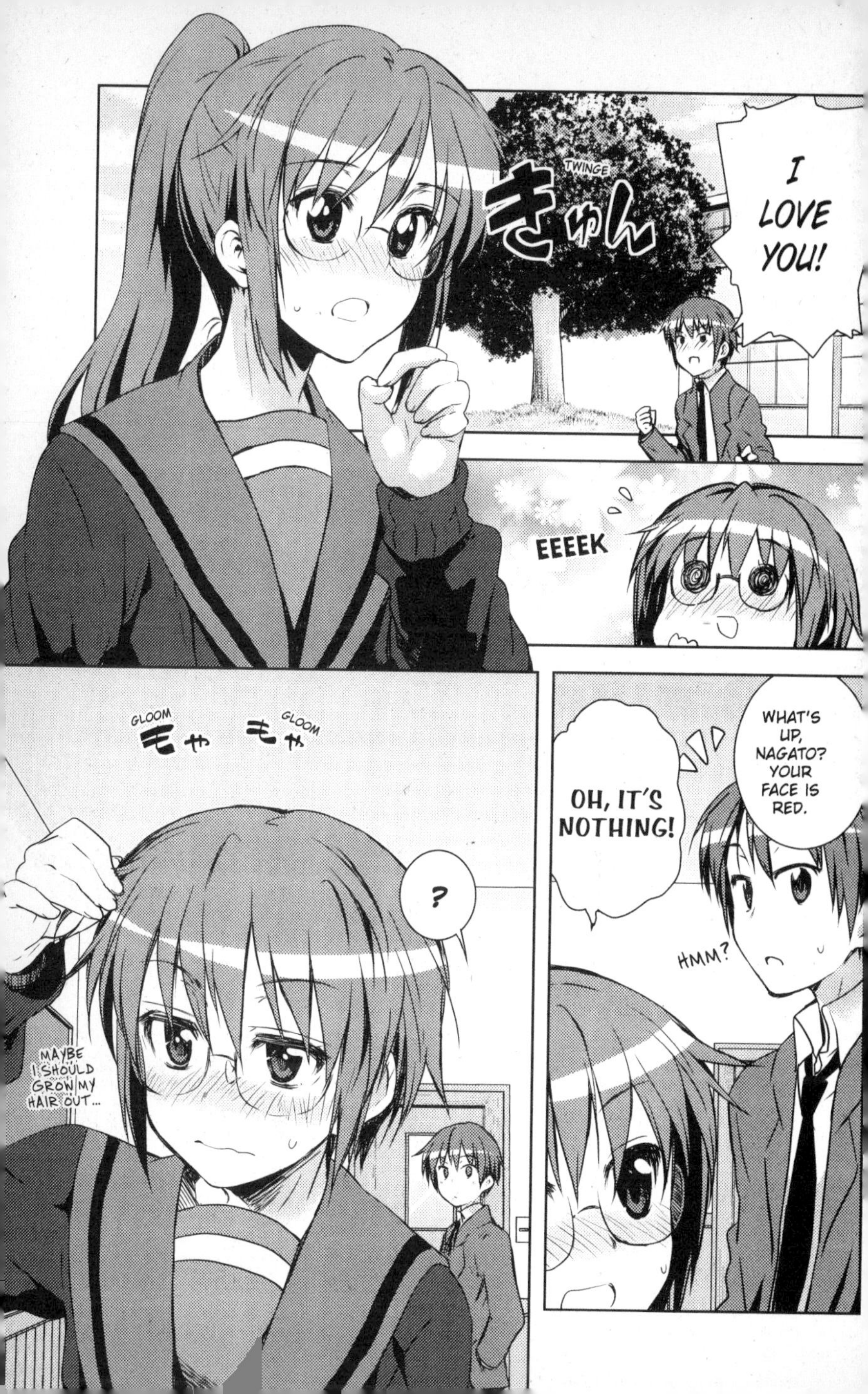
I LOVE YOU!
TWINGE
きゅん
EEEEK
WHAT'S UP, NAGATO? YOUR FACE IS RED.
OH, IT'S NOTHING!
HMM?
GLOOM
もや
GLOOM
もや
?
MAYBE I SHOULD GROW MY HAIR OUT...

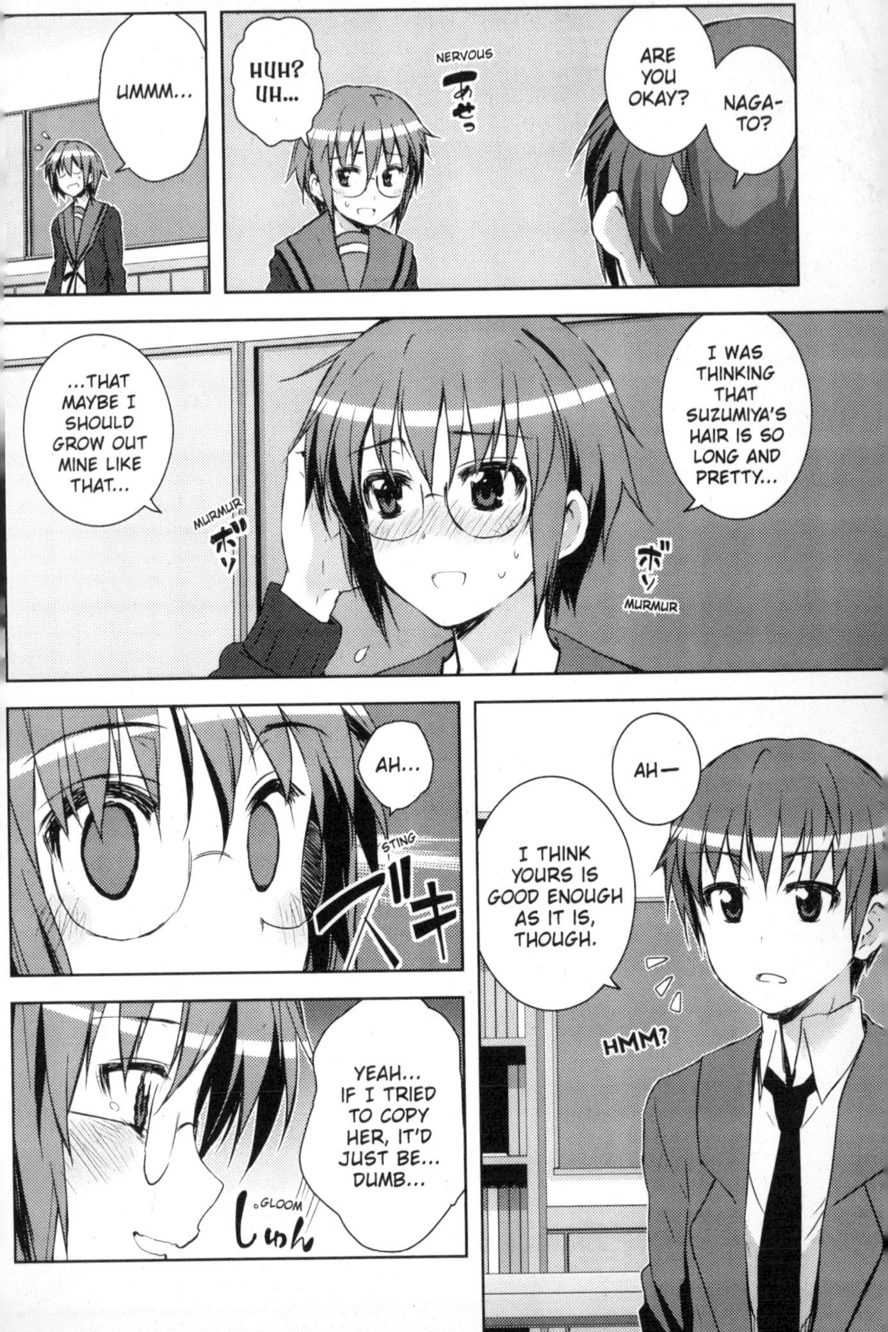
NAGA-TO?
ARE YOU OKAY?
NERVOUS
あせっ
HUH? UH...
UMMM...
I WAS THINKING THAT SUZUMIYA'S HAIR IS SO LONG AND PRETTY...
ボソ
MURMUR
...THAT MAYBE I SHOULD GROW OUT MINE LIKE THAT...
MURMUR
ボソ
AH—
I THINK YOURS IS GOOD ENOUGH AS IT IS, THOUGH.
HMM?
AH...
STING
ズキ
YEAH... IF I TRIED TO COPY HER, IT'D JUST BE... DUMB...
GLOOM
しゅん

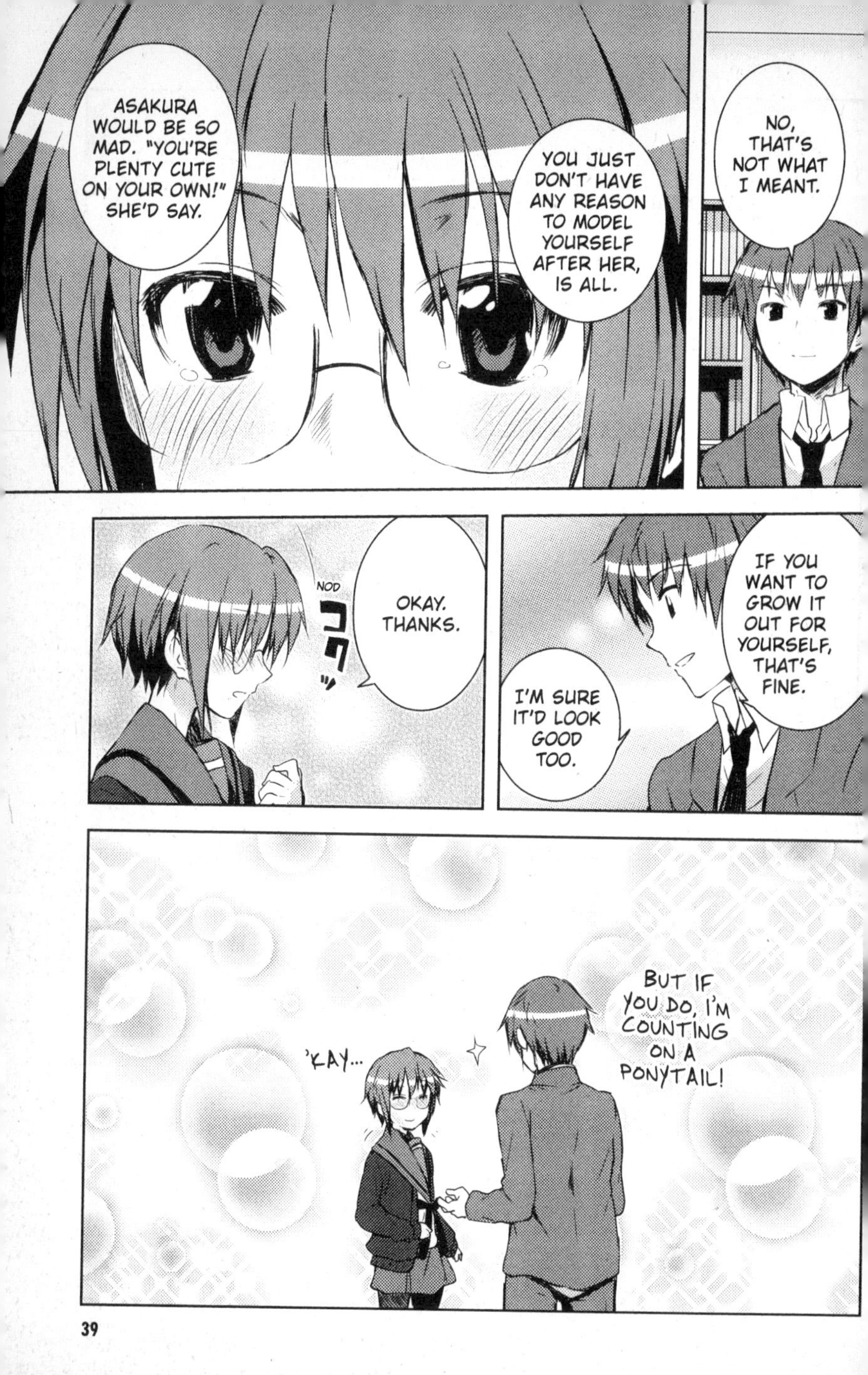
NO, THAT'S NOT WHAT I MEANT.
YOU JUST DON'T HAVE ANY REASON TO MODEL YOURSELF AFTER HER, IS ALL.
ASAKURA WOULD BE SO MAD. "YOU'RE PLENTY CUTE ON YOUR OWN!" SHE'D SAY.
IF YOU WANT TO GROW IT OUT FOR YOURSELF, THAT'S FINE.
I'M SURE IT'D LOOK GOOD TOO.
OKAY. THANKS.
NOD
コクッ
BUT IF YOU DO, I'M COUNTING ON A PONYTAIL!
'KAY...

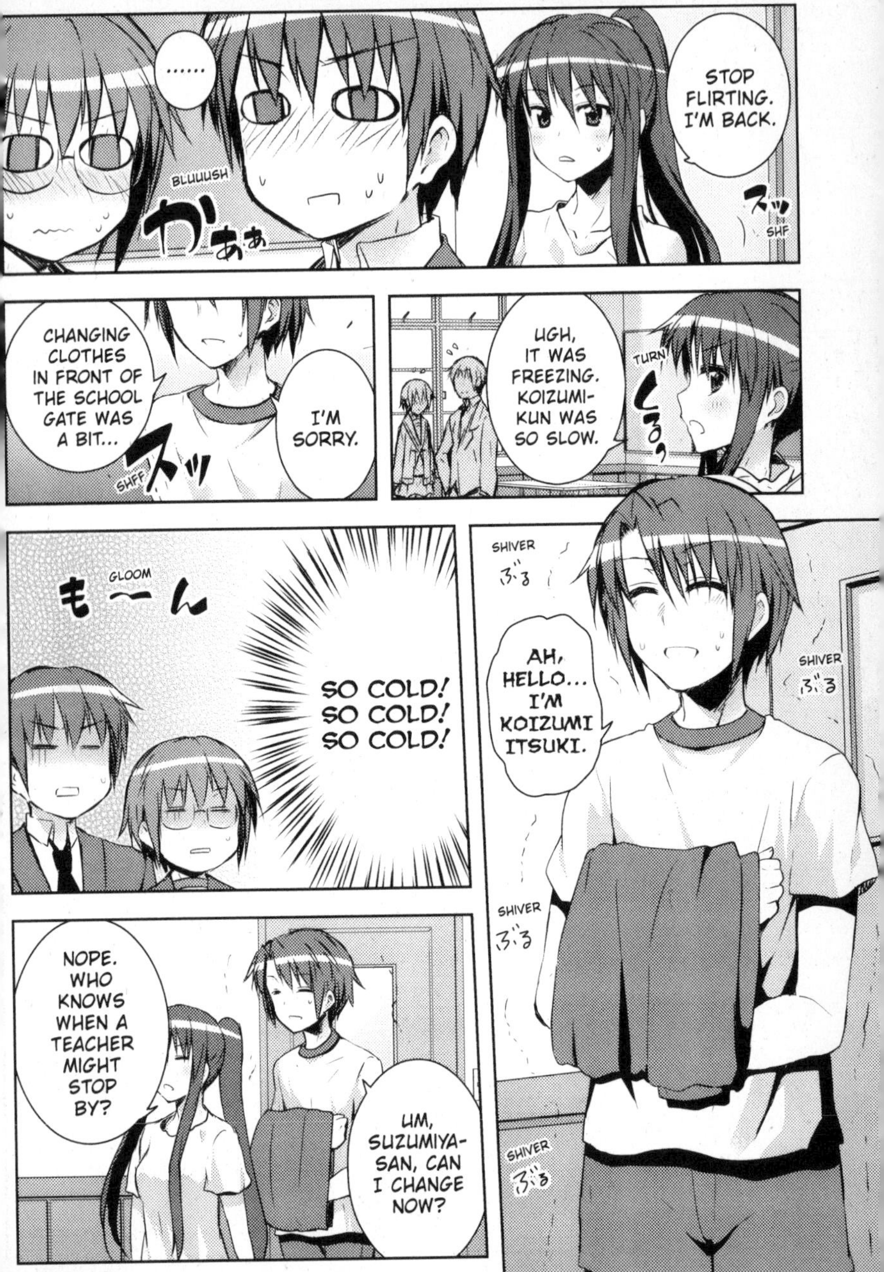
STOP FLIRTING. I'M BACK.
スッ
SHF
……
BLUUUSH
わぁぁ
TURN
くるっ
UGH, IT WAS FREEZING. KOIZUMI-KUN WAS SO SLOW.
I'M SORRY.
CHANGING CLOTHES IN FRONT OF THE SCHOOL GATE WAS A BIT...
SHFF
スッ
SHIVER
ぶる
AH, HELLO... I'M KOIZUMI ITSUKI.
SHIVER
ぶる
SHIVER
ぶる
SHIVER
ぶる
GLOOM
も～ん
SO COLD! SO COLD! SO COLD!
UM, SUZUMIYA-SAN, CAN I CHANGE NOW?
NOPE. WHO KNOWS WHEN A TEACHER MIGHT STOP BY?

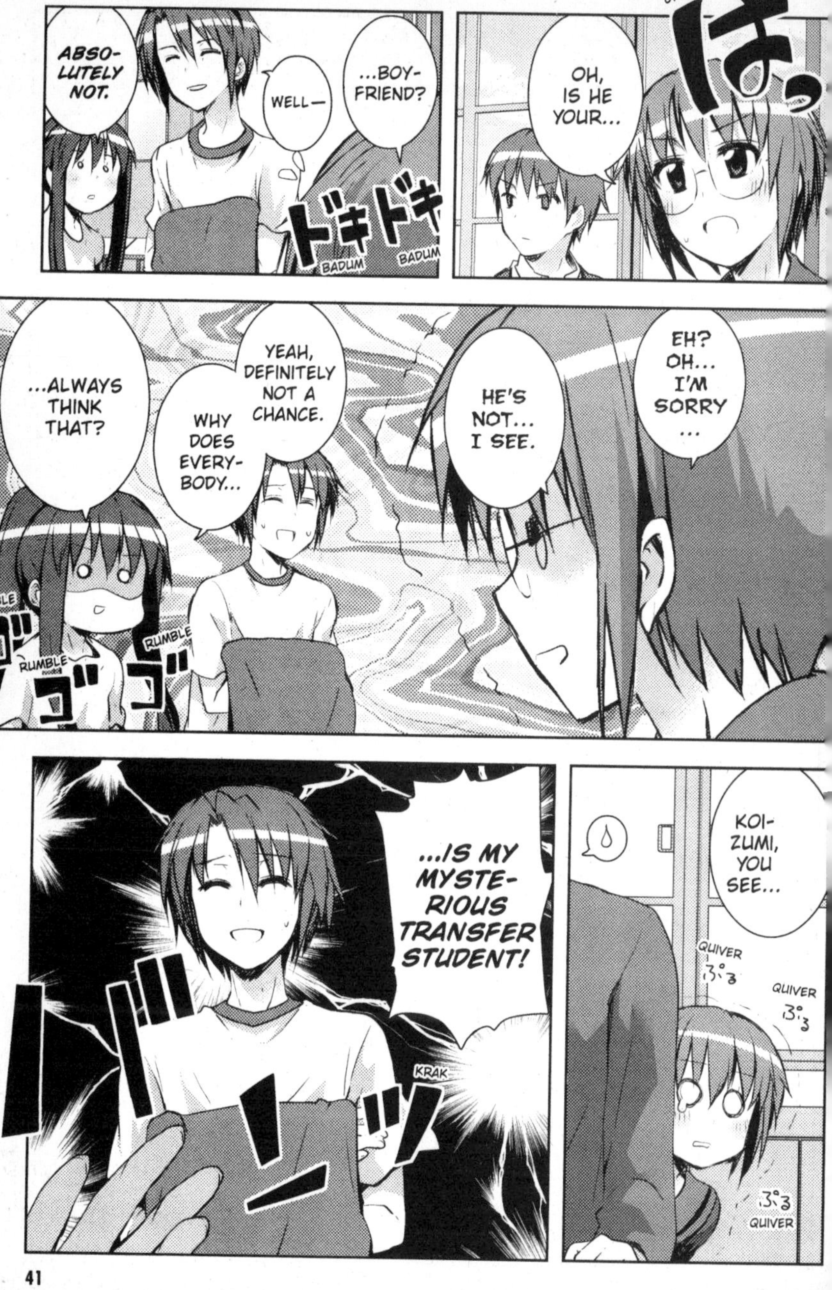
GASP
はっ
OH, IS HE YOUR...
...BOY-FRIEND?
WELL—
ABSO-LUTELY NOT.
ドキドキ
BADUM BADUM
EH? OH... I'M SORRY...
HE'S NOT... I SEE.
YEAH, DEFINITELY NOT A CHANCE.
WHY DOES EVERY-BODY...
...ALWAYS THINK THAT?
ゴゴゴ
RUMBLE RUMBLE RUMBLE
KOI-ZUMI, YOU SEE...
ぷる ぷる ぷる
QUIVER QUIVER QUIVER
...IS MY MYSTE-RIOUS TRANSFER STUDENT!
ドドン
KRAK

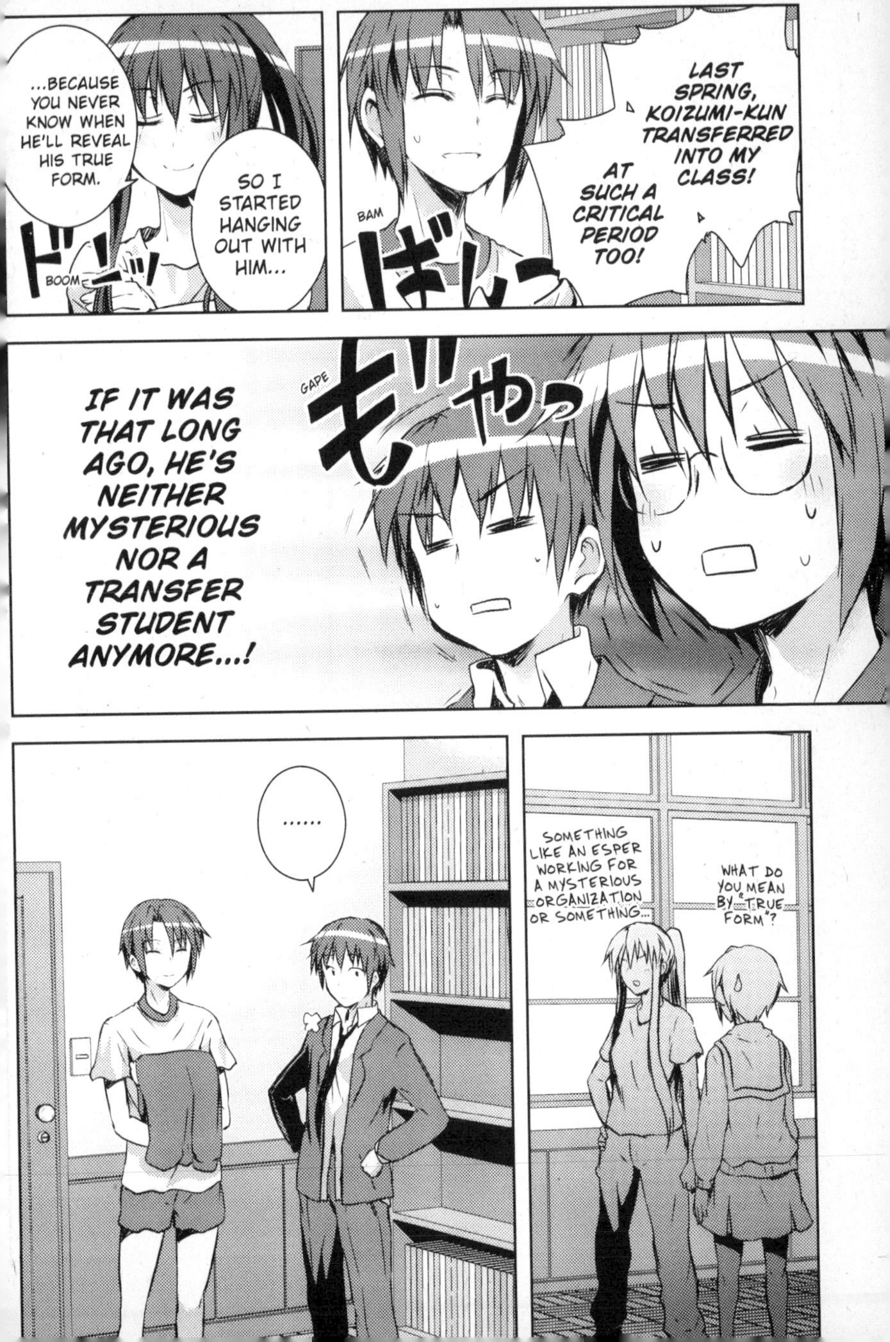
LAST SPRING, KOIZUMI-KUN TRANSFERRED INTO MY CLASS!
AT SUCH A CRITICAL PERIOD TOO!
ぎんっ
BAM
SO I STARTED HANGING OUT WITH HIM...
...BECAUSE YOU NEVER KNOW WHEN HE'LL REVEAL HIS TRUE FORM.
ドドンッ
BOOM
もやっ
GAPE
IF IT WAS THAT LONG AGO, HE'S NEITHER MYSTERIOUS NOR A TRANSFER STUDENT ANYMORE...!
WHAT DO YOU MEAN BY "TRUE FORM"?
SOMETHING LIKE AN ESPER WORKING FOR A MYSTERIOUS ORGANIZATION OR SOMETHING...
......

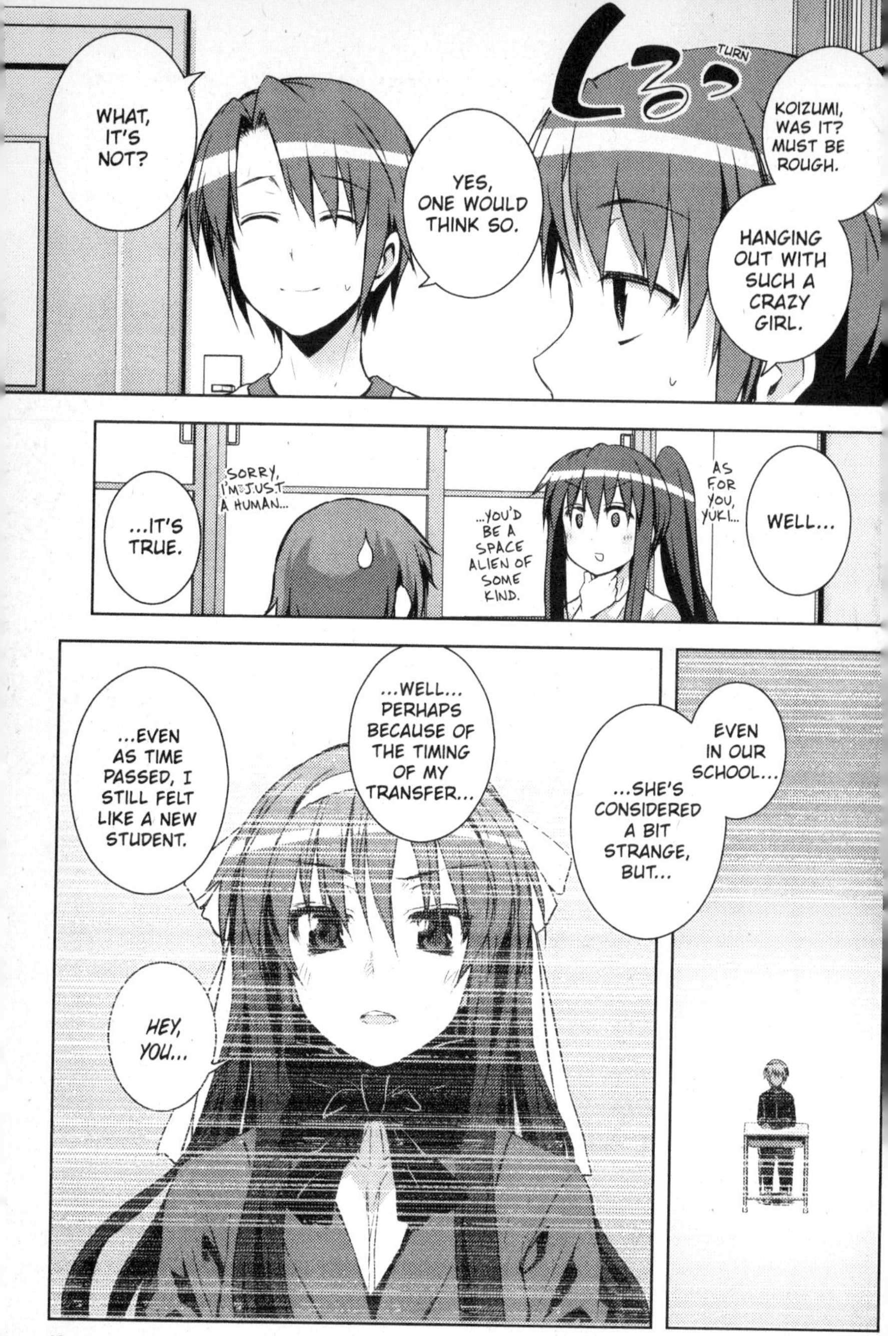

くるっ
TURN
KOIZUMI, WAS IT? MUST BE ROUGH.
HANGING OUT WITH SUCH A CRAZY GIRL.
YES, ONE WOULD THINK SO.
WHAT, IT'S NOT?
WELL...
AS FOR YOU, YUKI...
...YOU'D BE A SPACE ALIEN OF SOME KIND.
SORRY, I'M JUST A HUMAN...
...IT'S TRUE.
EVEN IN OUR SCHOOL...
...SHE'S CONSIDERED A BIT STRANGE, BUT...
...WELL... PERHAPS BECAUSE OF THE TIMING OF MY TRANSFER...
...EVEN AS TIME PASSED, I STILL FELT LIKE A NEW STUDENT.
HEY, YOU...

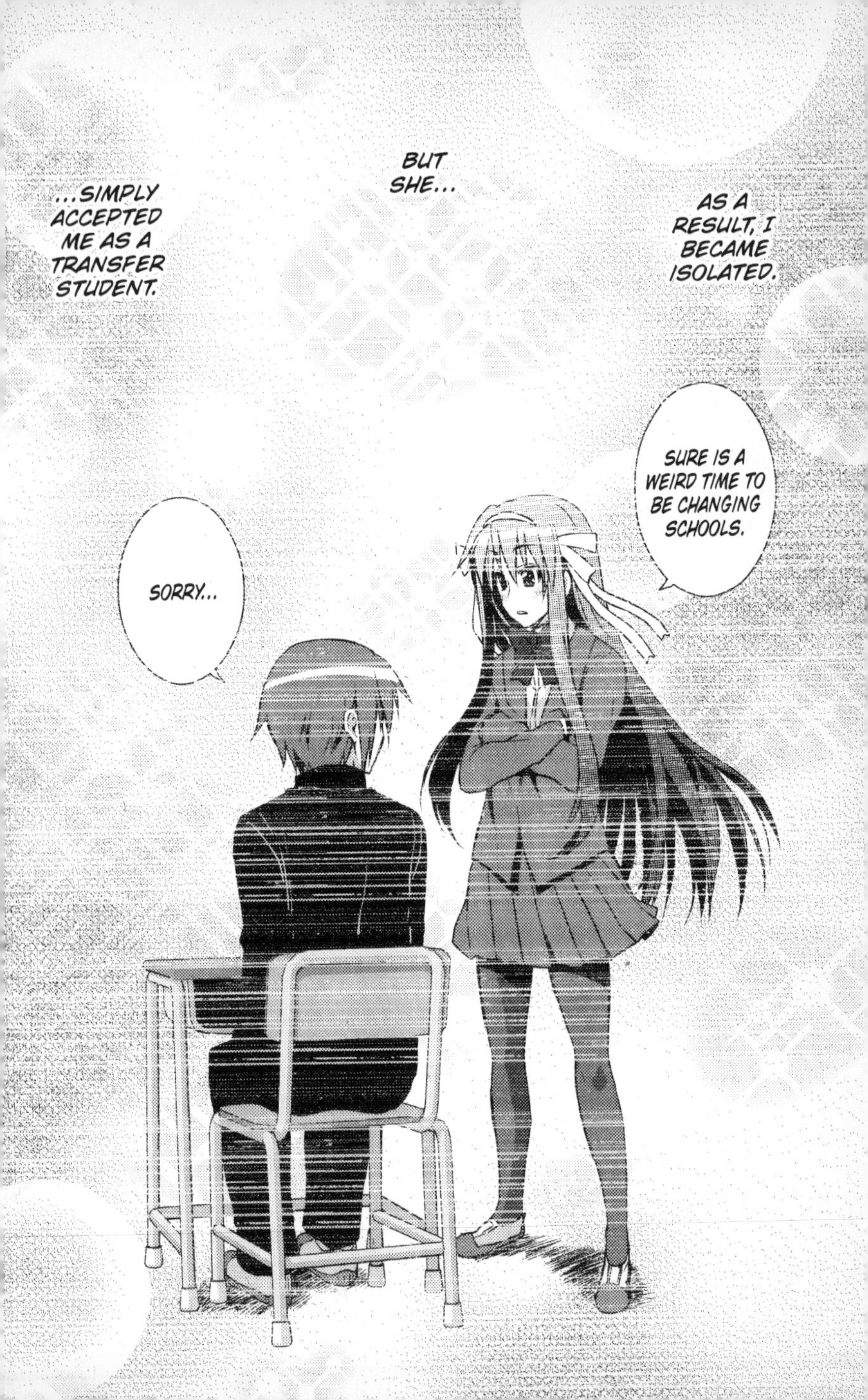
AS A RESULT, I BECAME ISOLATED.
BUT SHE...
...SIMPLY ACCEPTED ME AS A TRANSFER STUDENT.
SURE IS A WEIRD TIME TO BE CHANGING SCHOOLS.
SORRY...

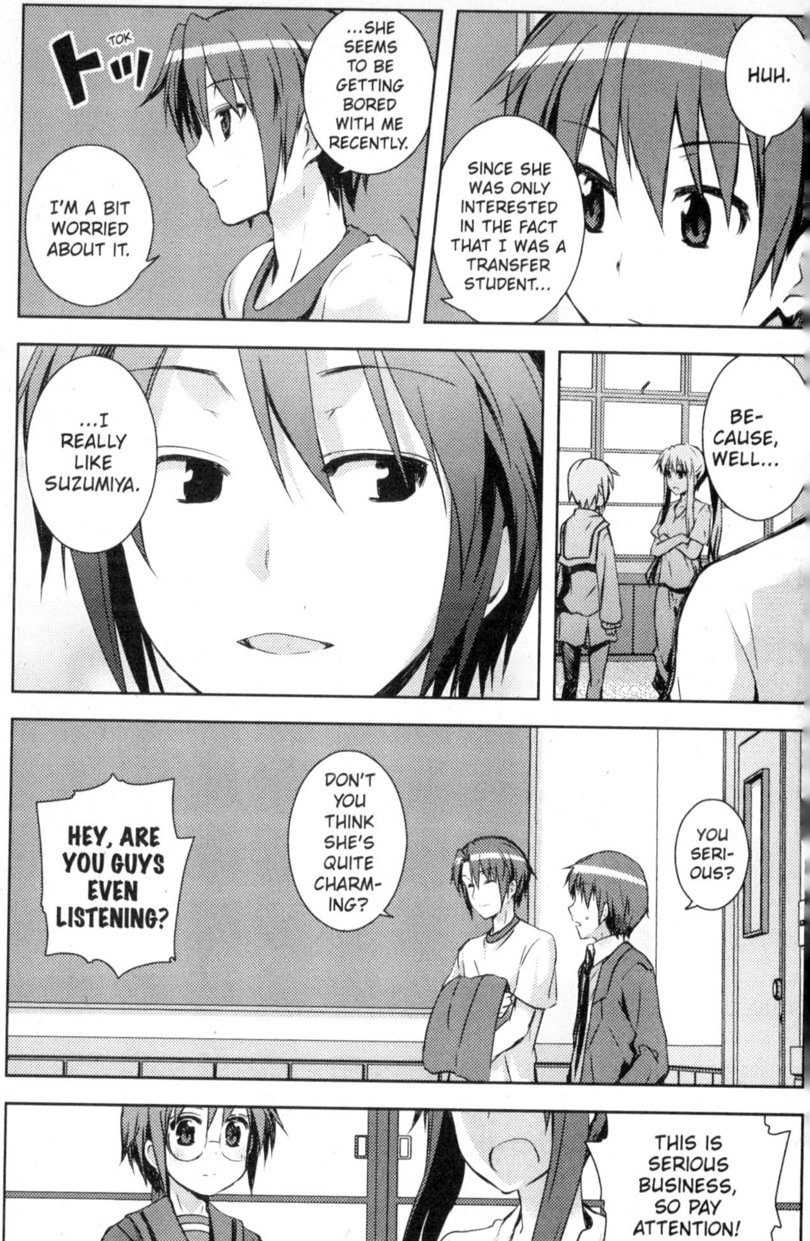
HUH.
SINCE SHE WAS ONLY INTERESTED IN THE FACT THAT I WAS A TRANSFER STUDENT...
TOK
...SHE SEEMS TO BE GETTING BORED WITH ME RECENTLY.
I'M A BIT WORRIED ABOUT IT.
BE-CAUSE, WELL...
...I REALLY LIKE SUZUMIYA.
YOU SERI-OUS?
DON'T YOU THINK SHE'S QUITE CHARM-ING?
HEY, ARE YOU GUYS EVEN LISTENING?
THIS IS SERIOUS BUSINESS, SO PAY ATTENTION!

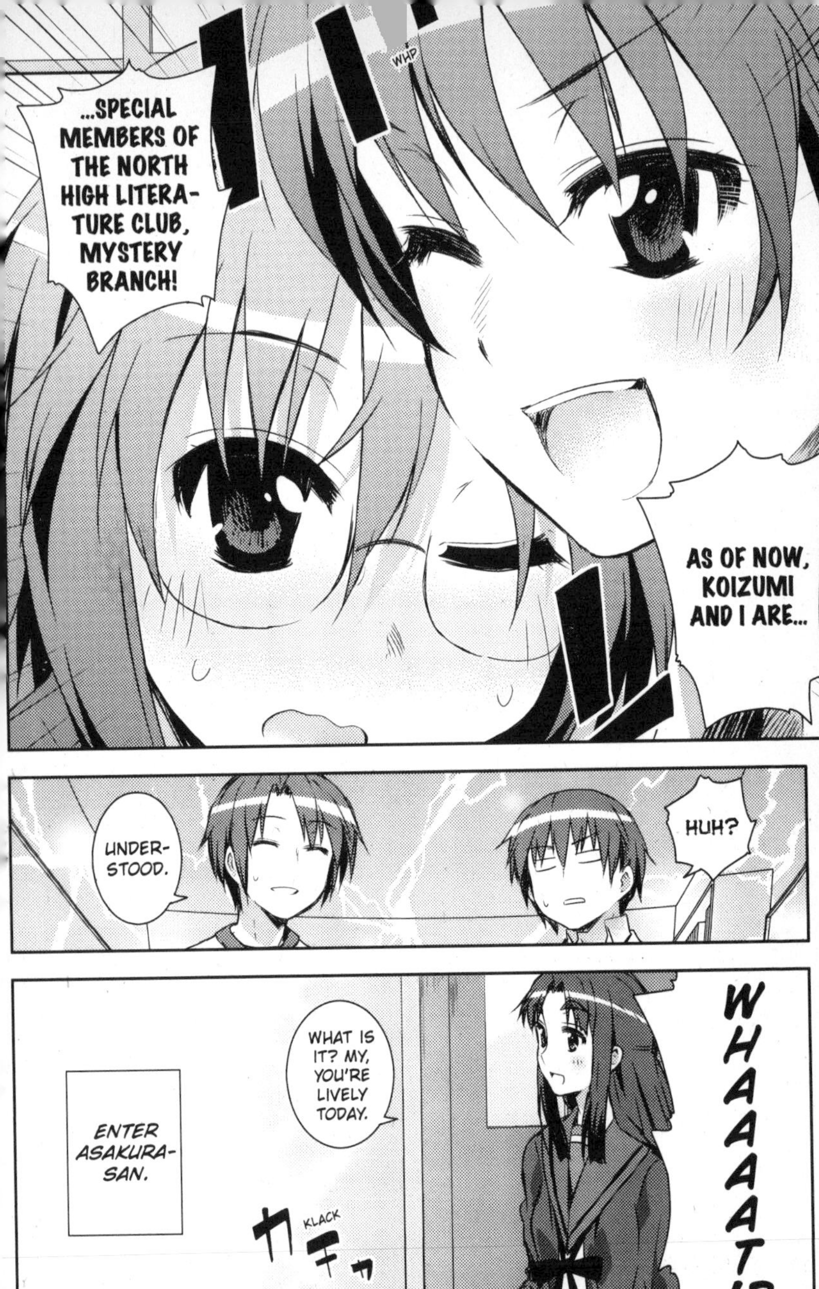
WHP
AS OF NOW, KOIZUMI AND I ARE...
...SPECIAL MEMBERS OF THE NORTH HIGH LITERATURE CLUB, MYSTERY BRANCH!
HUH?
UNDERSTOOD.
WHAAAAAT!?
WHAT IS IT? MY, YOU'RE LIVELY TODAY.
KLACK
ENTER ASAKURA-SAN.

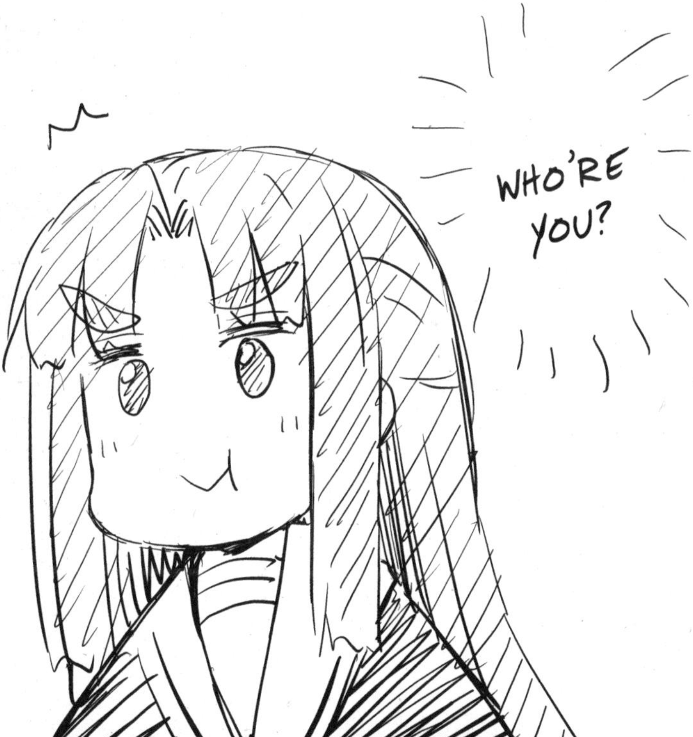
WHO'RE YOU?

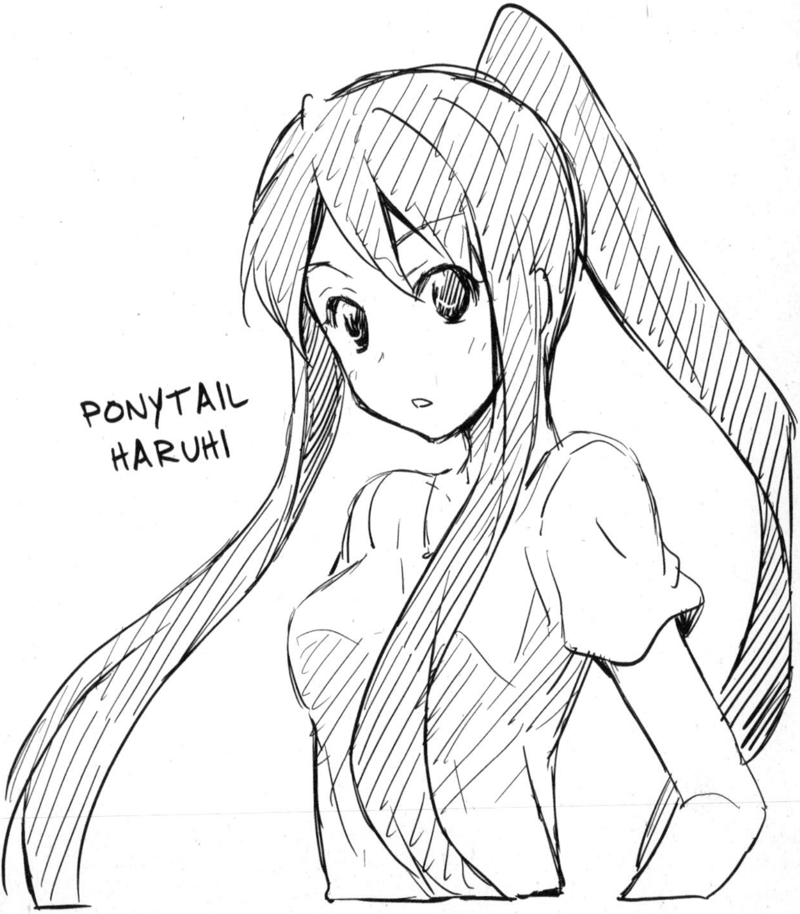
PONYTAIL
HARUHI

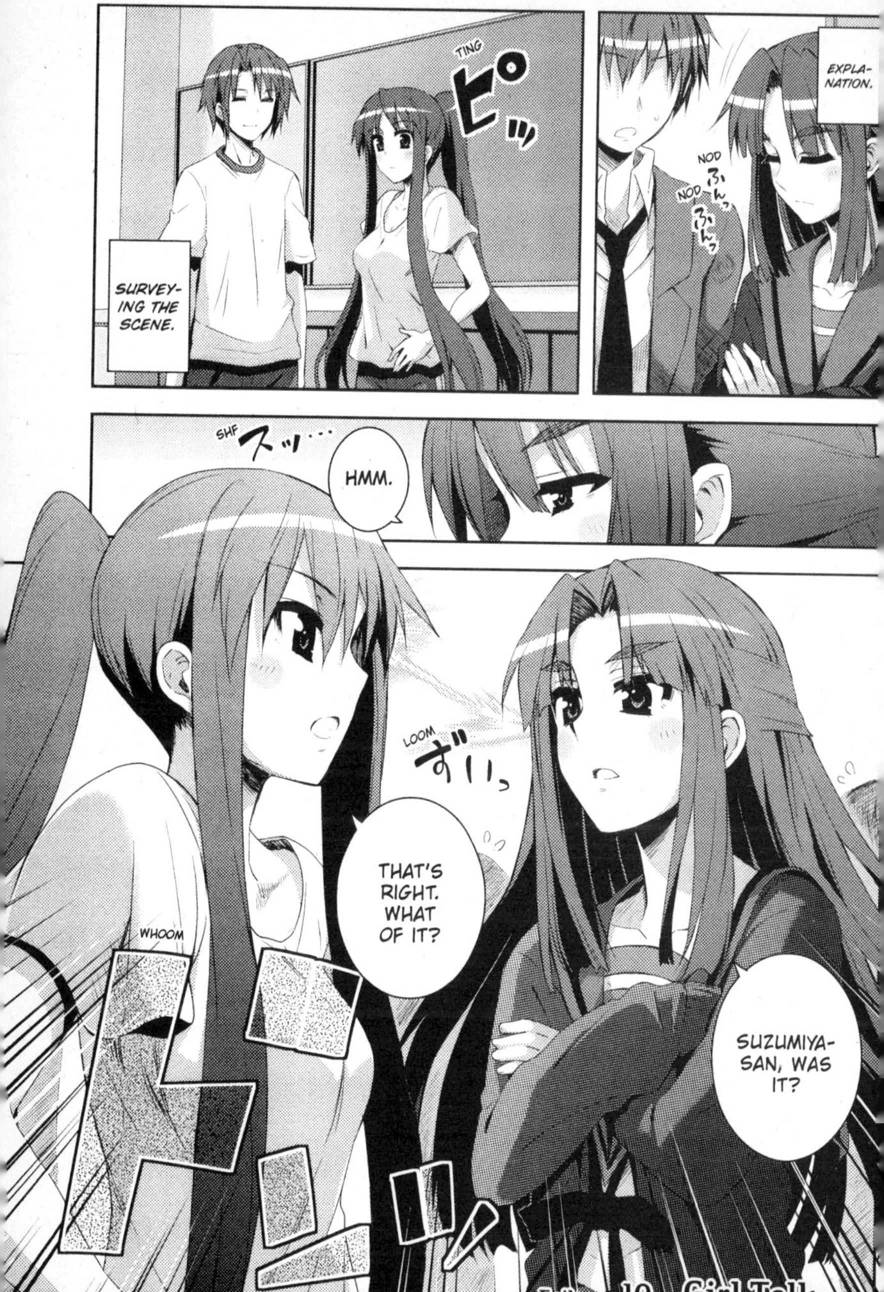
EXPLA-NATION.
NOD ふんっ
NOD ふんっ
TING ピッ
SURVEYING THE SCENE.
SHF スッ…
HMM.
SUZUMIYA-SAN, WAS IT?
LOOM ずいっ
THAT'S RIGHT. WHAT OF IT?
WHOOM

Epilogue 10>> Girl Talk

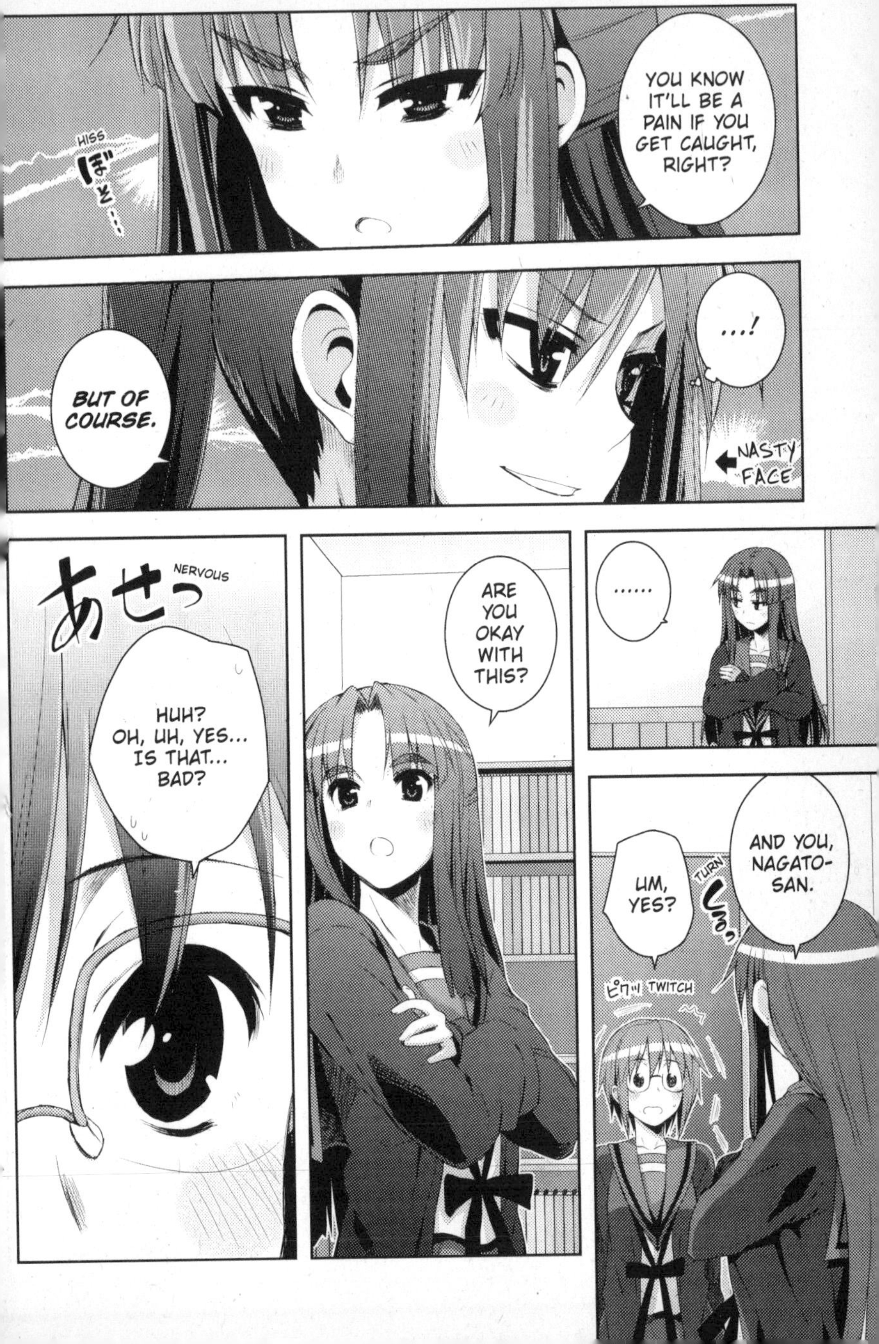
YOU KNOW IT'LL BE A PAIN IF YOU GET CAUGHT, RIGHT?
HISS ぼそ…
…!
NASTY FACE
BUT OF COURSE.
……
AND YOU, NAGATO-SAN.
TURN
UM, YES?
ピクッ!! TWITCH
ARE YOU OKAY WITH THIS?
あせっ NERVOUS
HUH? OH, UH, YES… IS THAT… BAD?

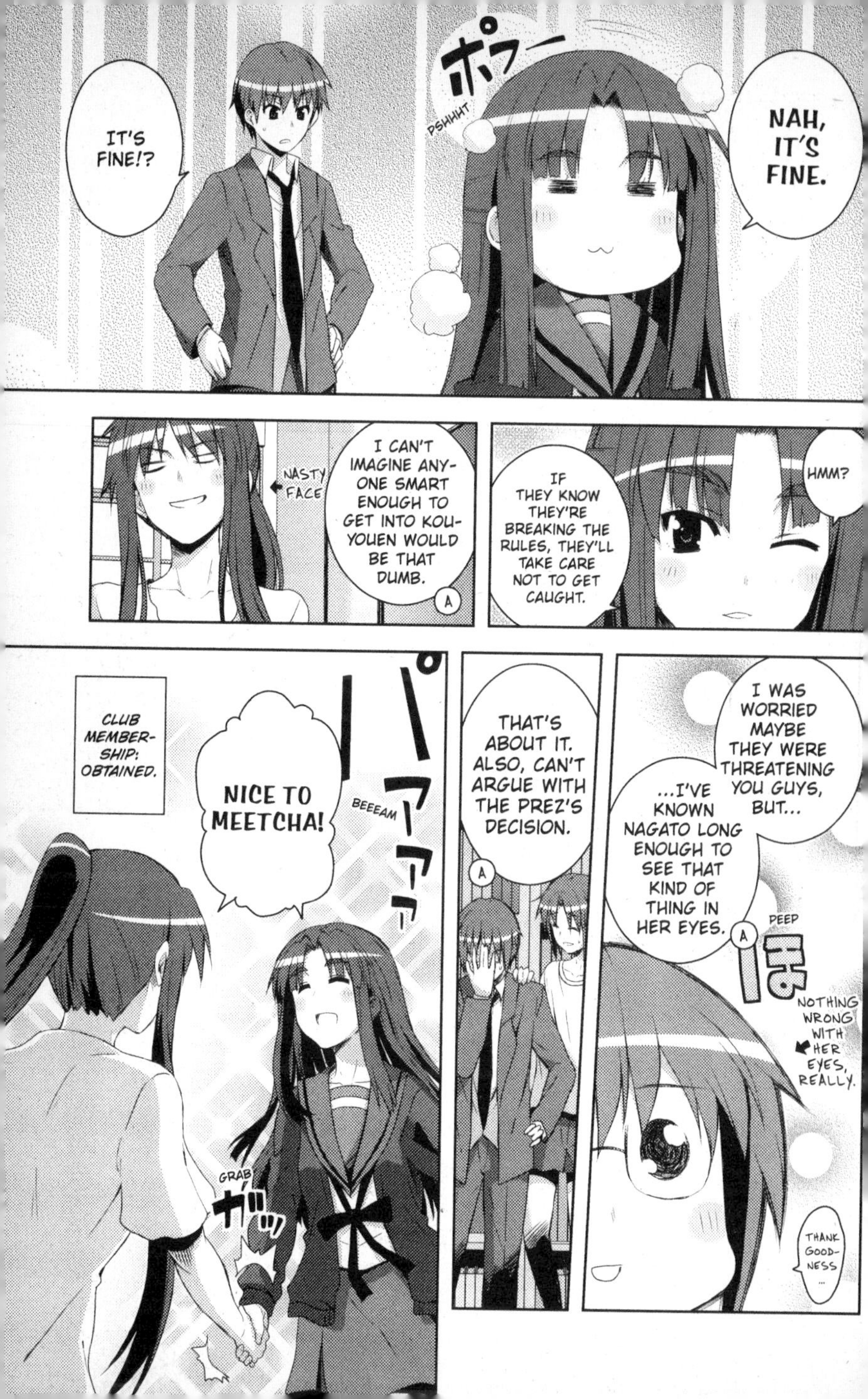
PSHHHT
NAH, IT'S FINE.
IT'S FINE!?
HMM?
IF THEY KNOW THEY'RE BREAKING THE RULES, THEY'LL TAKE CARE NOT TO GET CAUGHT.
I CAN'T IMAGINE ANYONE SMART ENOUGH TO GET INTO KOUYOUEN WOULD BE THAT DUMB.
A
NASTY FACE
I WAS WORRIED MAYBE THEY WERE THREATENING YOU GUYS, BUT...
...I'VE KNOWN NAGATO LONG ENOUGH TO SEE THAT KIND OF THING IN HER EYES.
A
PEEP
NOTHING WRONG WITH HER EYES, REALLY.
THANK GOODNESS...
THAT'S ABOUT IT. ALSO, CAN'T ARGUE WITH THE PREZ'S DECISION.
A
BEEEAM
NICE TO MEETCHA!
CLUB MEMBERSHIP: OBTAINED.
GRAB

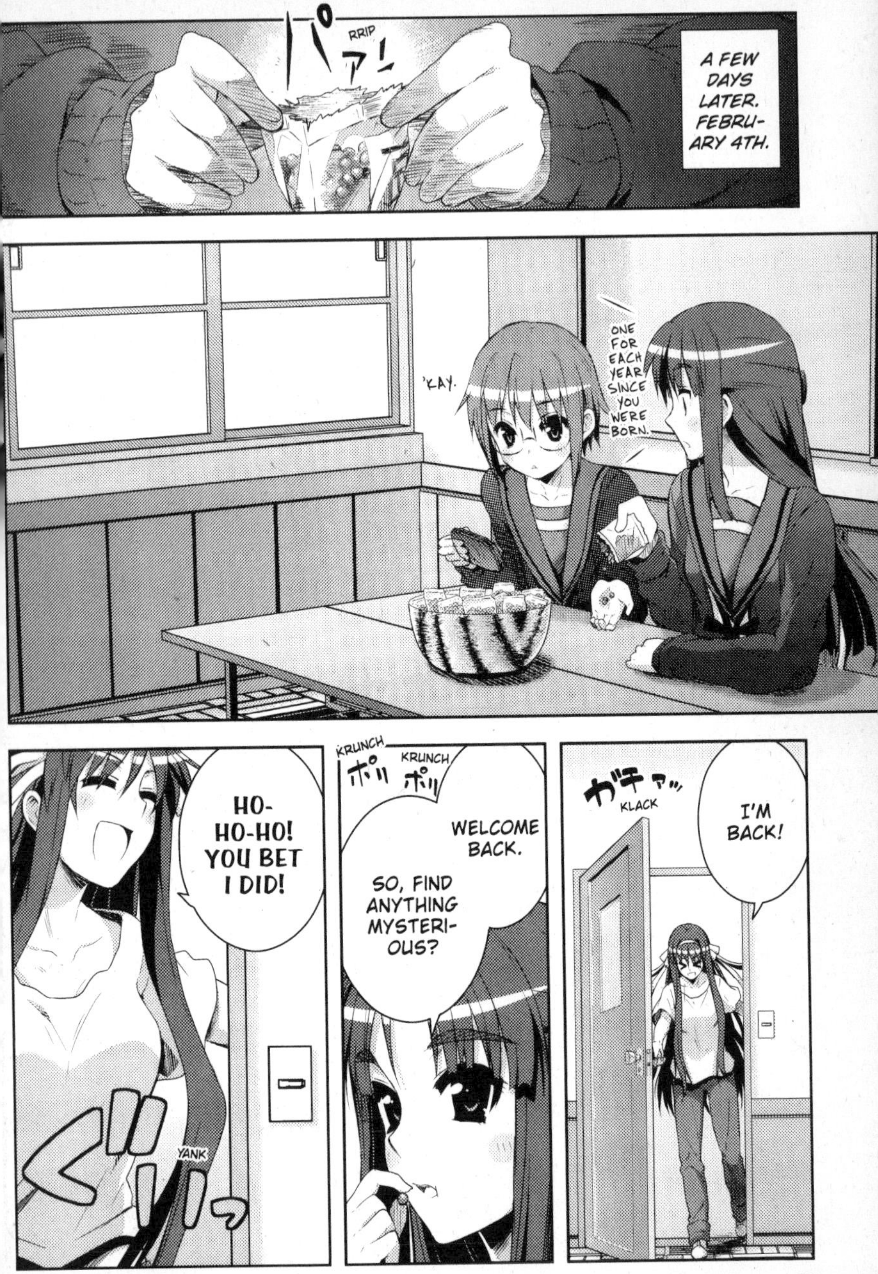
A FEW DAYS LATER. FEBRUARY 4TH.
RRIP
ONE FOR EACH YEAR SINCE YOU WERE BORN.
'KAY.
KLACK
I'M BACK!
KRUNCH
KRUNCH
WELCOME BACK.
SO, FIND ANYTHING MYSTERIOUS?
HO-HO-HO! YOU BET I DID!
YANK

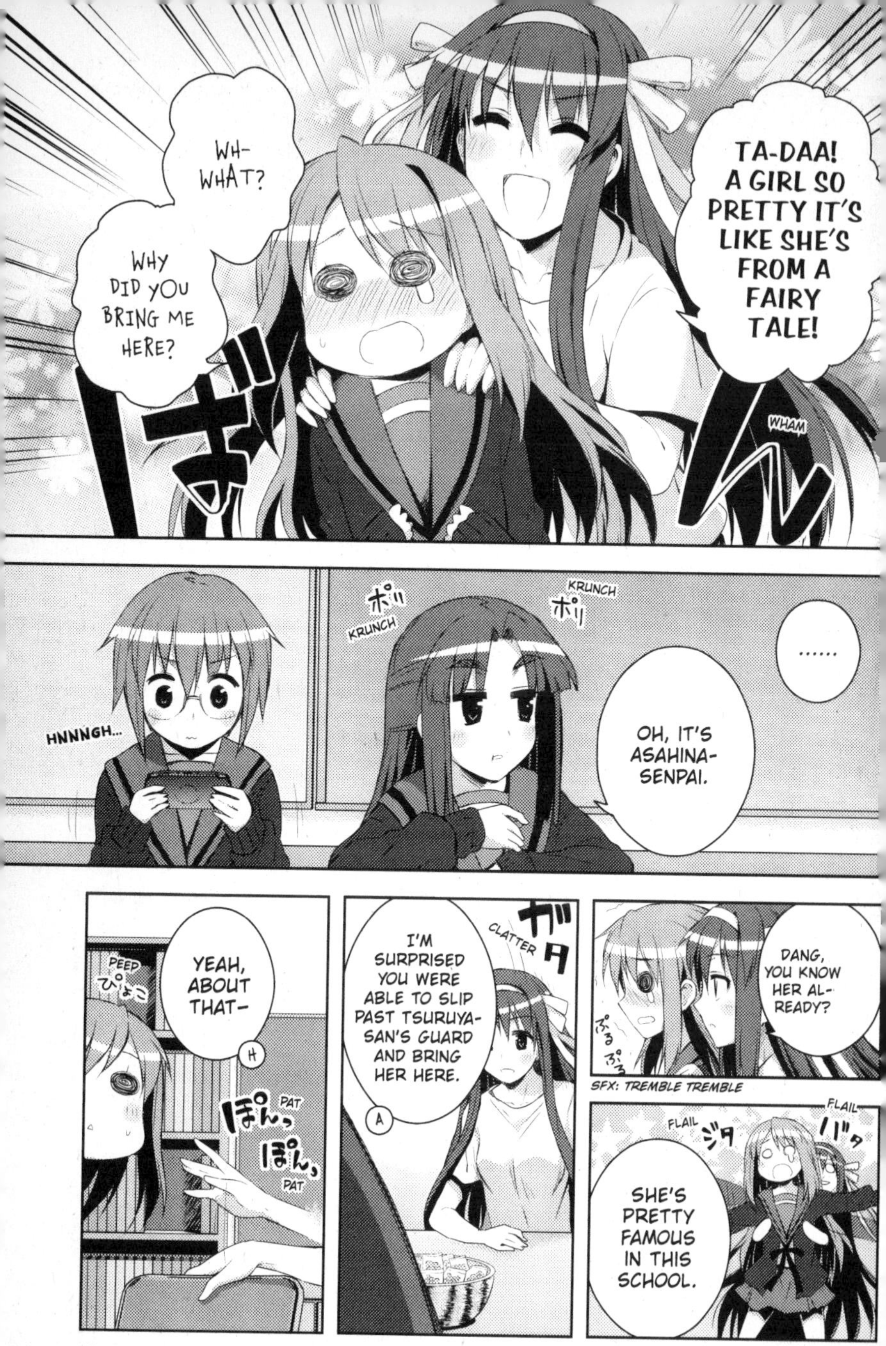
TA-DAA! A GIRL SO PRETTY IT'S LIKE SHE'S FROM A FAIRY TALE!
WHAM
WH- WHAT?
WHY DID YOU BRING ME HERE?
......
OH, IT'S ASAHINA-SENPAI.
KRUNCH
ポリ
KRUNCH
ポリ
HNNNGH...
DANG, YOU KNOW HER AL- READY?
SFX: TREMBLE TREMBLE
FLAIL
FLAIL
SHE'S PRETTY FAMOUS IN THIS SCHOOL.
ガタ
CLATTER
I'M SURPRISED YOU WERE ABLE TO SLIP PAST TSURUYA-SAN'S GUARD AND BRING HER HERE.
YEAH, ABOUT THAT—
PEEP
ぴょこ
PAT
PAT

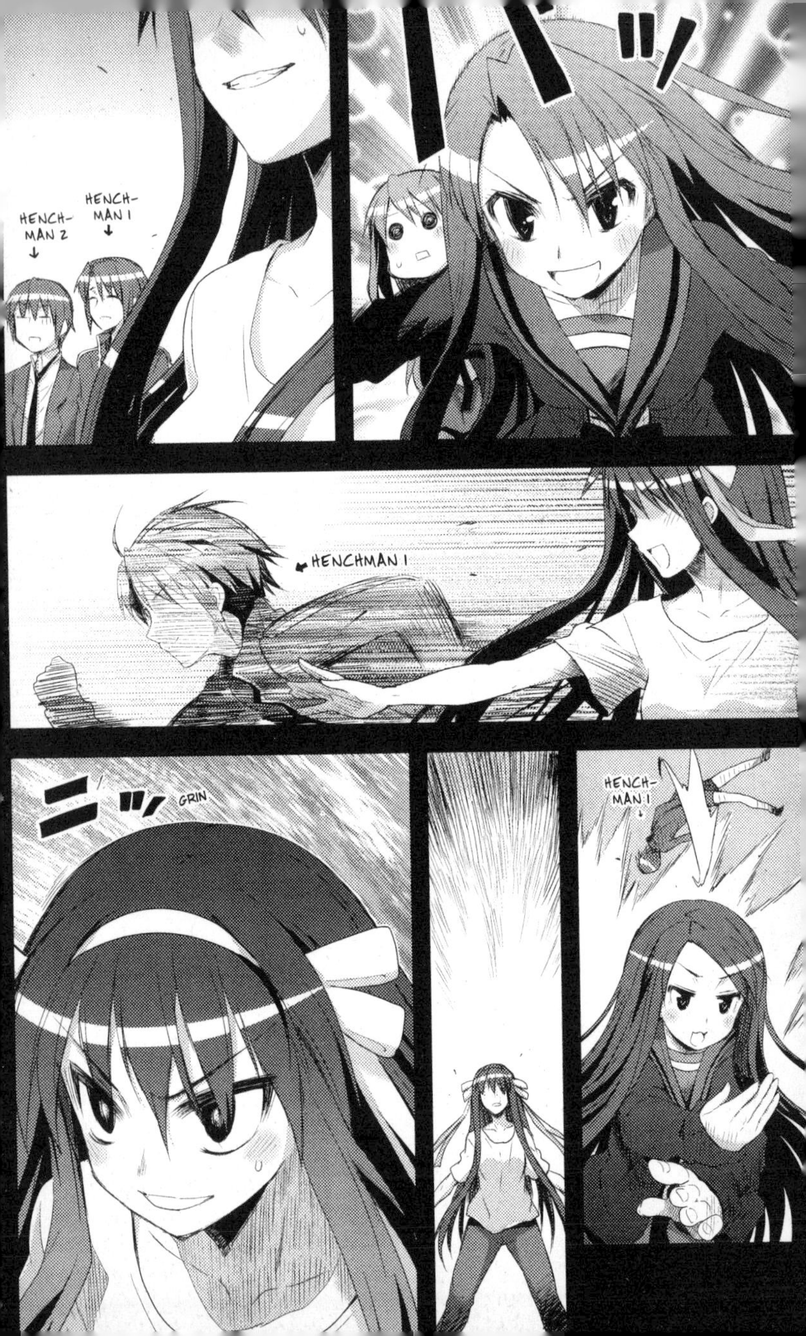
HENCH-MAN 1
HENCH-MAN 2
HENCHMAN 1
HENCH-MAN 1
GRIN

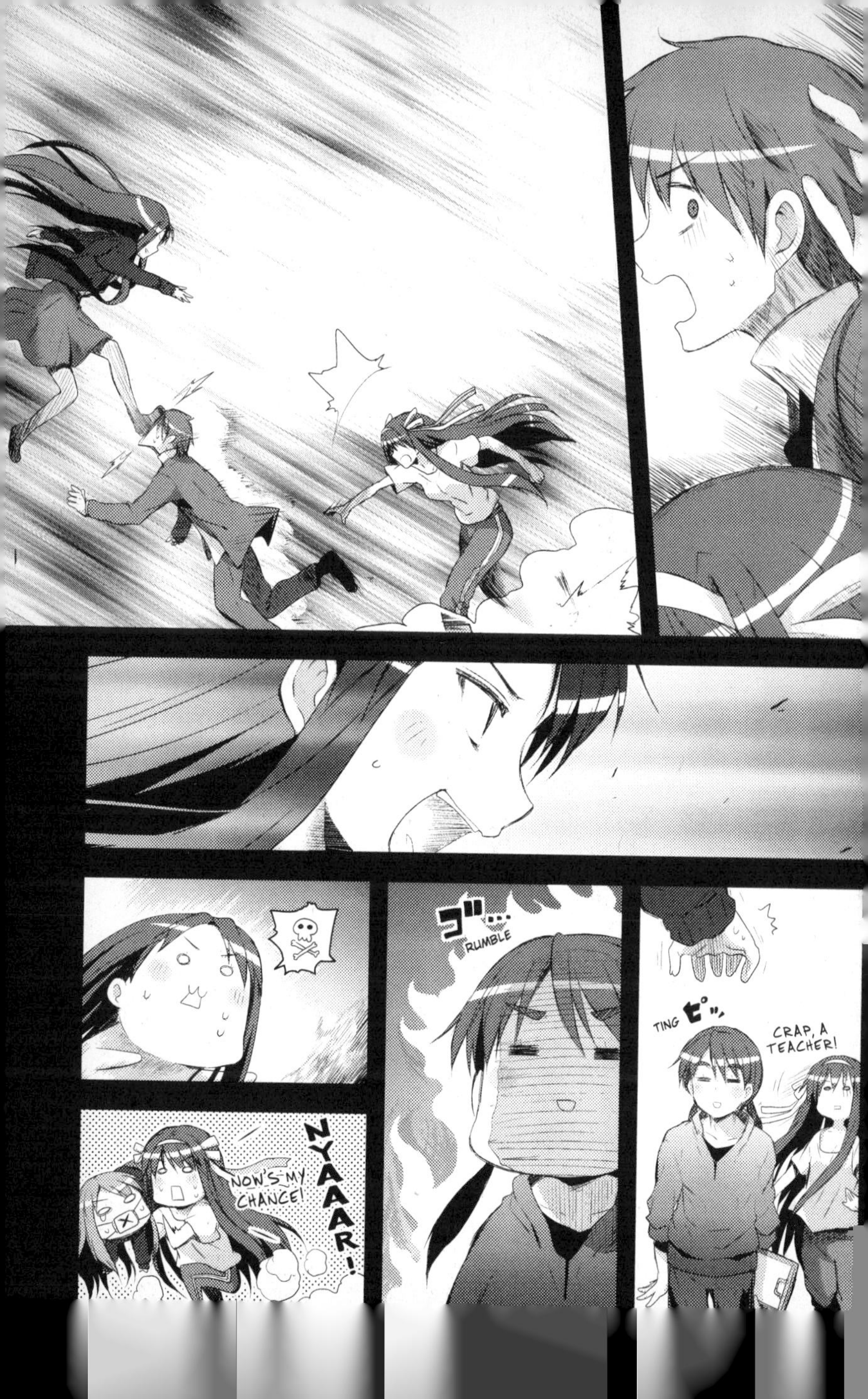
TING
CRAP, A TEACHER!
RUMBLE
NOW'S MY CHANCE!
NYAAAR!

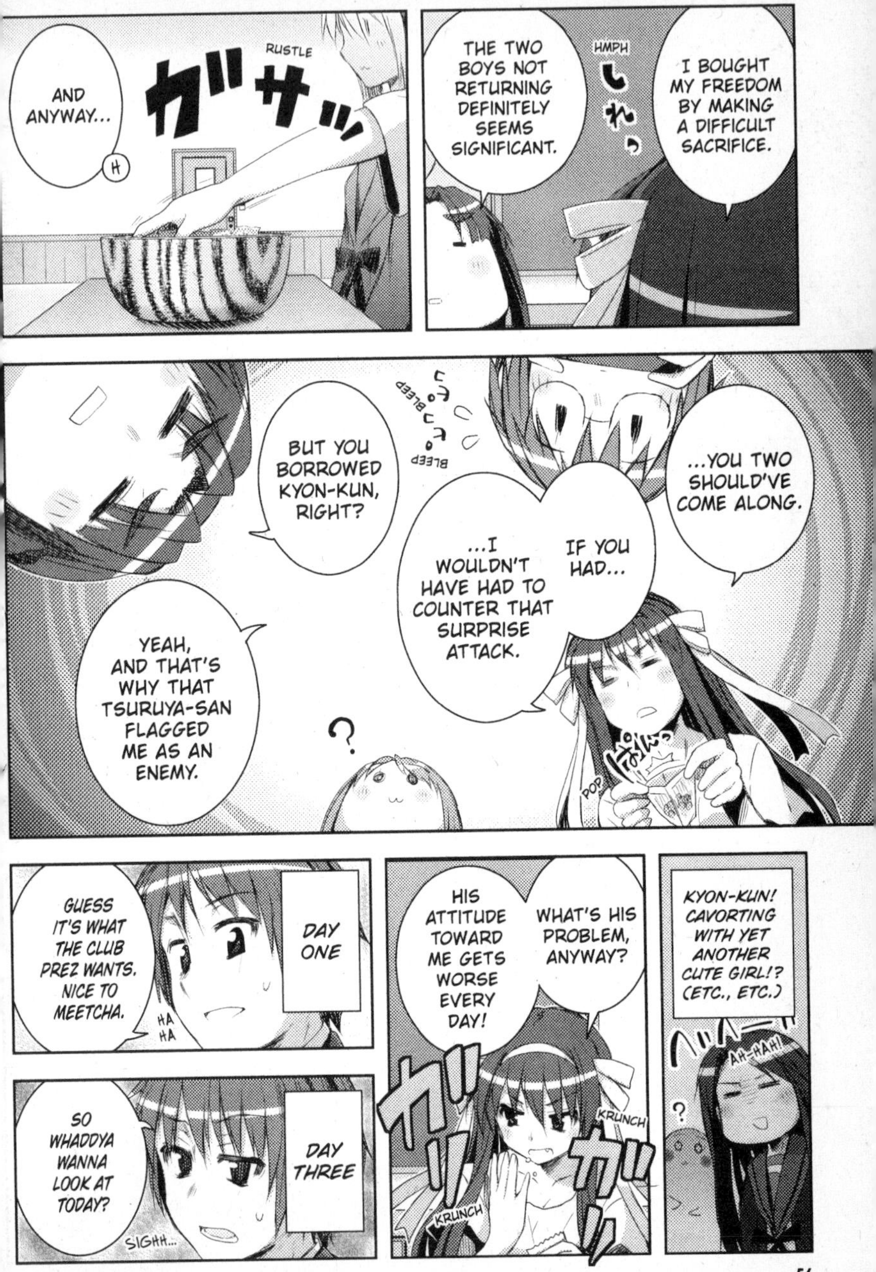
I BOUGHT MY FREEDOM BY MAKING A DIFFICULT SACRIFICE.
HMPH
THE TWO BOYS NOT RETURNING DEFINITELY SEEMS SIGNIFICANT.
RUSTLE
AND ANYWAY...
H
...YOU TWO SHOULD'VE COME ALONG.
IF YOU HAD...
...I WOULDN'T HAVE HAD TO COUNTER THAT SURPRISE ATTACK.
POP
BLEEP
BLEEP
BUT YOU BORROWED KYON-KUN, RIGHT?
?
YEAH, AND THAT'S WHY THAT TSURUYA-SAN FLAGGED ME AS AN ENEMY.
KYON-KUN! CAVORTING WITH YET ANOTHER CUTE GIRL!? (ETC., ETC.)
AH-HAH!
?
WHAT'S HIS PROBLEM, ANYWAY?
HIS ATTITUDE TOWARD ME GETS WORSE EVERY DAY!
KRUNCH
KRUNCH
DAY ONE
GUESS IT'S WHAT THE CLUB PREZ WANTS. NICE TO MEETCHA.
HA HA
DAY THREE
SO WHADDYA WANNA LOOK AT TODAY?
SIGHH...

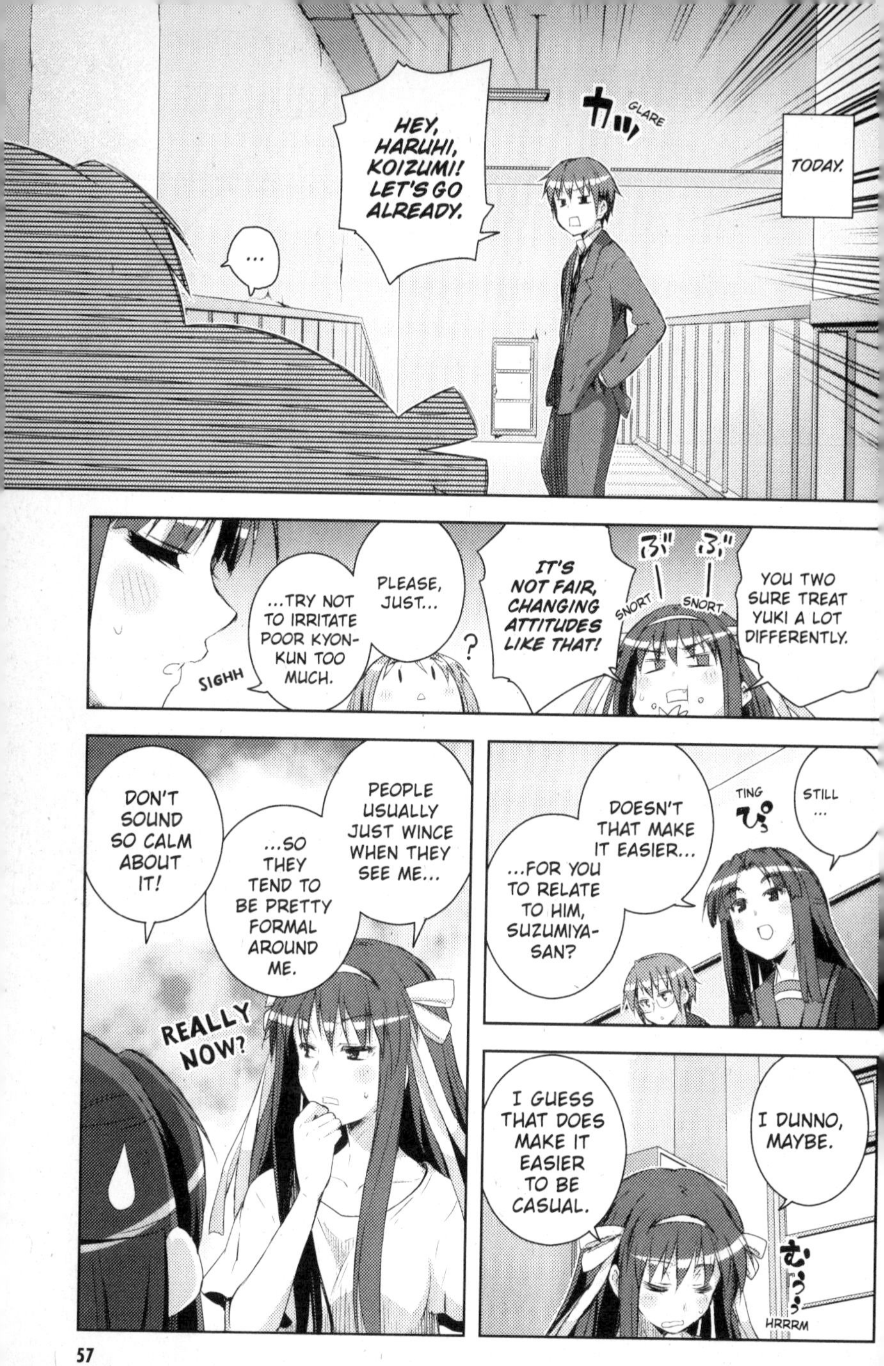
TODAY.
GLARE
HEY, HARUHI, KOIZUMI! LET'S GO ALREADY.
...
YOU TWO SURE TREAT YUKI A LOT DIFFERENTLY.
SNORT
SNORT
IT'S NOT FAIR, CHANGING ATTITUDES LIKE THAT!
?
PLEASE, JUST...
...TRY NOT TO IRRITATE POOR KYON-KUN TOO MUCH.
SIGHH
STILL ...
TING
DOESN'T THAT MAKE IT EASIER...
...FOR YOU TO RELATE TO HIM, SUZUMIYA-SAN?
I DUNNO, MAYBE.
I GUESS THAT DOES MAKE IT EASIER TO BE CASUAL.
HRRRM
PEOPLE USUALLY JUST WINCE WHEN THEY SEE ME...
...SO THEY TEND TO BE PRETTY FORMAL AROUND ME.
DON'T SOUND SO CALM ABOUT IT!
REALLY NOW?

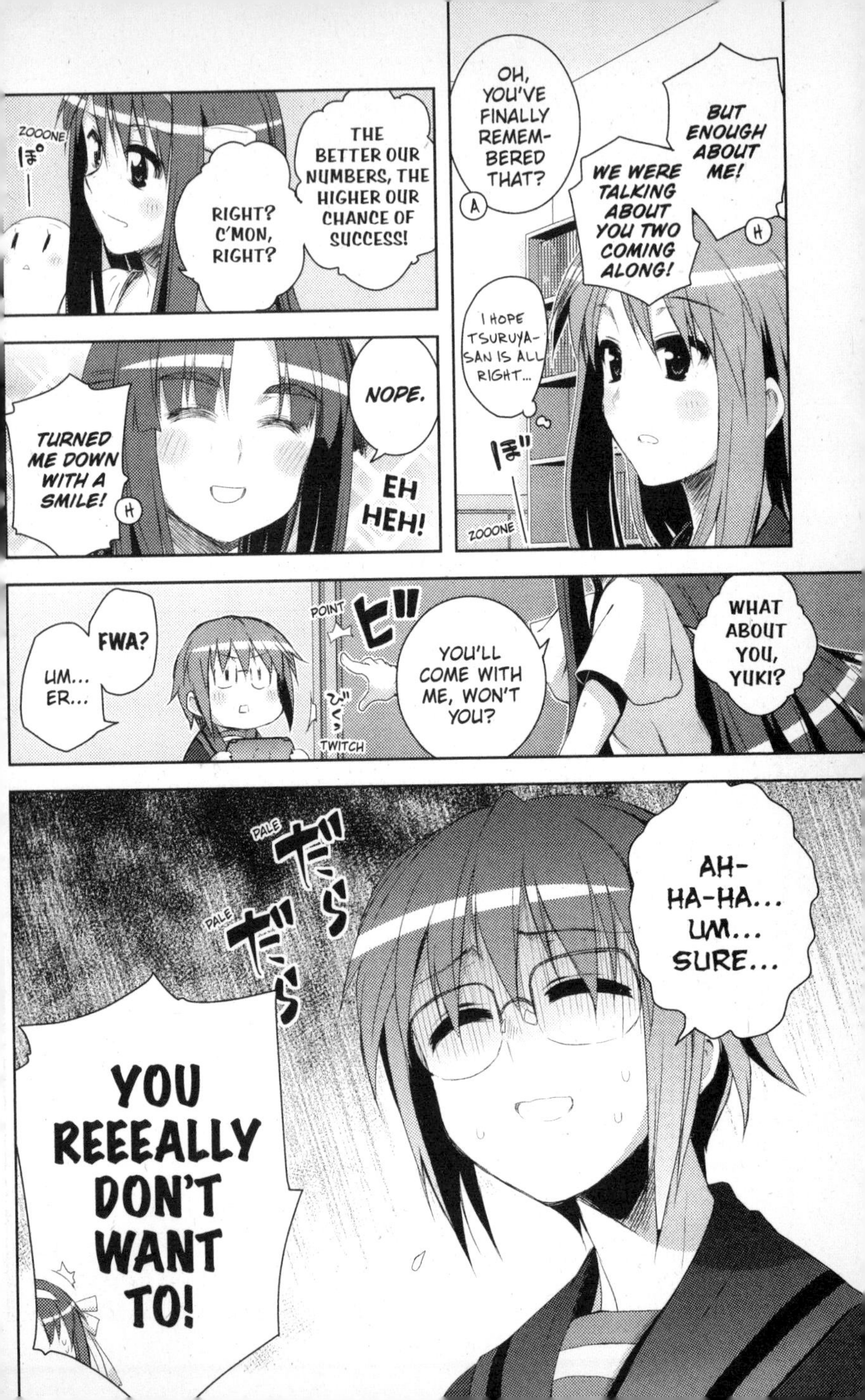
BUT ENOUGH ABOUT ME!
WE WERE TALKING ABOUT YOU TWO COMING ALONG!
OH, YOU'VE FINALLY REMEM-BERED THAT?
I HOPE TSURUYA-SAN IS ALL RIGHT...
ぼ"
ZOOONE
THE BETTER OUR NUMBERS, THE HIGHER OUR CHANCE OF SUCCESS!
RIGHT? C'MON, RIGHT?
ZOOONE
ぽー
NOPE.
EH HEH!
TURNED ME DOWN WITH A SMILE!
WHAT ABOUT YOU, YUKI?
YOU'LL COME WITH ME, WON'T YOU?
ビッ
POINT
びくっ
TWITCH
FWA?
UM... ER...
AH-HA-HA... UM... SURE...
だら
PALE
だら
PALE
YOU REEEALLY DON'T WANT TO!

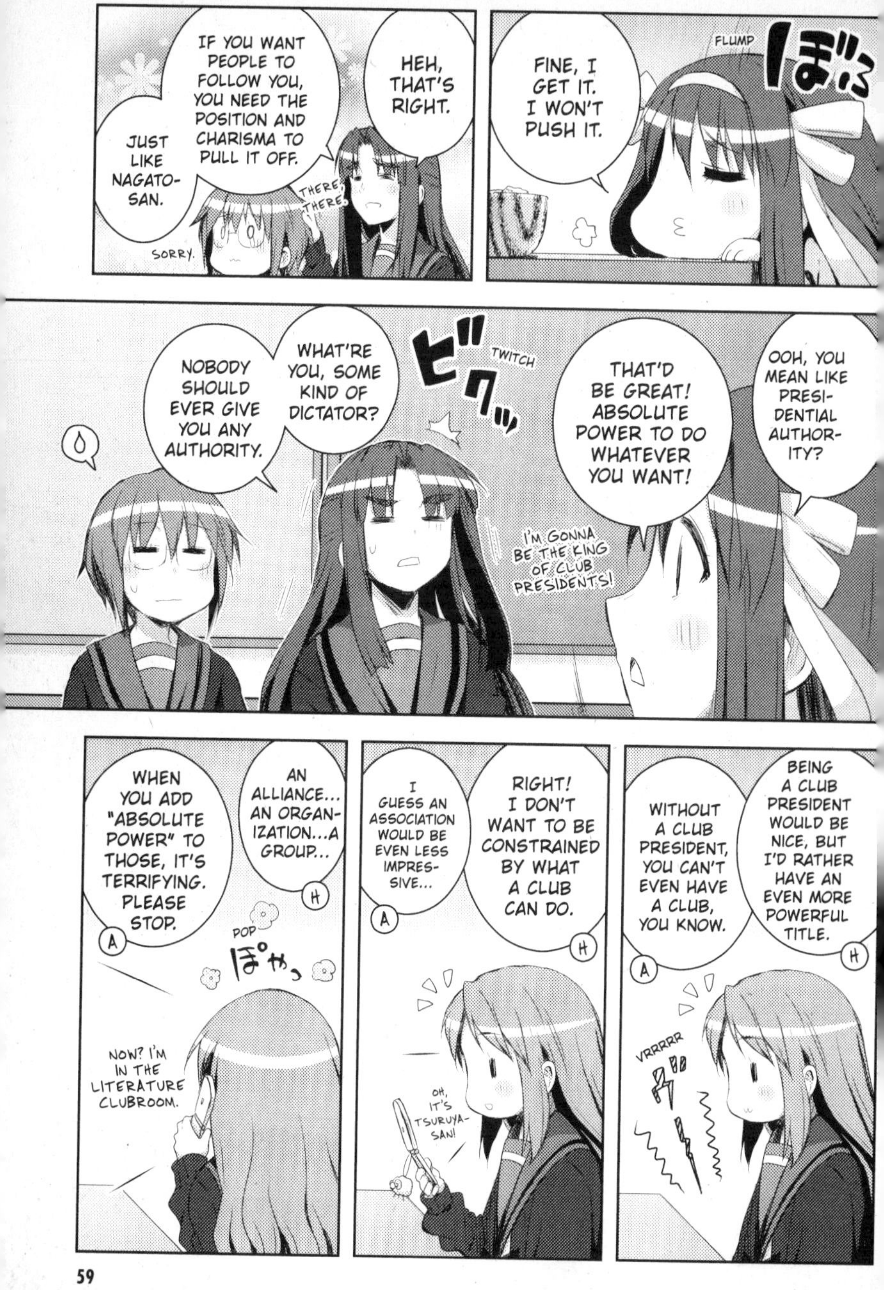
FLUMP
ぼふ
FINE, I GET IT. I WON'T PUSH IT.
HEH, THAT'S RIGHT.
IF YOU WANT PEOPLE TO FOLLOW YOU, YOU NEED THE POSITION AND CHARISMA TO PULL IT OFF.
JUST LIKE NAGATO-SAN.
THERE, THERE.
SORRY.
OOH, YOU MEAN LIKE PRESIDENTIAL AUTHORITY?
THAT'D BE GREAT! ABSOLUTE POWER TO DO WHATEVER YOU WANT!
I'M GONNA BE THE KING OF CLUB PRESIDENTS!
ビクッ
TWITCH
WHAT'RE YOU, SOME KIND OF DICTATOR?
NOBODY SHOULD EVER GIVE YOU ANY AUTHORITY.
BEING A CLUB PRESIDENT WOULD BE NICE, BUT I'D RATHER HAVE AN EVEN MORE POWERFUL TITLE.
WITHOUT A CLUB PRESIDENT, YOU CAN'T EVEN HAVE A CLUB, YOU KNOW.
VRRRRR
RIGHT! I DON'T WANT TO BE CONSTRAINED BY WHAT A CLUB CAN DO.
I GUESS AN ASSOCIATION WOULD BE EVEN LESS IMPRESSIVE...
OH, IT'S TSURUYA-SAN!
AN ALLIANCE... AN ORGANIZATION...A GROUP...
WHEN YOU ADD "ABSOLUTE POWER" TO THOSE, IT'S TERRIFYING. PLEASE STOP.
POP
ぽやっ
NOW? I'M IN THE LITERATURE CLUBROOM.

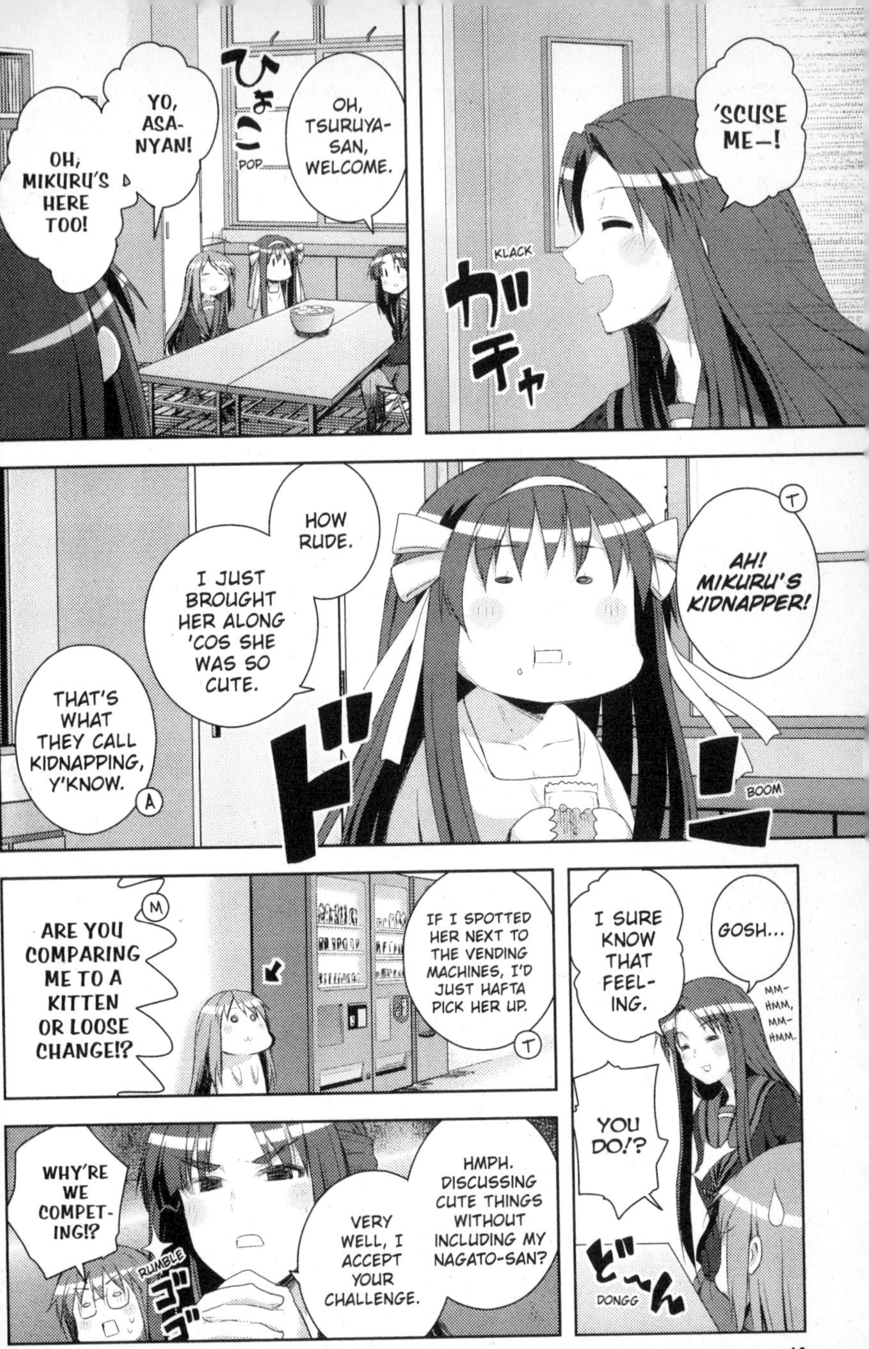
'SCUSE ME—!
KLACK
OH, TSURUYA-SAN, WELCOME.
POP
YO, ASA-NYAN!
OH, MIKURU'S HERE TOO!
AH! MIKURU'S KIDNAPPER!
BOOM
HOW RUDE.
I JUST BROUGHT HER ALONG 'COS SHE WAS SO CUTE.
THAT'S WHAT THEY CALL KIDNAPPING, Y'KNOW.
GOSH...
I SURE KNOW THAT FEEL-ING.
MM-HMM, MM-HMM.
YOU DO!?
DONGG
IF I SPOTTED HER NEXT TO THE VENDING MACHINES, I'D JUST HAFTA PICK HER UP.
ARE YOU COMPARING ME TO A KITTEN OR LOOSE CHANGE!?
HMPH. DISCUSSING CUTE THINGS WITHOUT INCLUDING MY NAGATO-SAN?
VERY WELL, I ACCEPT YOUR CHALLENGE.
WHY'RE WE COMPET-ING!?
RUMBLE

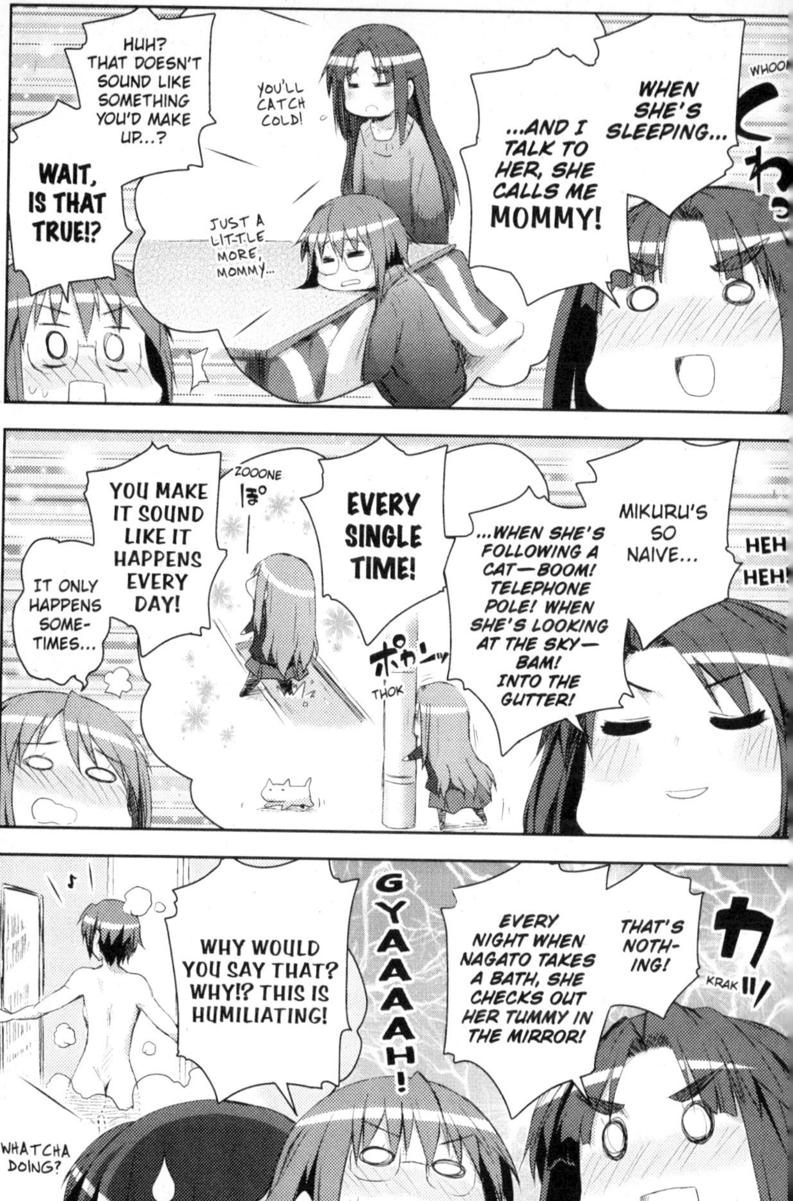
WHOO
WHEN SHE'S SLEEPING...
...AND I TALK TO HER, SHE CALLS ME MOMMY!
YOU'LL CATCH COLD!
HUH? THAT DOESN'T SOUND LIKE SOMETHING YOU'D MAKE UP...?
JUST A LIT-TLE MORE, MOMMY...
WAIT, IS THAT TRUE!?
HEH HEH
MIKURU'S SO NAIVE...
...WHEN SHE'S FOLLOWING A CAT—BOOM! TELEPHONE POLE! WHEN SHE'S LOOKING AT THE SKY—BAM! INTO THE GUTTER!
EVERY SINGLE TIME!
ZOOONE
THOK
YOU MAKE IT SOUND LIKE IT HAPPENS EVERY DAY!
IT ONLY HAPPENS SOME-TIMES...
KRAK
THAT'S NOTH-ING!
EVERY NIGHT WHEN NAGATO TAKES A BATH, SHE CHECKS OUT HER TUMMY IN THE MIRROR!
GYAAAAH!
WHY WOULD YOU SAY THAT? WHY!? THIS IS HUMILIATING!
WHATCHA DOING?

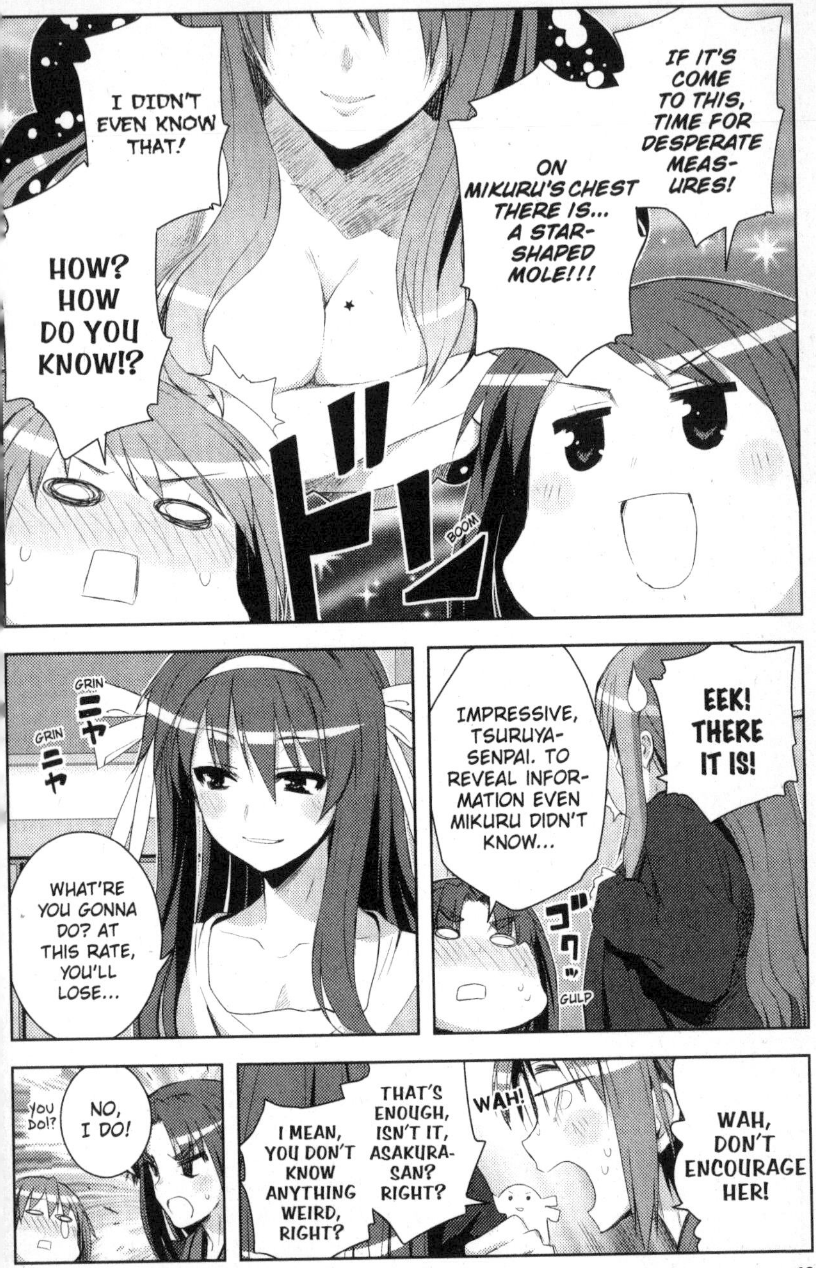
IF IT'S COME TO THIS, TIME FOR DESPERATE MEAS-URES!
ON MIKURU'S CHEST THERE IS... A STAR-SHAPED MOLE!!!
I DIDN'T EVEN KNOW THAT!
HOW? HOW DO YOU KNOW!?
ドン
BOOM
EEK! THERE IT IS!
IMPRESSIVE, TSURUYA-SENPAI. TO REVEAL INFOR-MATION EVEN MIKURU DIDN'T KNOW...
ゴクッ
GULP
ニヤ
GRIN
ニヤ
GRIN
WHAT'RE YOU GONNA DO? AT THIS RATE, YOU'LL LOSE...
WAH, DON'T ENCOURAGE HER!
WAH!
THAT'S ENOUGH, ISN'T IT, ASAKURA-SAN? RIGHT?
I MEAN, YOU DON'T KNOW ANYTHING WEIRD, RIGHT?
NO, I DO!
YOU DO!?

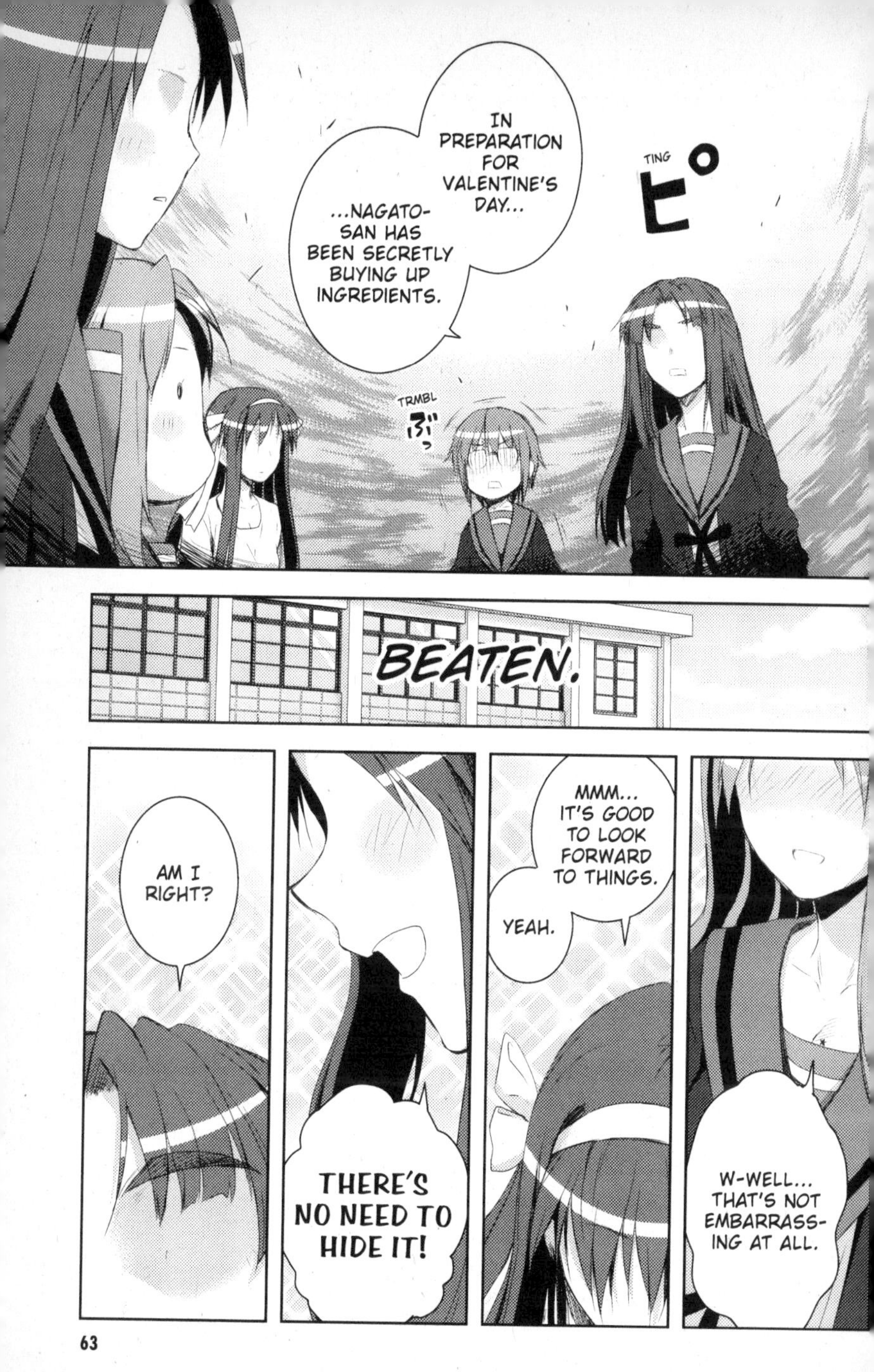
TING
ピ
IN PREPARATION FOR VALENTINE'S DAY...
...NAGATO-SAN HAS BEEN SECRETLY BUYING UP INGREDIENTS.
TRMBL
BEATEN.
W-WELL... THAT'S NOT EMBARRASS-ING AT ALL.
MMM... IT'S GOOD TO LOOK FORWARD TO THINGS.
YEAH.
THERE'S NO NEED TO HIDE IT!
AM I RIGHT?

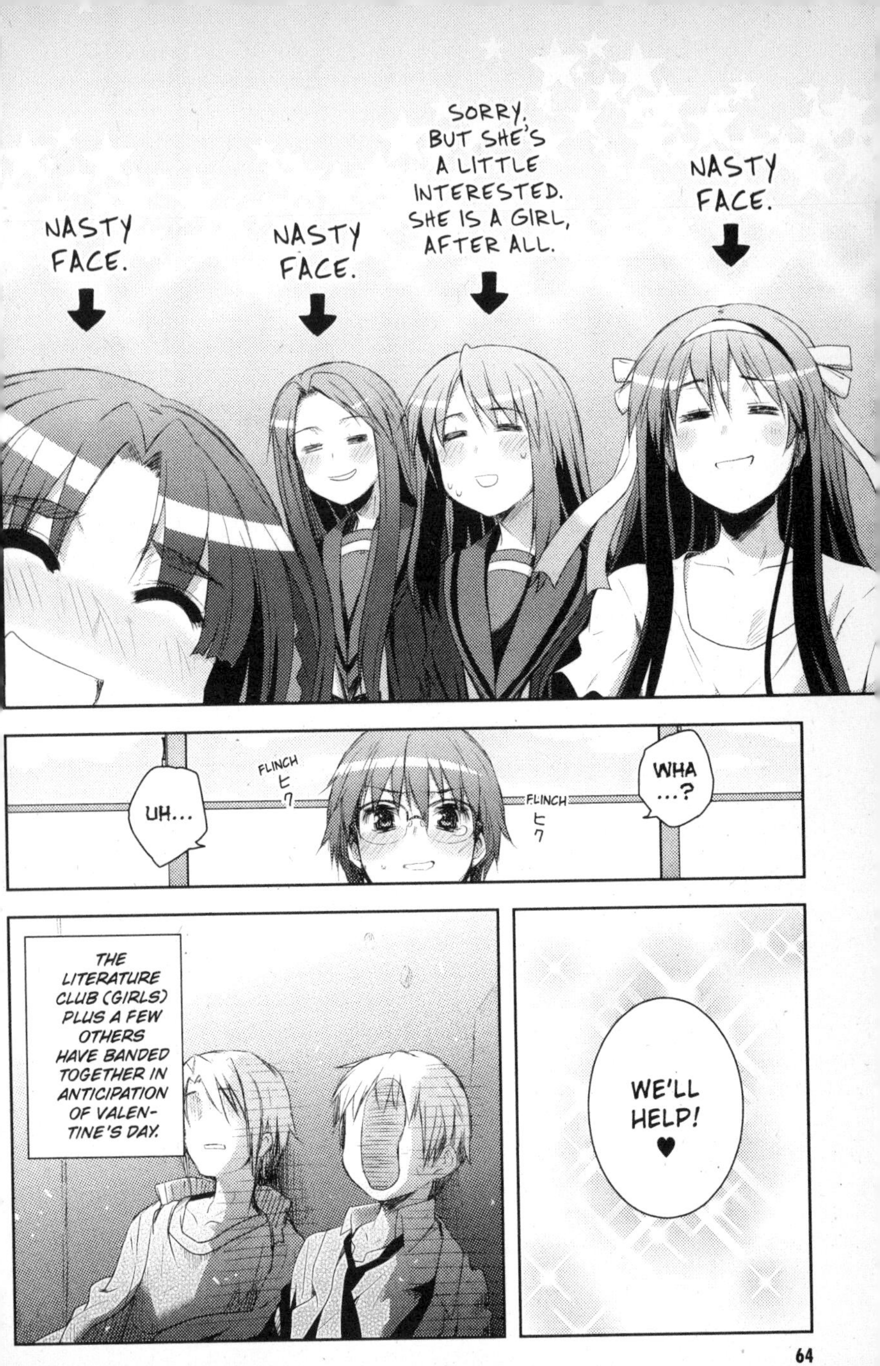
NASTY FACE.
SORRY. BUT SHE'S A LITTLE INTERESTED. SHE IS A GIRL, AFTER ALL.
NASTY FACE.
NASTY FACE.
WHA ...?
FLINCH ヒク
FLINCH ヒク
UH...
WE'LL HELP! ♥
THE LITERATURE CLUB (GIRLS) PLUS A FEW OTHERS HAVE BANDED TOGETHER IN ANTICIPATION OF VALENTINE'S DAY.

WELCOME HOME!

YOUNG WIFE
NAGATO
(ARTIST'S
CONCEPTION)

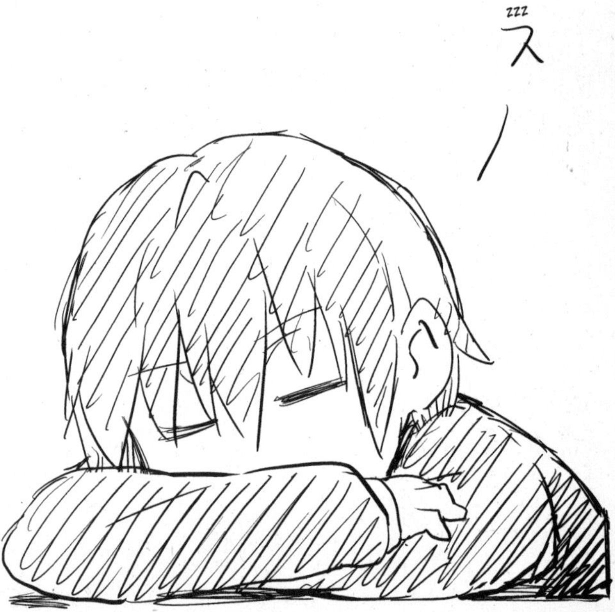
zzz
スー

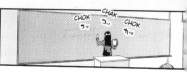

CHOK CHAK CHOK

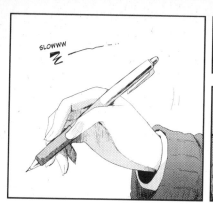

SLOWWW

ZZZZZ

KYON-KUN, KYON-KUN.

WHISPER

WHISPER

HEY.

OW!

TWITCH

STAB

Epilogue 11>> Valentine's Day: The Day Before

ABOUT THAT...

THAT ACTUALLY HURT!

WHADDAYA WANT?

CLATTER

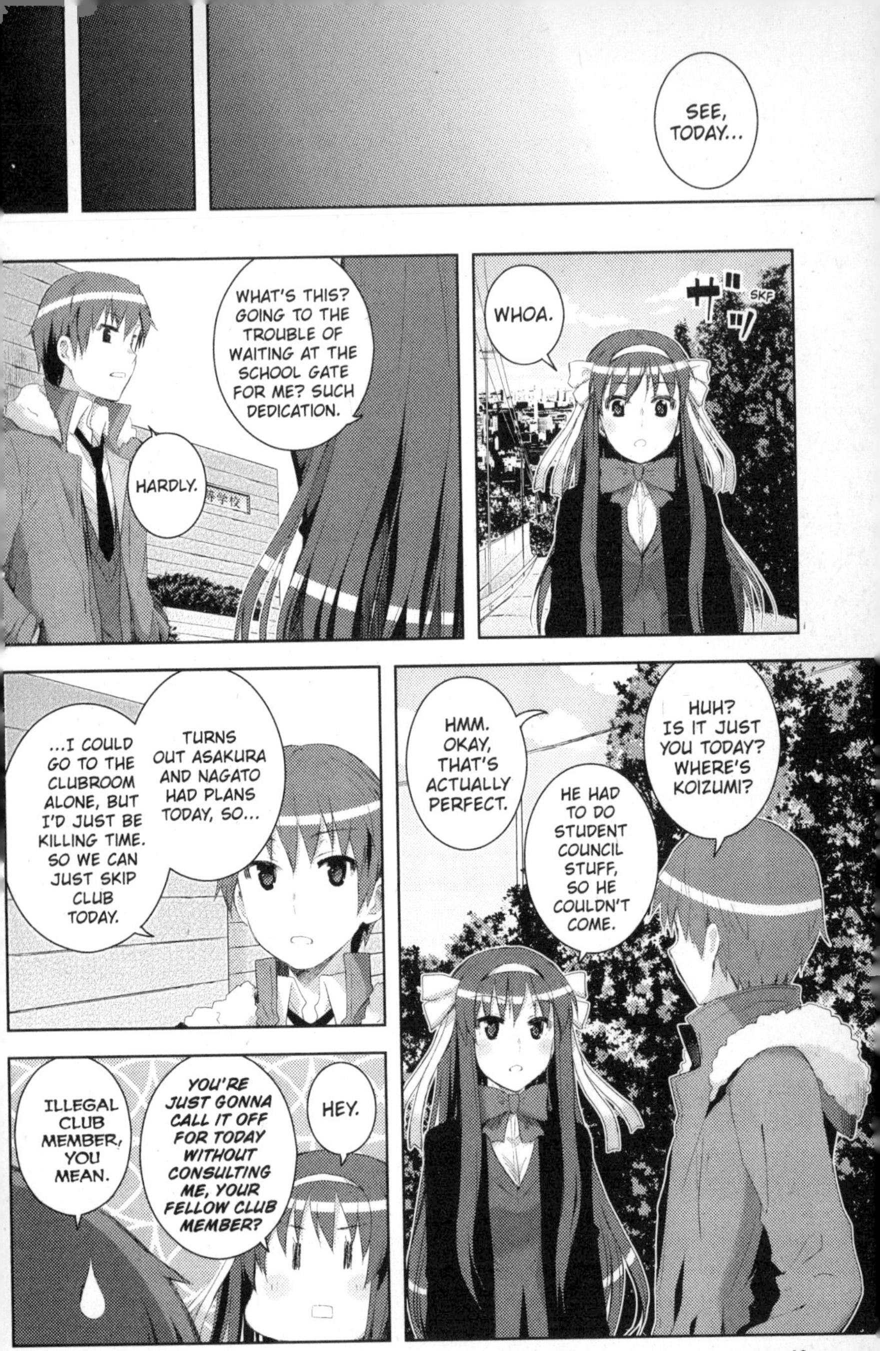
SEE, TODAY...
ザッ
SKP
WHOA.
WHAT'S THIS? GOING TO THE TROUBLE OF WAITING AT THE SCHOOL GATE FOR ME? SUCH DEDICATION.
HARDLY.
HUH? IS IT JUST YOU TODAY? WHERE'S KOIZUMI?
HE HAD TO DO STUDENT COUNCIL STUFF, SO HE COULDN'T COME.
HMM. OKAY, THAT'S ACTUALLY PERFECT.
TURNS OUT ASAKURA AND NAGATO HAD PLANS TODAY, SO...
...I COULD GO TO THE CLUBROOM ALONE, BUT I'D JUST BE KILLING TIME. SO WE CAN JUST SKIP CLUB TODAY.
HEY.
YOU'RE JUST GONNA CALL IT OFF FOR TODAY WITHOUT CONSULTING ME, YOUR FELLOW CLUB MEMBER?
ILLEGAL CLUB MEMBER, YOU MEAN.

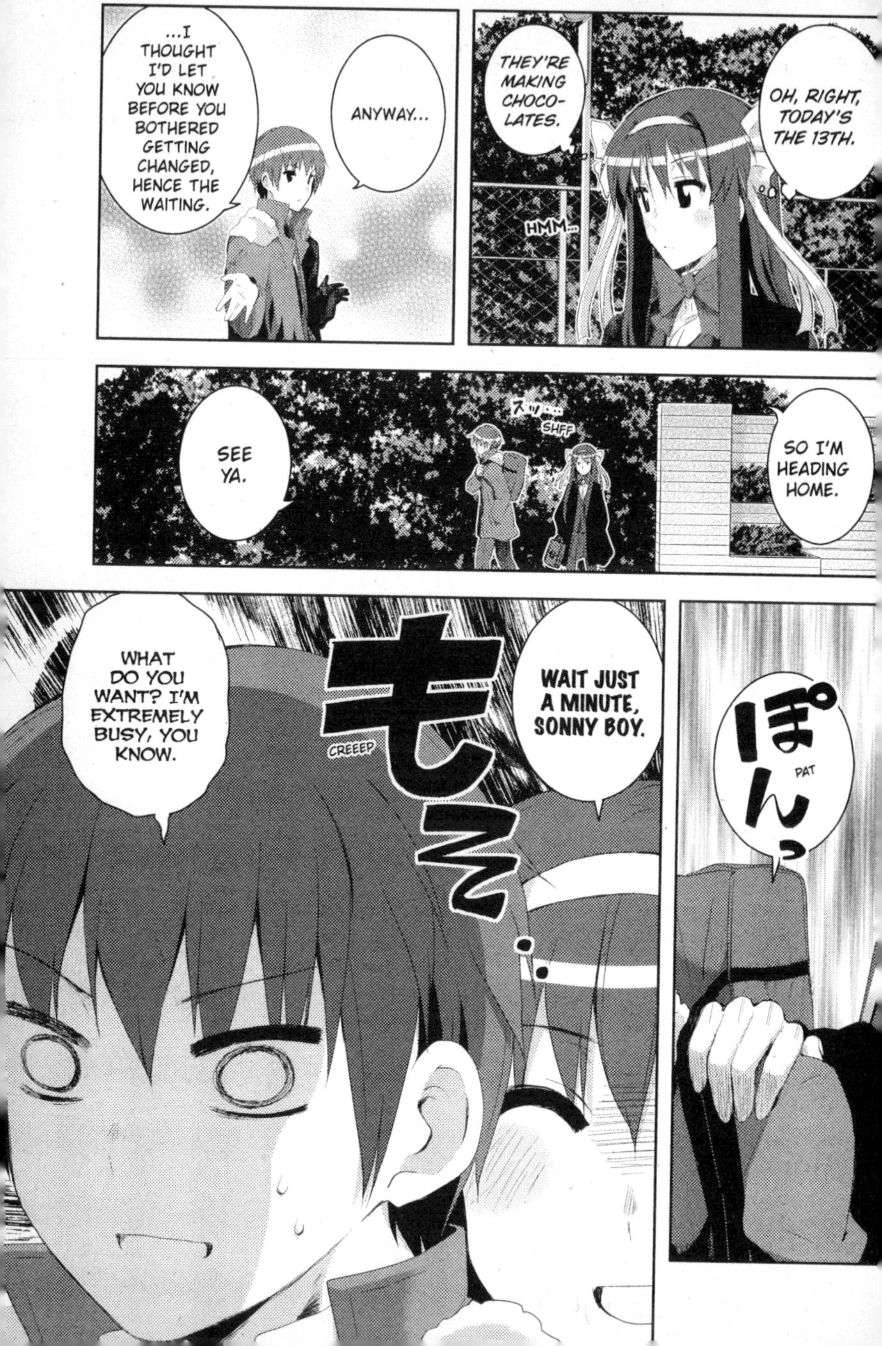
OH, RIGHT, TODAY'S THE 13TH.
THEY'RE MAKING CHOCO-LATES.
HMM...
ANYWAY...
...I THOUGHT I'D LET YOU KNOW BEFORE YOU BOTHERED GETTING CHANGED, HENCE THE WAITING.
SO I'M HEADING HOME.
スッ…
SHFF
SEE YA.
ぽんっ
PAT
WAIT JUST A MINUTE, SONNY BOY.
もぞ…
CREEEP
WHAT DO YOU WANT? I'M EXTREMELY BUSY, YOU KNOW.

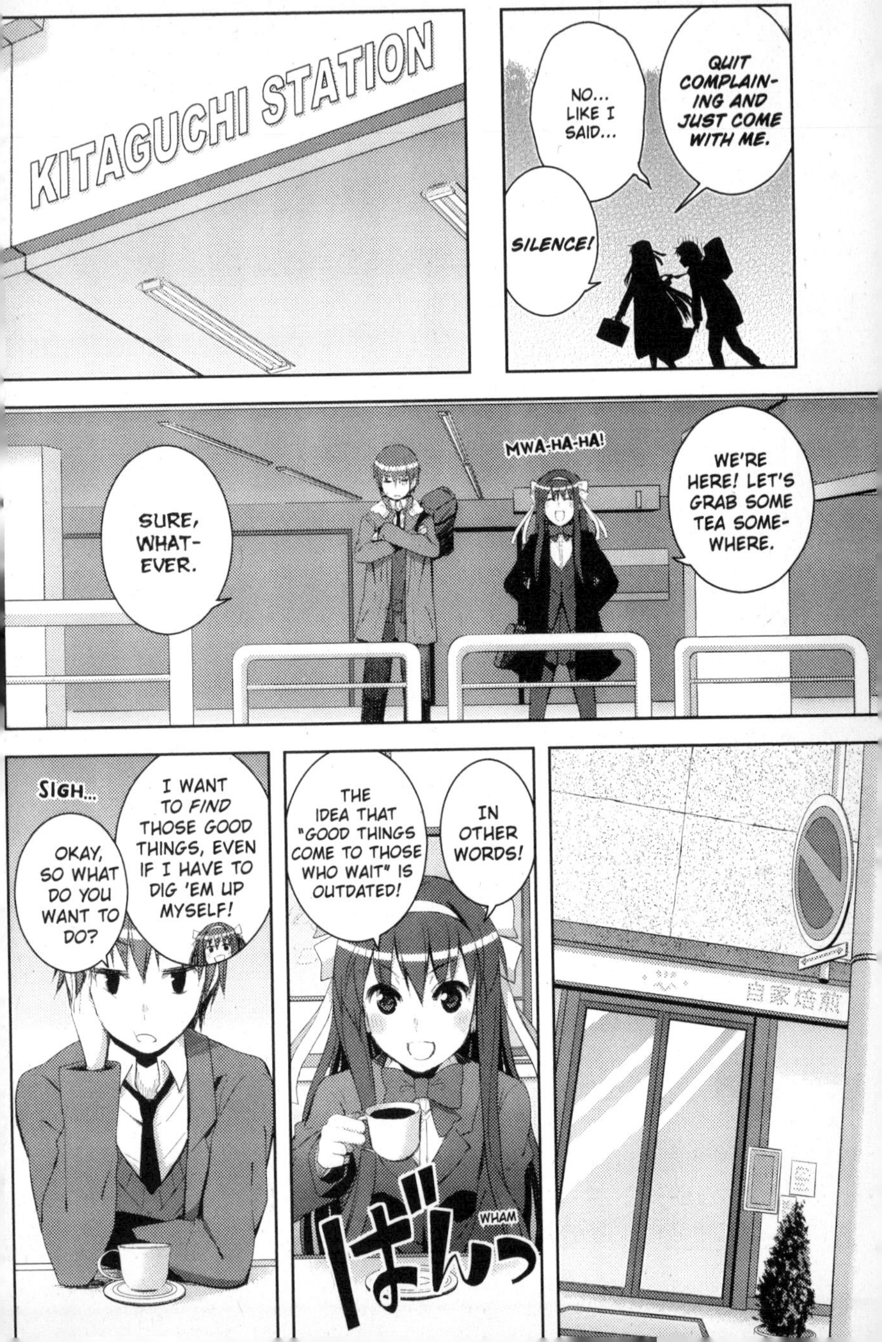
QUIT COMPLAINING AND JUST COME WITH ME.
NO... LIKE I SAID...
SILENCE!
KITAGUCHI STATION
WE'RE HERE! LET'S GRAB SOME TEA SOMEWHERE.
MWA-HA-HA!
SURE, WHATEVER.
自家焙煎
IN OTHER WORDS!
THE IDEA THAT "GOOD THINGS COME TO THOSE WHO WAIT" IS OUTDATED!
ばんっ
WHAM
I WANT TO *FIND* THOSE GOOD THINGS, EVEN IF I HAVE TO DIG 'EM UP MYSELF!
SIGH...
OKAY, SO WHAT DO YOU WANT TO DO?

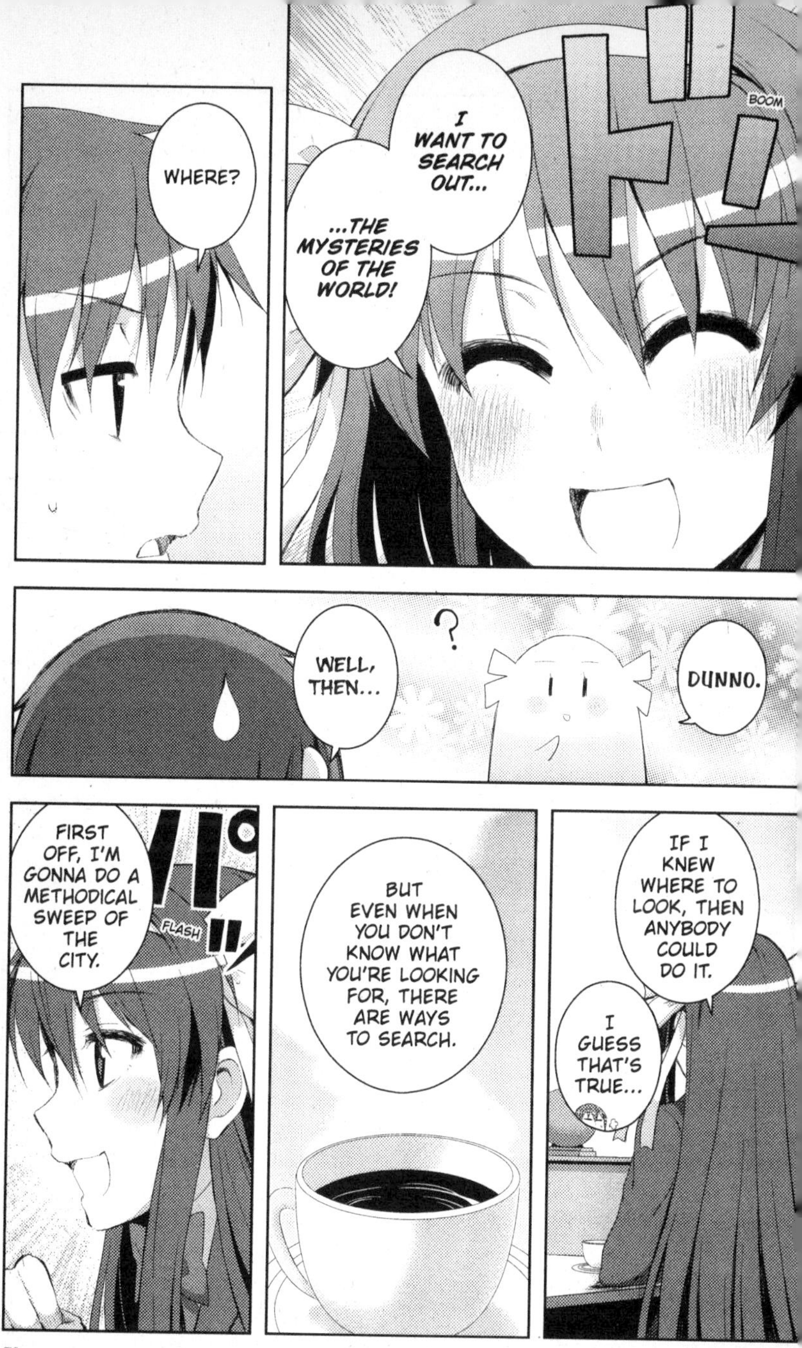
BOOM
I WANT TO SEARCH OUT...
...THE MYSTERIES OF THE WORLD!
WHERE?
DUNNO.
?
WELL, THEN...
IF I KNEW WHERE TO LOOK, THEN ANYBODY COULD DO IT.
I GUESS THAT'S TRUE...
BUT EVEN WHEN YOU DON'T KNOW WHAT YOU'RE LOOKING FOR, THERE ARE WAYS TO SEARCH.
FIRST OFF, I'M GONNA DO A METHODICAL SWEEP OF THE CITY.
FLASH

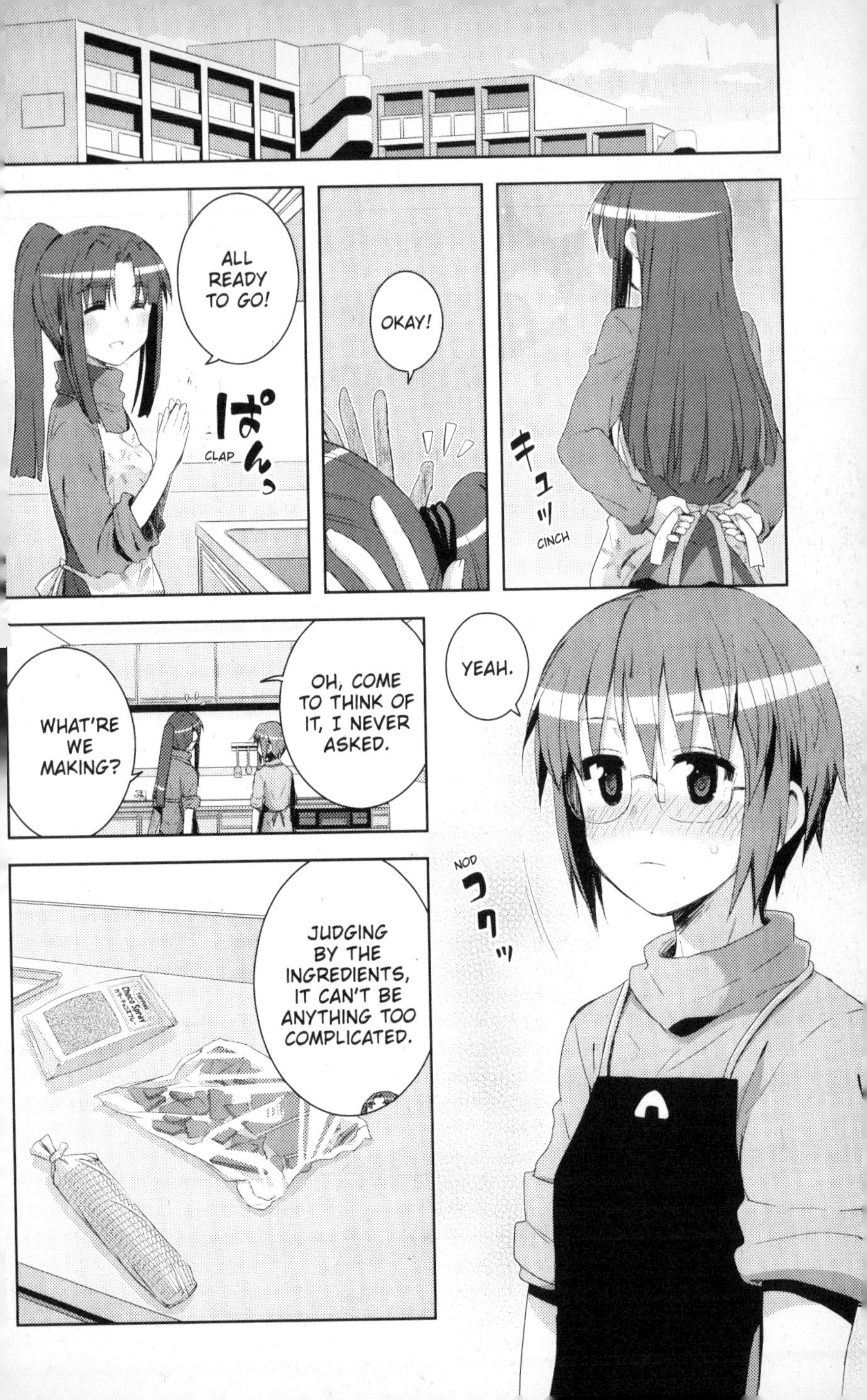
キュッ
CINCH
OKAY!
ALL READY TO GO!
ぽんっ
CLAP
YEAH.
NOD
コクッ
OH, COME TO THINK OF IT, I NEVER ASKED.
WHAT'RE WE MAKING?
JUDGING BY THE INGREDIENTS, IT CAN'T BE ANYTHING TOO COMPLICATED.

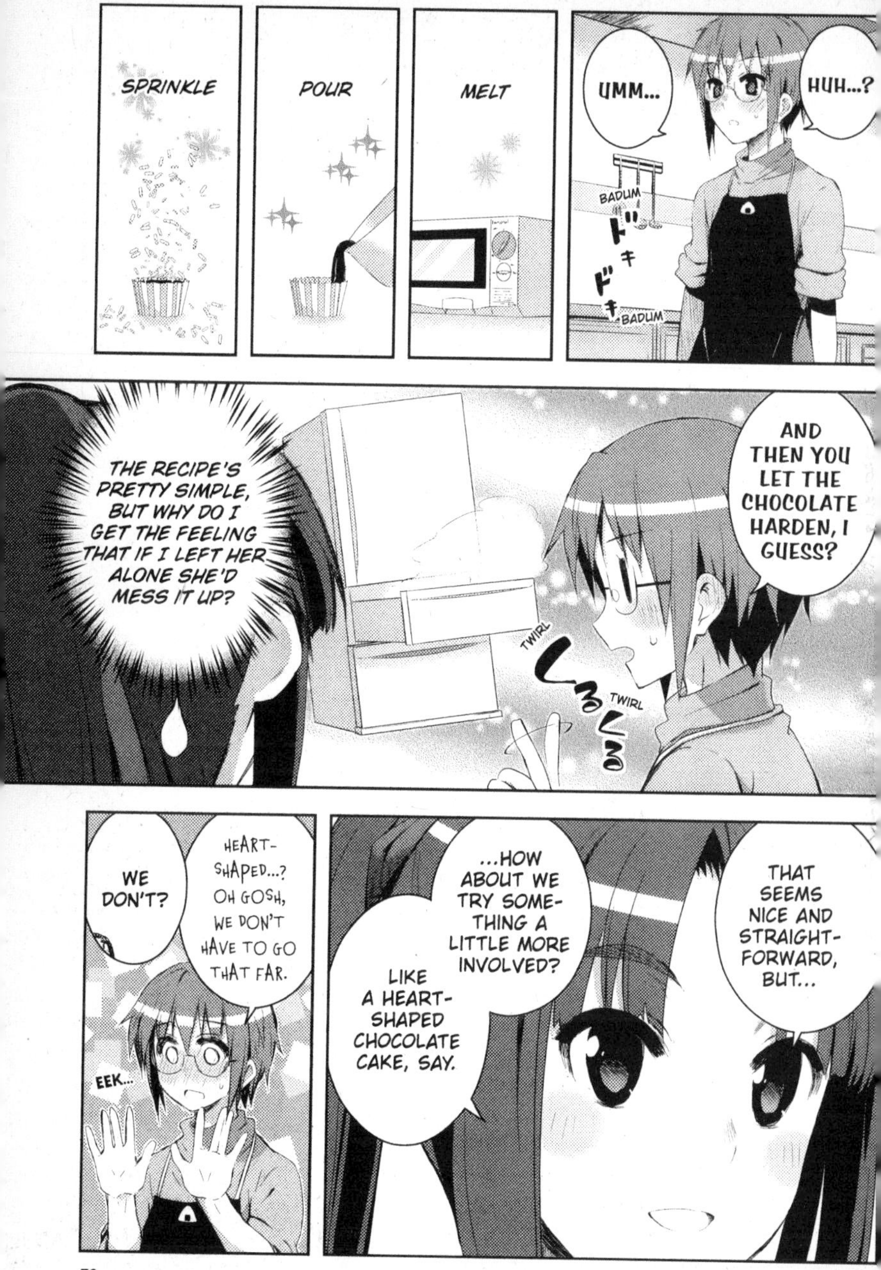
HUH...?
UMM...
BADUM
ドキ
ドキ
BADUM
MELT
POUR
SPRINKLE
AND THEN YOU LET THE CHOCOLATE HARDEN, I GUESS?
TWIRL
くるくる
TWIRL
THE RECIPE'S PRETTY SIMPLE, BUT WHY DO I GET THE FEELING THAT IF I LEFT HER ALONE SHE'D MESS IT UP?
THAT SEEMS NICE AND STRAIGHT-FORWARD, BUT...
...HOW ABOUT WE TRY SOME-THING A LITTLE MORE INVOLVED?
LIKE A HEART-SHAPED CHOCOLATE CAKE, SAY.
HEART-SHAPED...? OH GOSH, WE DON'T HAVE TO GO THAT FAR.
WE DON'T?
EEK...

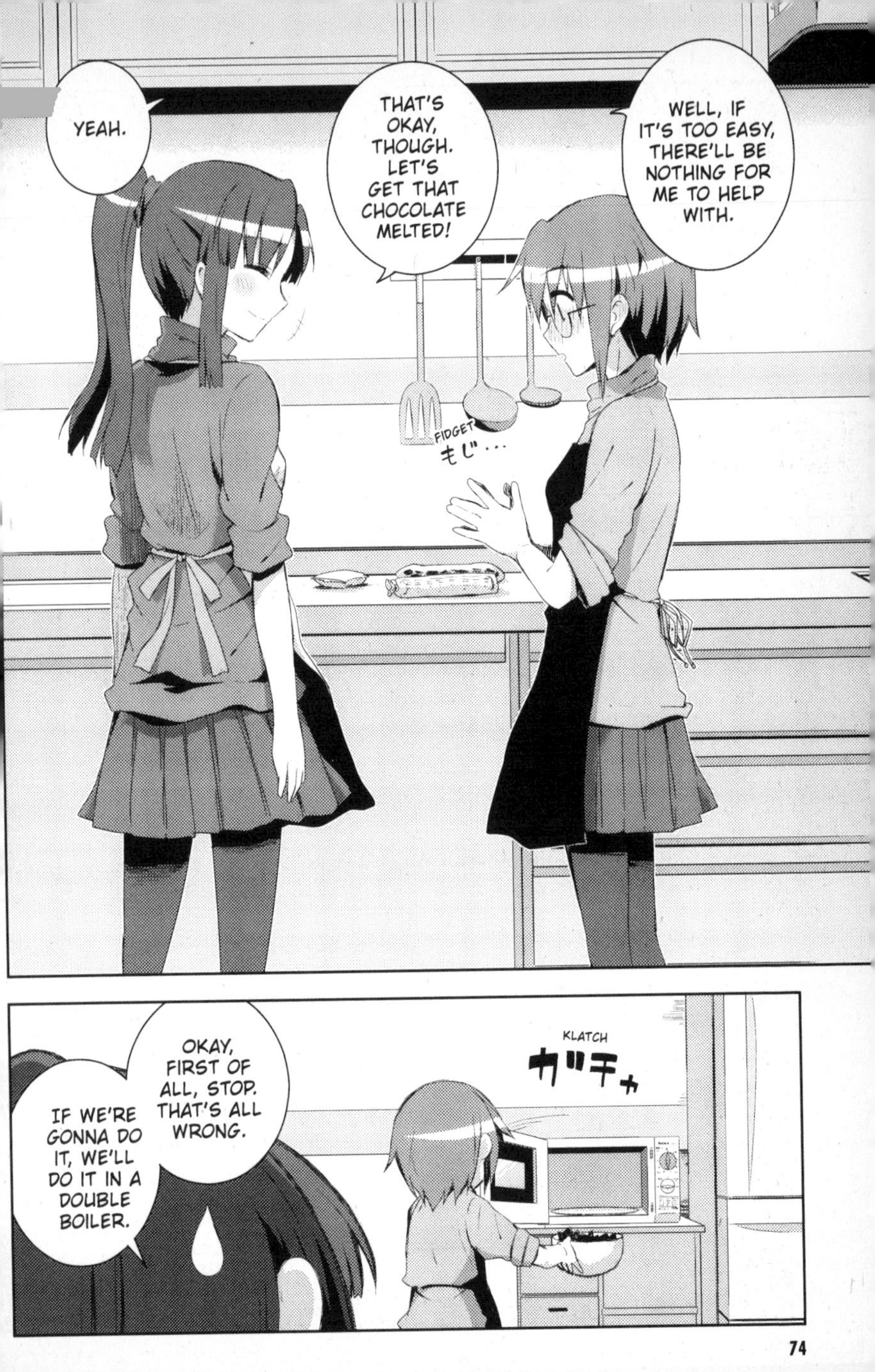
WELL, IF IT'S TOO EASY, THERE'LL BE NOTHING FOR ME TO HELP WITH.
THAT'S OKAY, THOUGH. LET'S GET THAT CHOCOLATE MELTED!
YEAH.
FIDGET
もじ…
KLATCH
ガチャ
OKAY, FIRST OF ALL, STOP. THAT'S ALL WRONG.
IF WE'RE GONNA DO IT, WE'LL DO IT IN A DOUBLE BOILER.

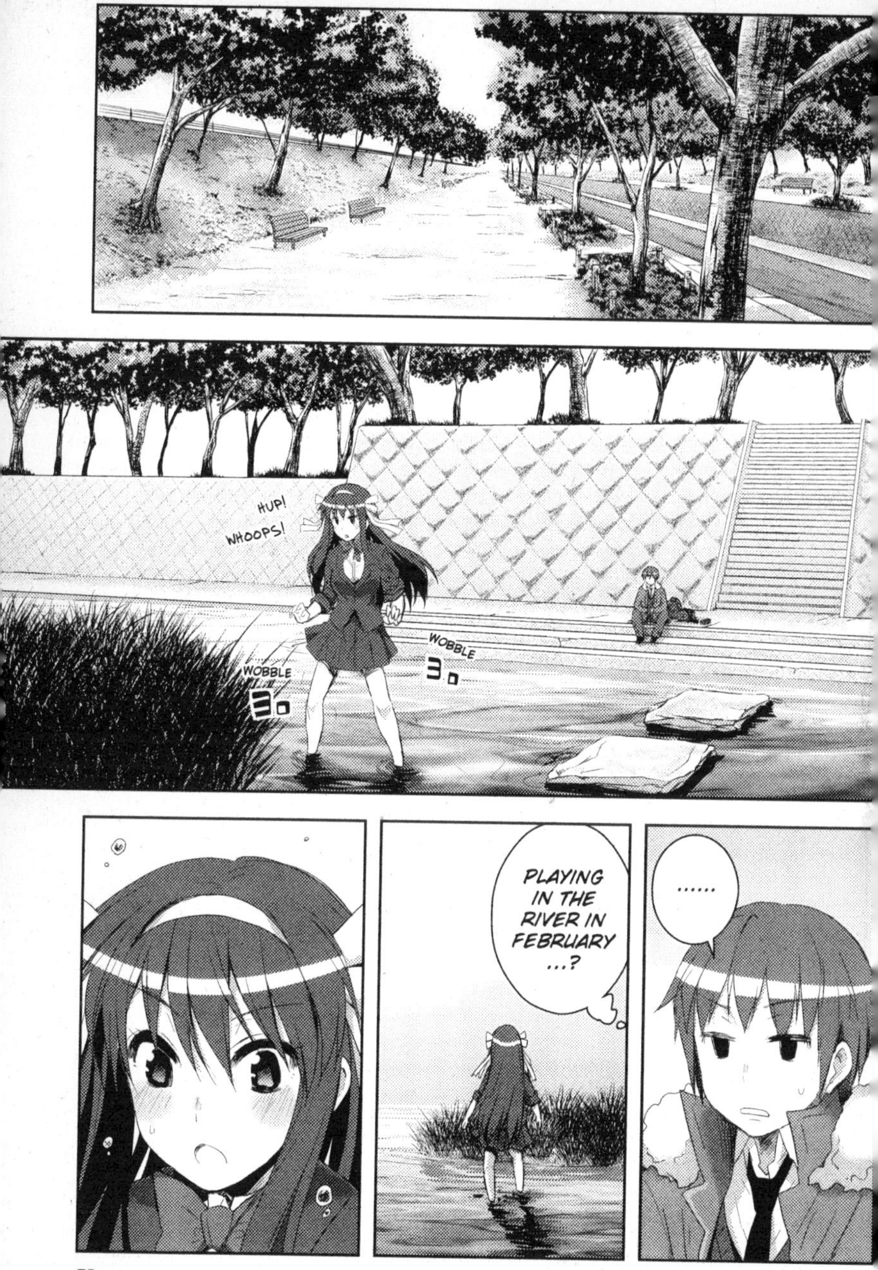
HUP!
WHOOPS!
WOBBLE
WOBBLE
......
PLAYING IN THE RIVER IN FEBRUARY ...?

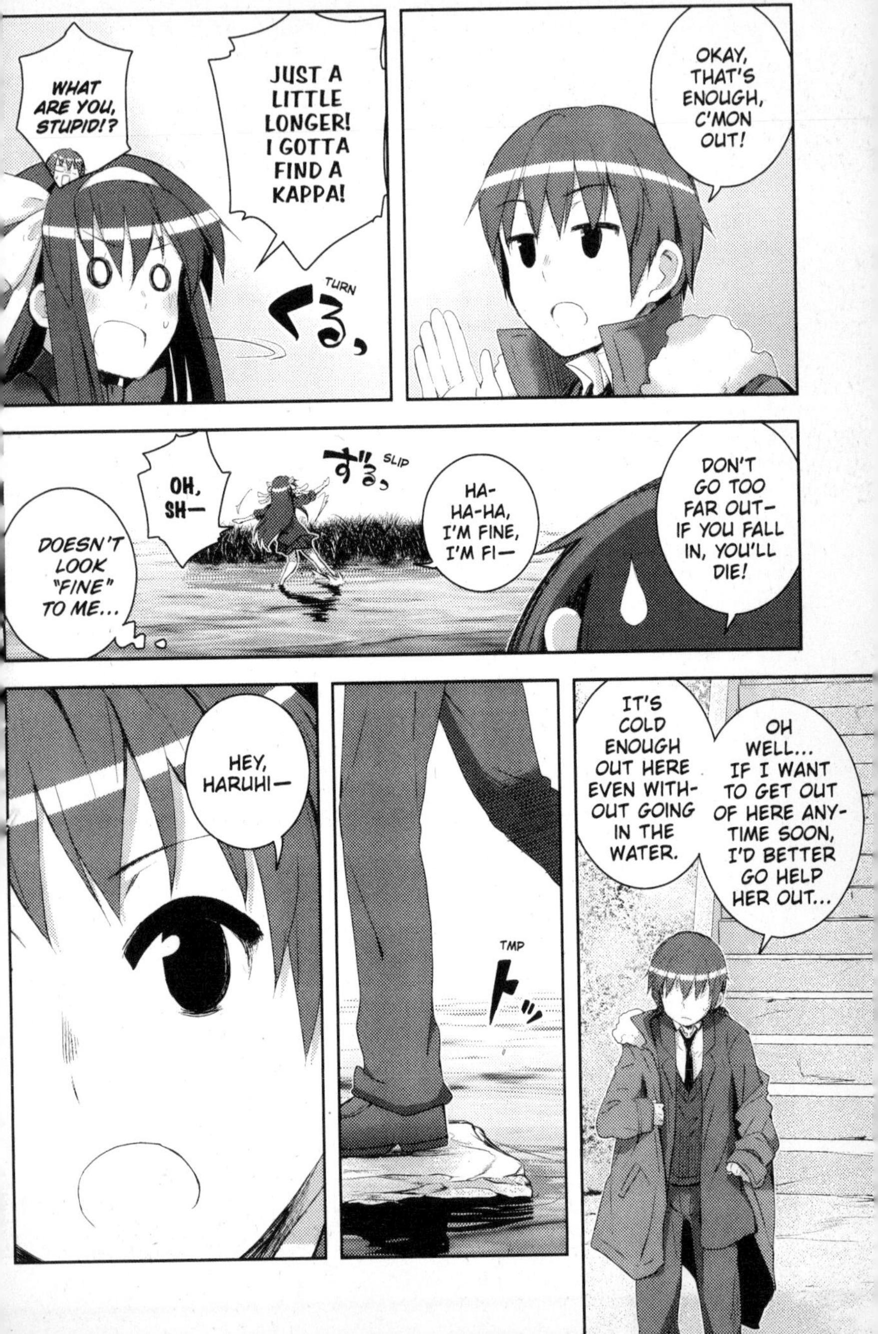
OKAY, THAT'S ENOUGH, C'MON OUT!
JUST A LITTLE LONGER! I GOTTA FIND A KAPPA!
くる
TURN
WHAT ARE YOU, STUPID!?
DON'T GO TOO FAR OUT— IF YOU FALL IN, YOU'LL DIE!
HA-HA-HA, I'M FINE, I'M FI—
ずる
SLIP
OH, SH—
DOESN'T LOOK "FINE" TO ME...
OH WELL... IF I WANT TO GET OUT OF HERE ANY-TIME SOON, I'D BETTER GO HELP HER OUT...
IT'S COLD ENOUGH OUT HERE EVEN WITH-OUT GOING IN THE WATER.
TMP
HEY, HARUHI—

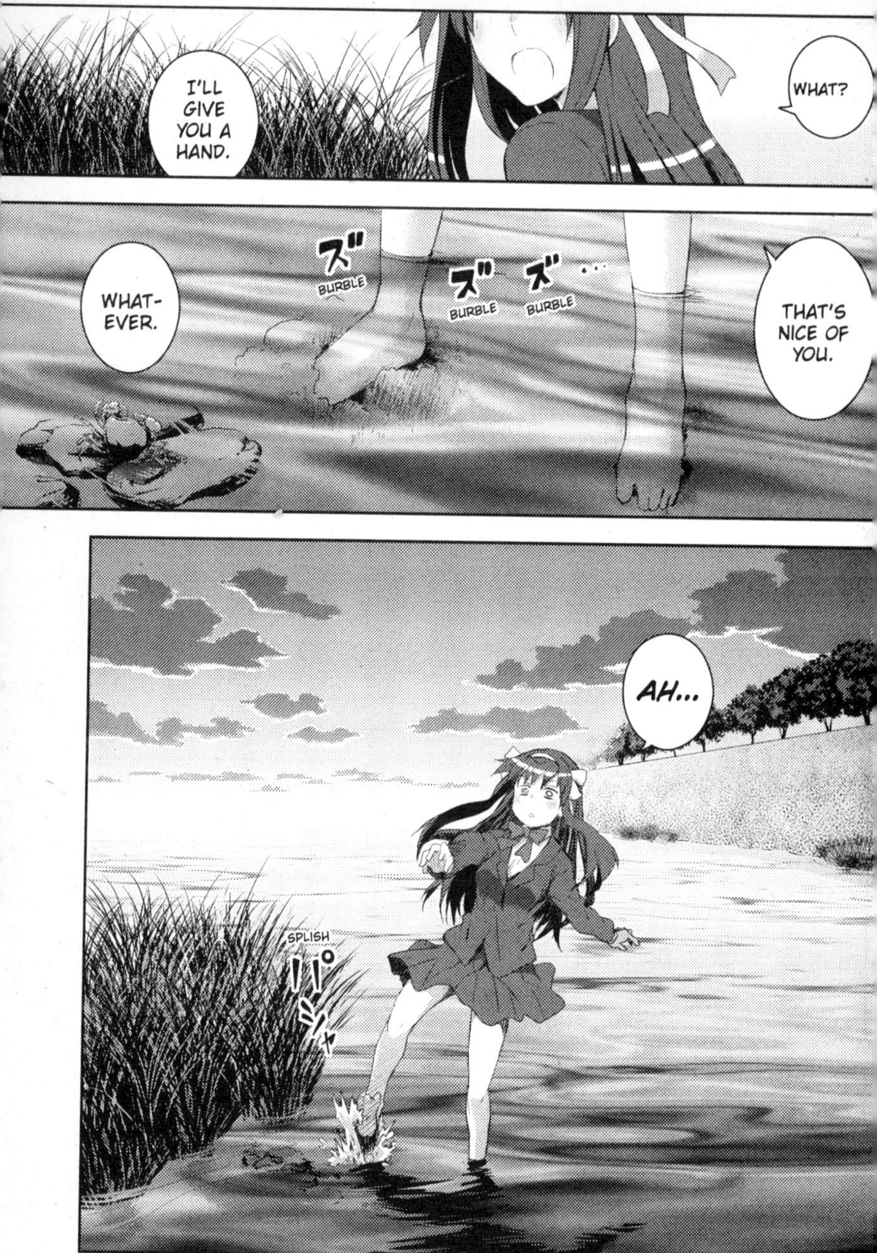
WHAT?
I'LL GIVE YOU A HAND.
THAT'S NICE OF YOU.
ズ BURBLE
ズ BURBLE
ズ BURBLE
WHAT-EVER.
AH...
SPLISH パシャ

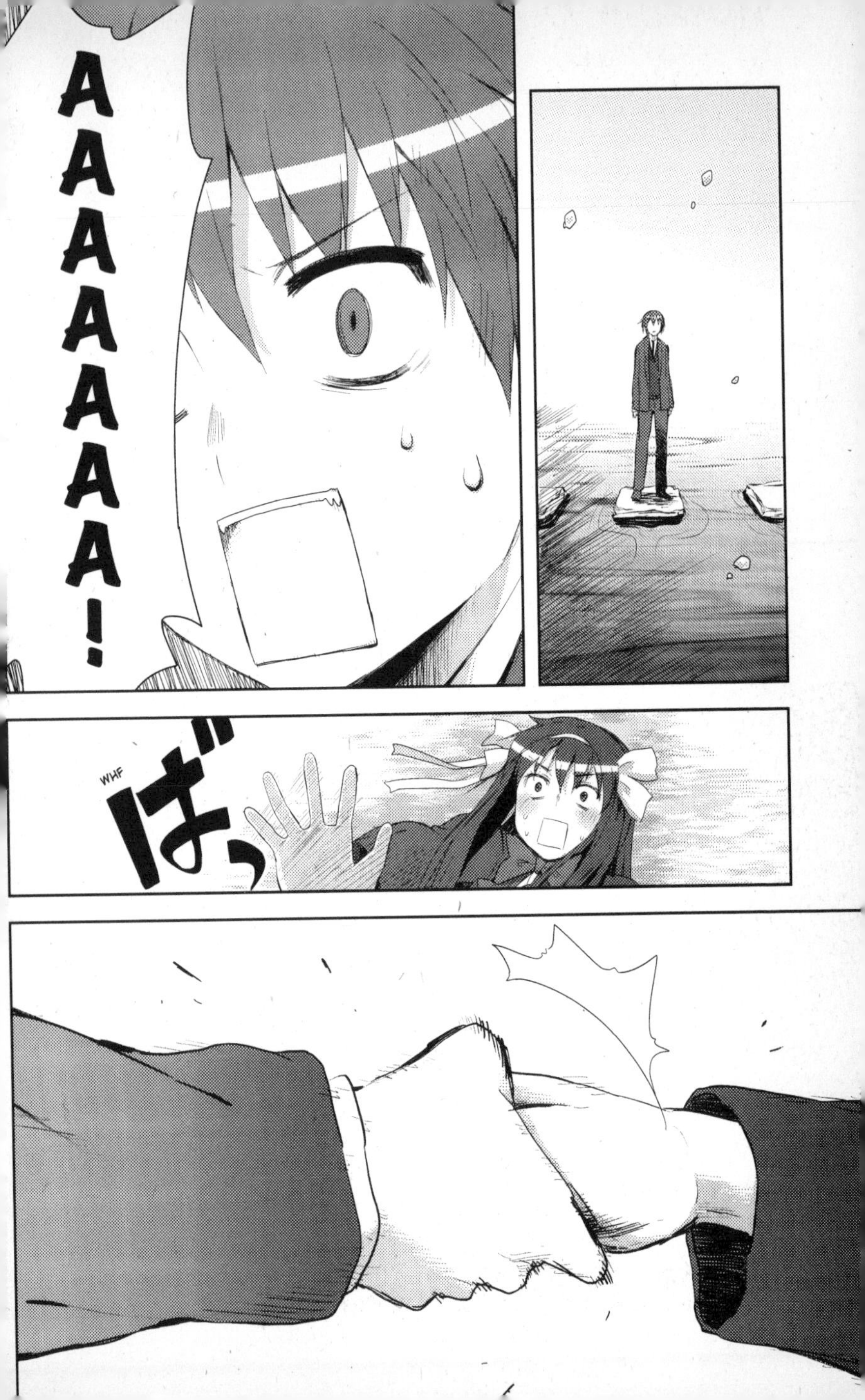
AAAAAAAAA!
WHF
ばっ

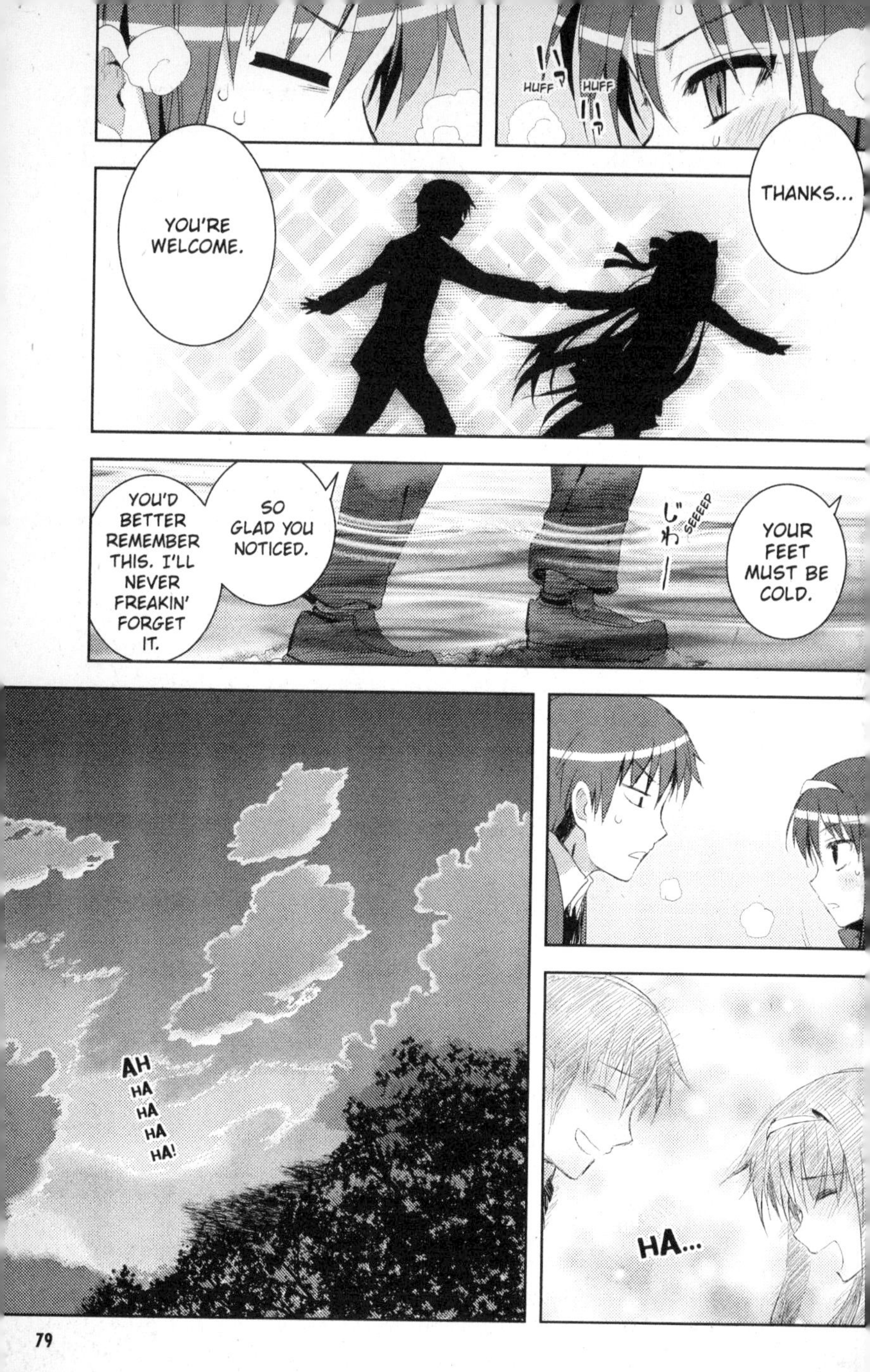
HUFF
HUFF
THANKS...
YOU'RE WELCOME.
YOUR FEET MUST BE COLD.
じわー
SEEEEP
SO GLAD YOU NOTICED.
YOU'D BETTER REMEMBER THIS. I'LL NEVER FREAKIN' FORGET IT.
HA...
AH HA HA HA HA!

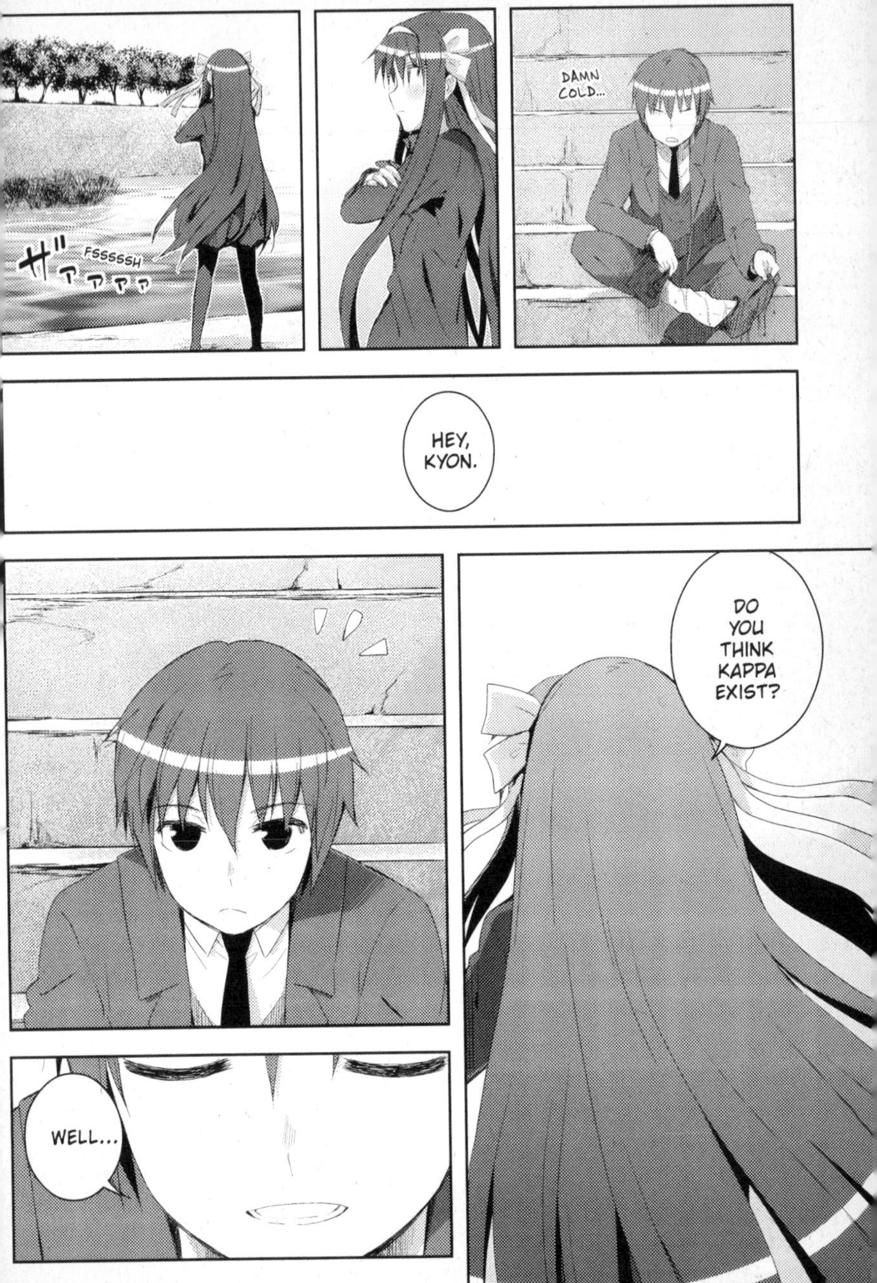
DAMN COLD...
ザァァァァ
FSSSSSH
HEY, KYON.
DO YOU THINK KAPPA EXIST?
WELL...

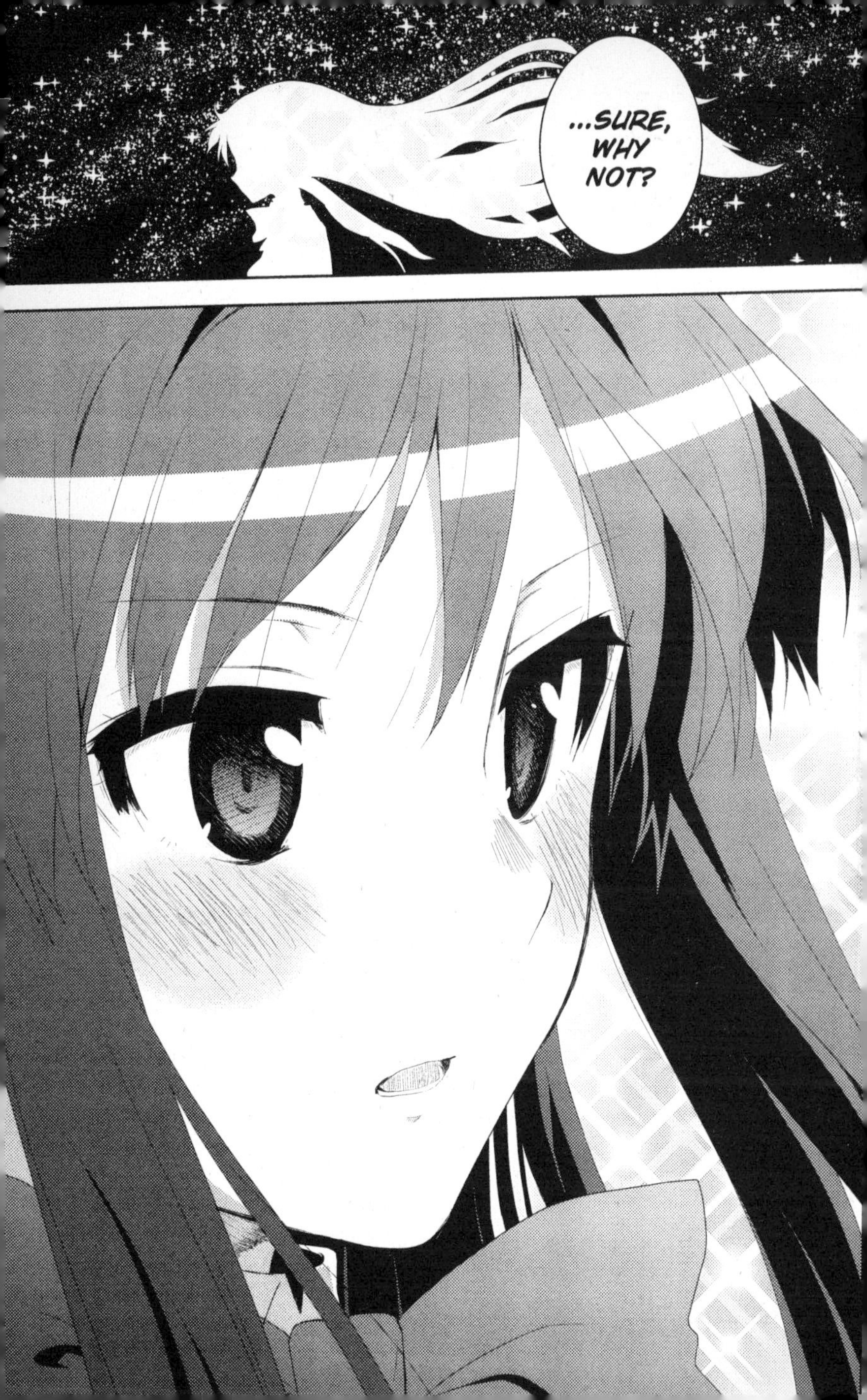
...SURE, WHY NOT?

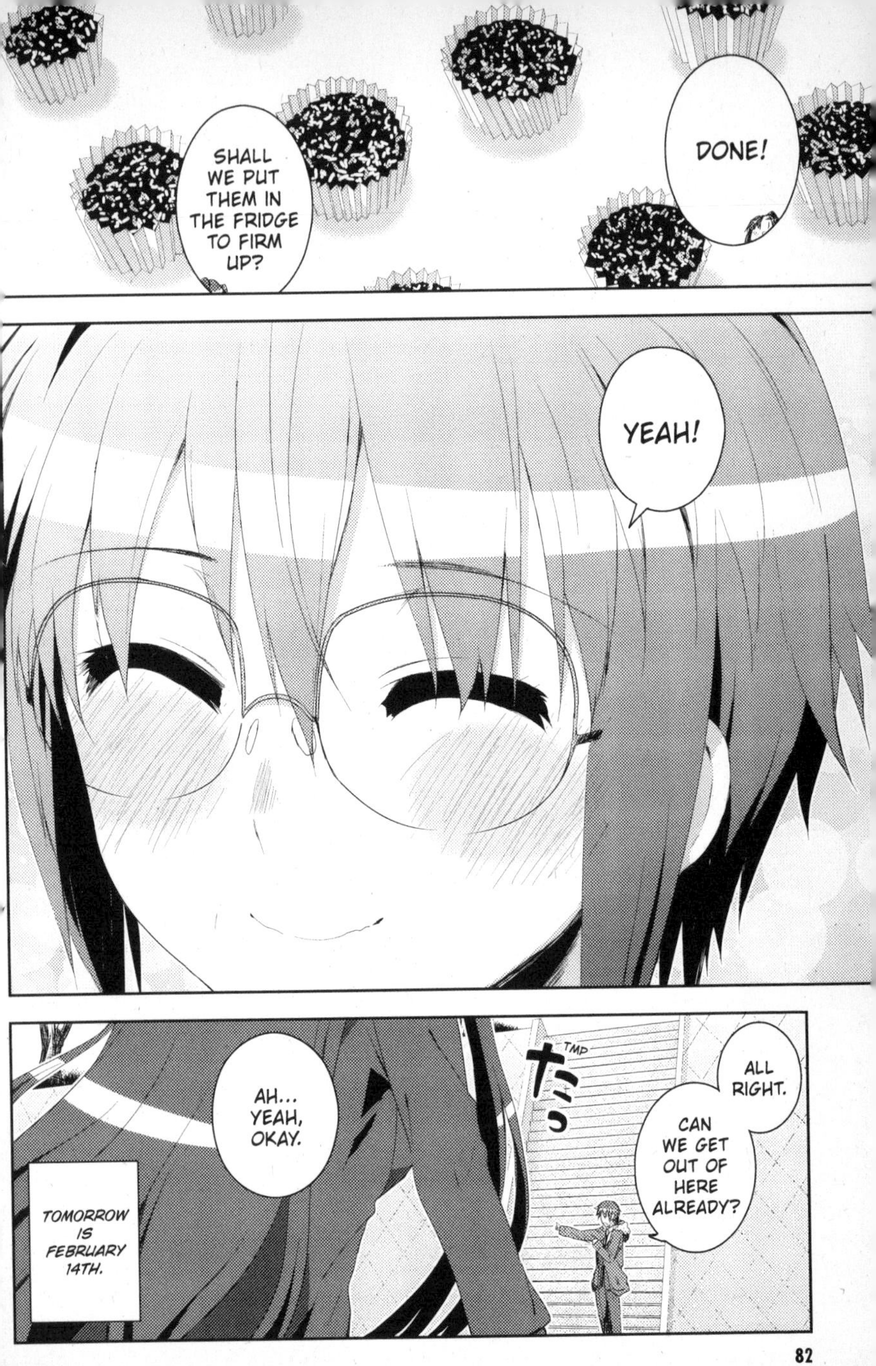
DONE!
SHALL WE PUT THEM IN THE FRIDGE TO FIRM UP?
YEAH!
ALL RIGHT.
CAN WE GET OUT OF HERE ALREADY?
TMP
AH... YEAH, OKAY.
TOMORROW IS FEBRUARY 14TH.

PAJAMAS

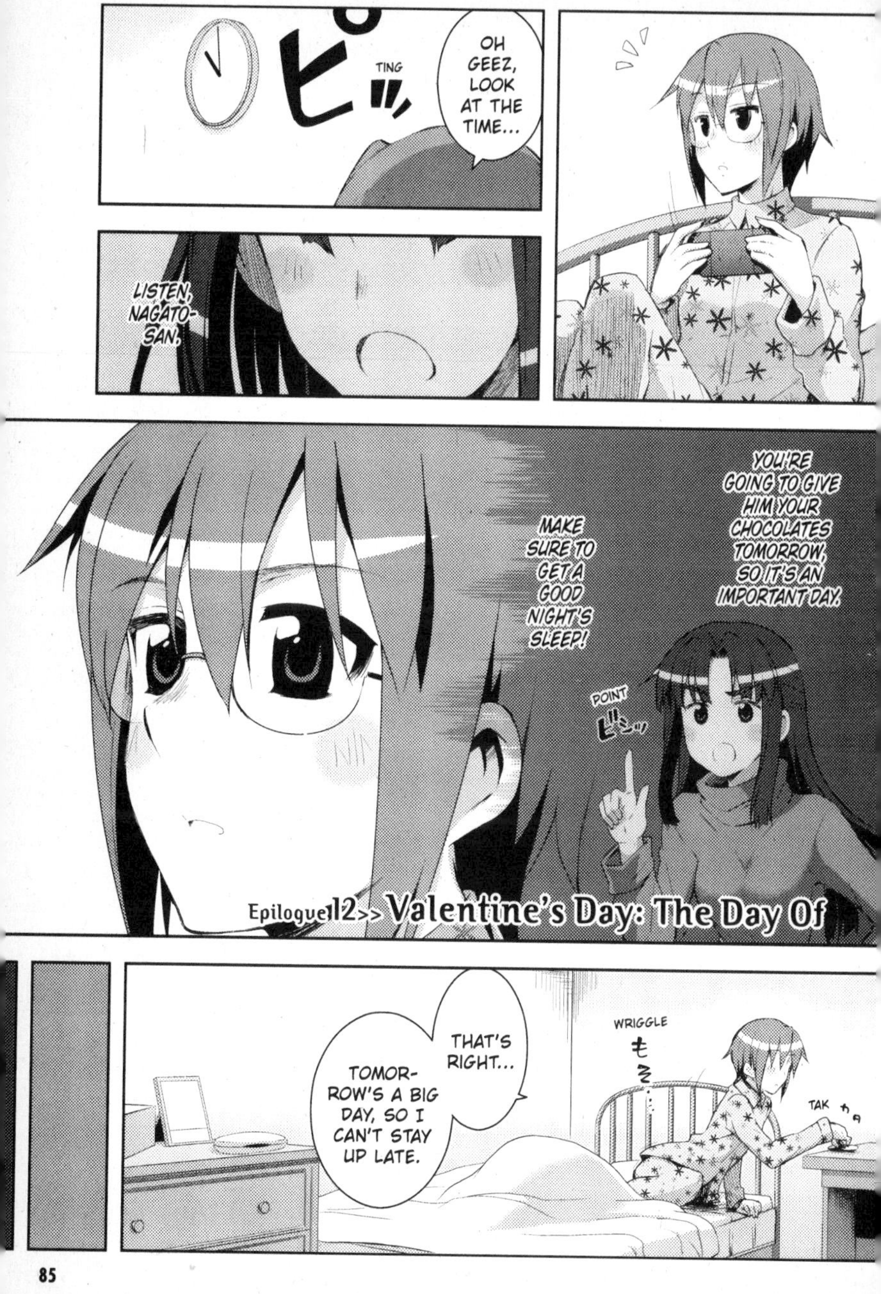
TING
OH GEEZ, LOOK AT THE TIME...
LISTEN, NAGATO-SAN.
YOU'RE GOING TO GIVE HIM YOUR CHOCOLATES TOMORROW, SO IT'S AN IMPORTANT DAY.
MAKE SURE TO GET A GOOD NIGHT'S SLEEP!
POINT
Epilogue 12>> Valentine's Day: The Day Of
WRIGGLE
TAK
THAT'S RIGHT...
TOMORROW'S A BIG DAY, SO I CAN'T STAY UP LATE.

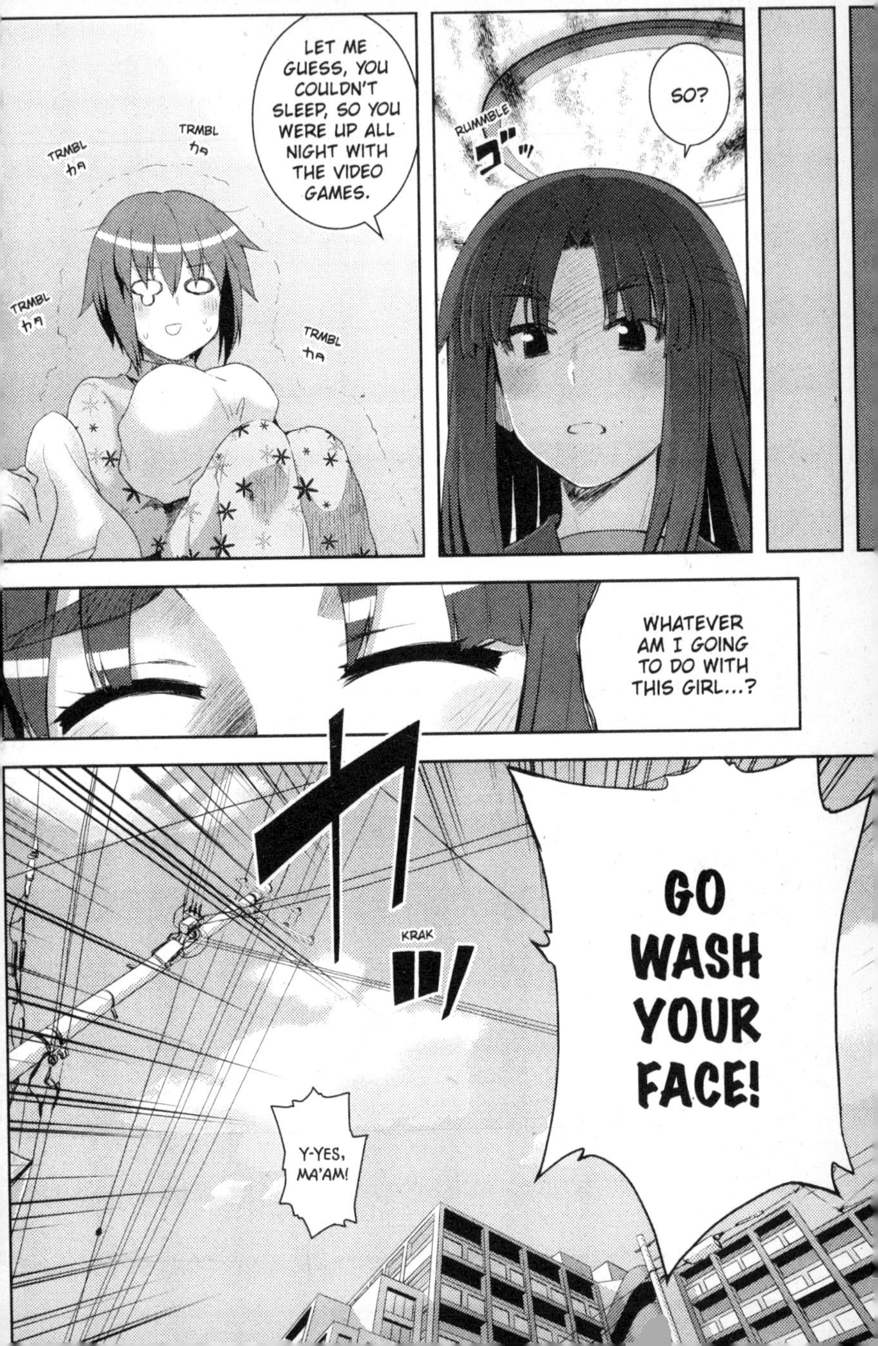

RUMMBLE
SO?
LET ME GUESS, YOU COULDN'T SLEEP, SO YOU WERE UP ALL NIGHT WITH THE VIDEO GAMES.
TRMBL
TRMBL
TRMBL
TRMBL
WHATEVER AM I GOING TO DO WITH THIS GIRL...?
GO WASH YOUR FACE!
KRAK
Y-YES, MA'AM!

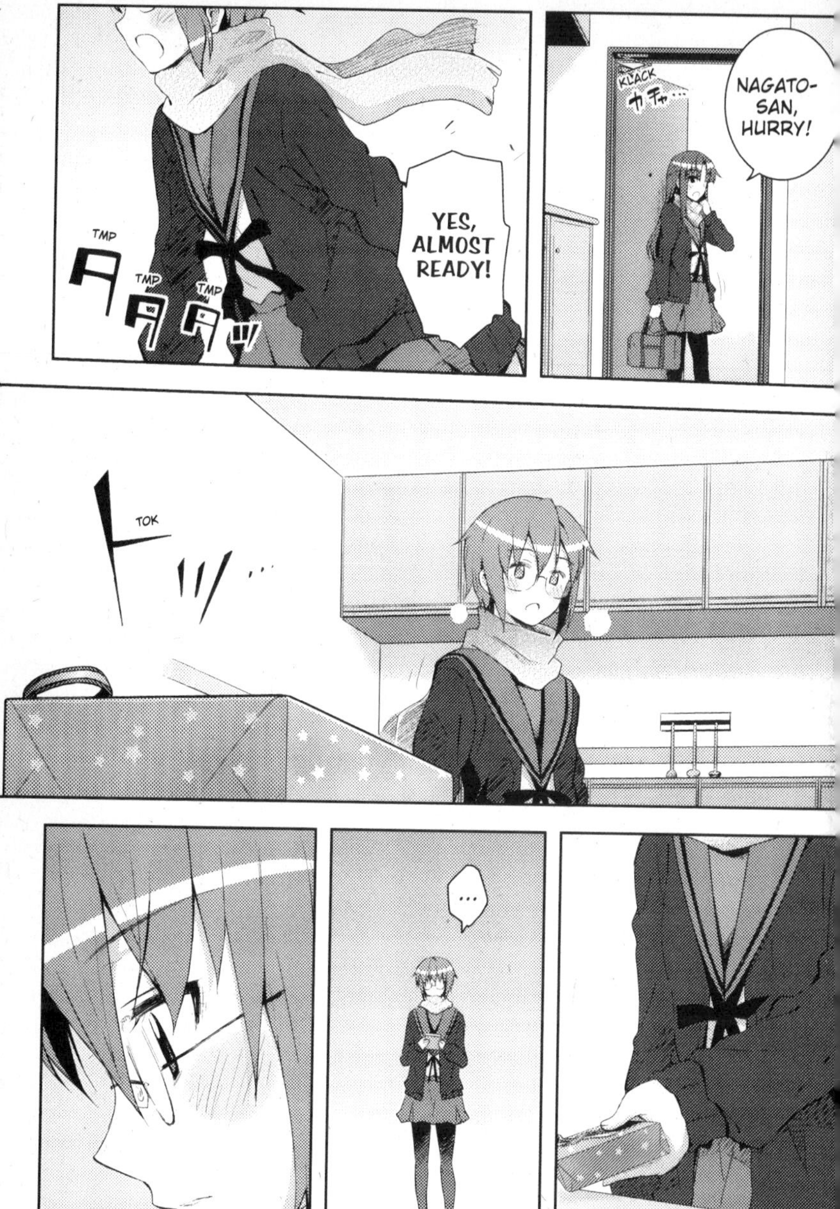
KLACK
カチャ…
NAGATO-SAN, HURRY!
YES, ALMOST READY!
TMP
タタタッ
TMP
TMP
TOK
トッ…
…

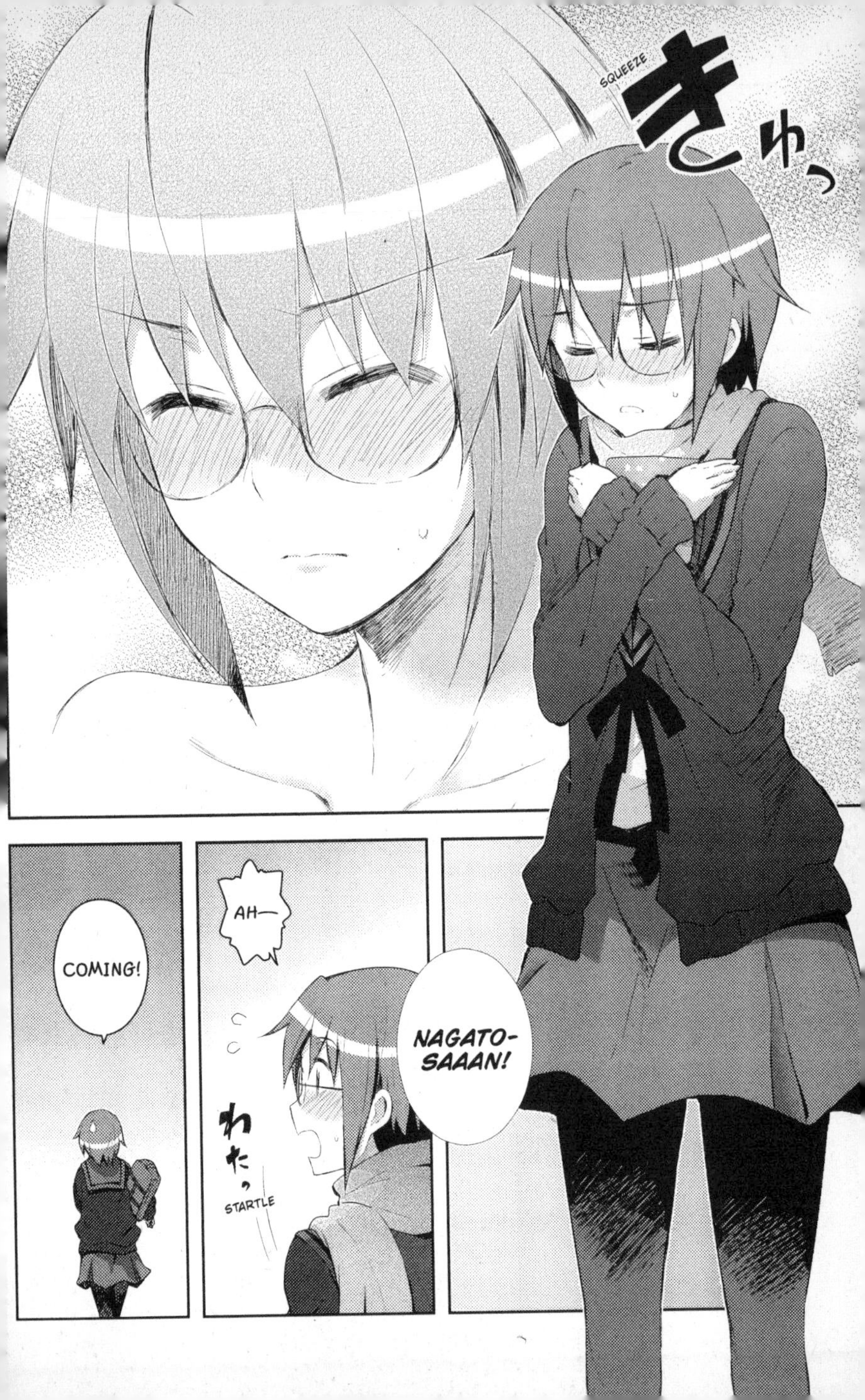
SQUEEZE
きゅっ
NAGATO-SAAAN!
AH—
わたっ
STARTLE
COMING!

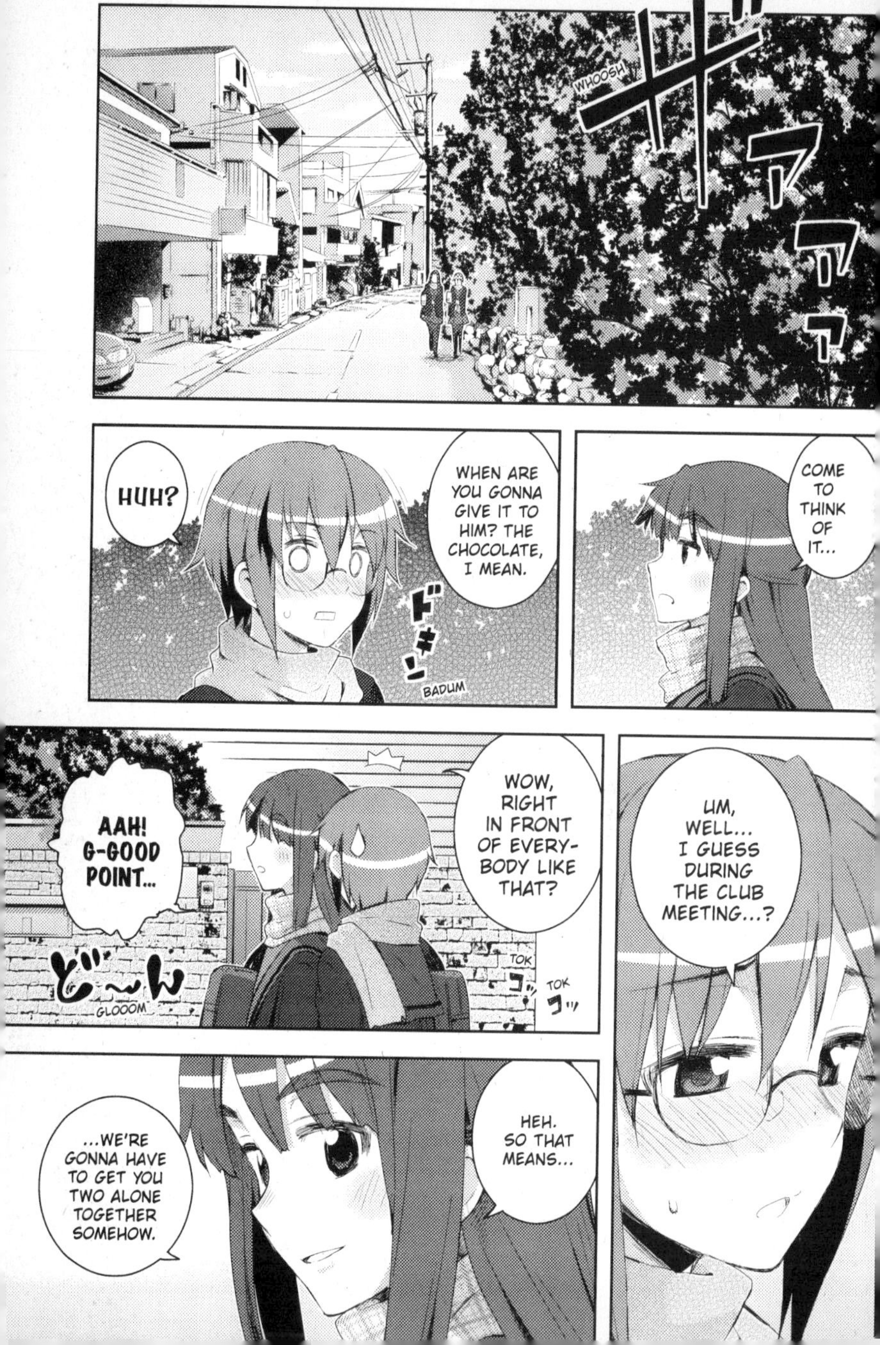

ザァァァ
WHOOSH
COME TO THINK OF IT...
WHEN ARE YOU GONNA GIVE IT TO HIM? THE CHOCOLATE, I MEAN.
HUH?
ドキン
BADUM
UM, WELL... I GUESS DURING THE CLUB MEETING...?
WOW, RIGHT IN FRONT OF EVERY-BODY LIKE THAT?
コッ
TOK
コッ
TOK
AAH! G-GOOD POINT...
ど~ん
GLOOOM
HEH. SO THAT MEANS...
...WE'RE GONNA HAVE TO GET YOU TWO ALONE TOGETHER SOMEHOW.

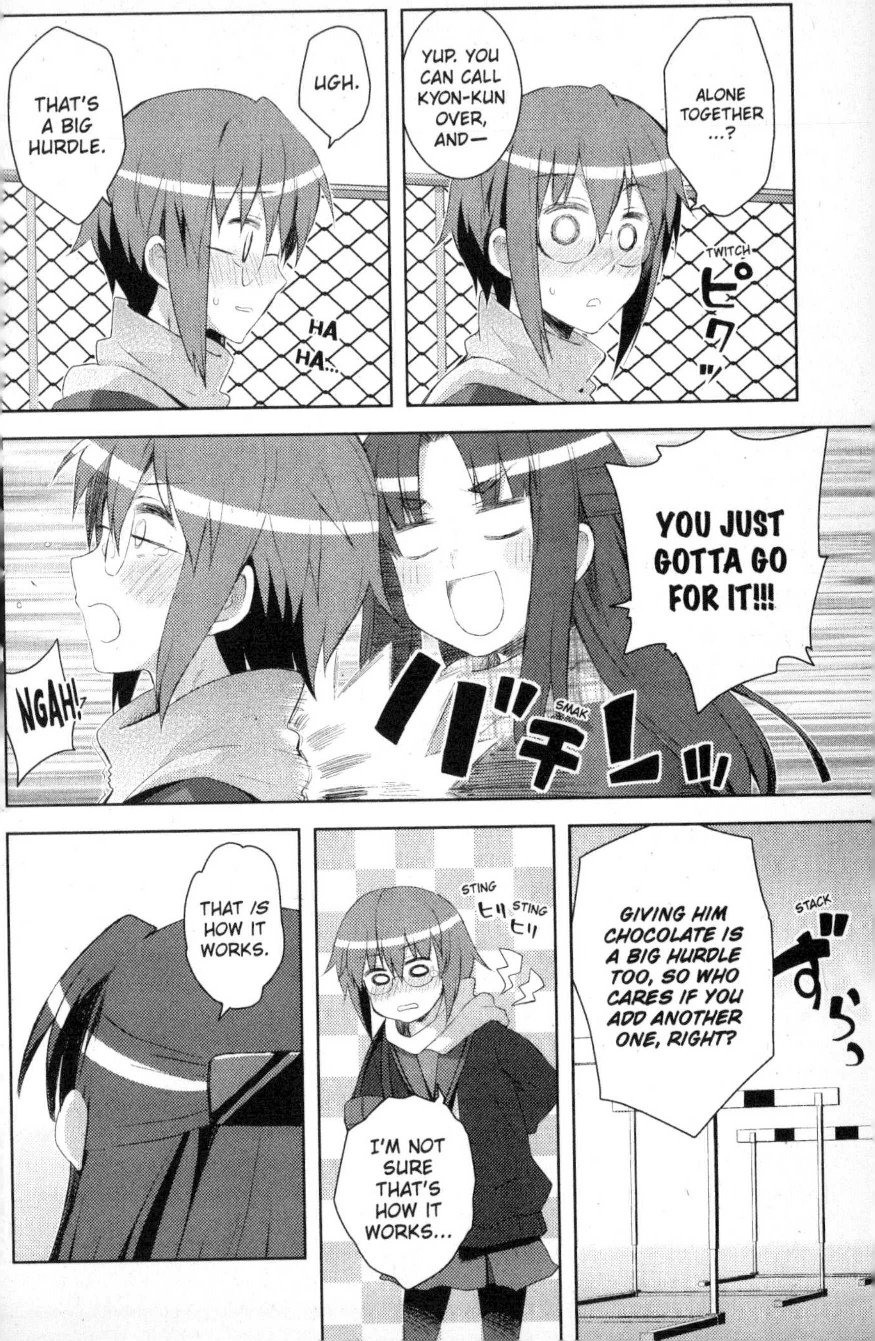
YUP. YOU CAN CALL KYON-KUN OVER, AND—
ALONE TOGETHER ...?
TWITCH
ピクッ
UGH.
THAT'S A BIG HURDLE.
HA HA...
YOU JUST GOTTA GO FOR IT!!!
SMAK
バチンッ
NGAH!
GIVING HIM CHOCOLATE IS A BIG HURDLE TOO, SO WHO CARES IF YOU ADD ANOTHER ONE, RIGHT?
STACK
ずらっ
STING
ヒリ
STING
ヒリ
I'M NOT SURE THAT'S HOW IT WORKS...
THAT IS HOW IT WORKS.

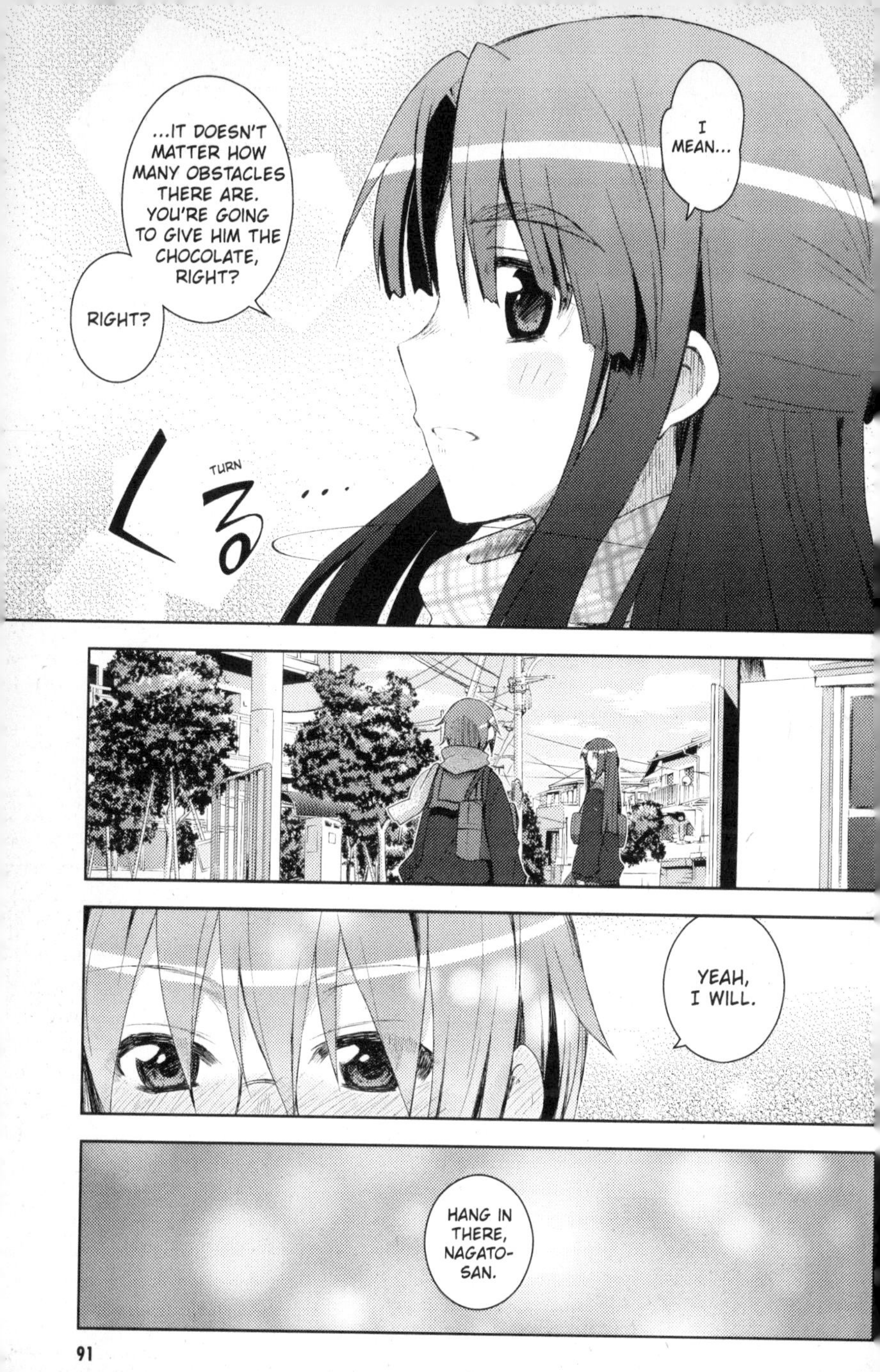
I MEAN...
...IT DOESN'T MATTER HOW MANY OBSTACLES THERE ARE. YOU'RE GOING TO GIVE HIM THE CHOCOLATE, RIGHT?
RIGHT?
TURN
くる
...
YEAH, I WILL.
HANG IN THERE, NAGATO-SAN.

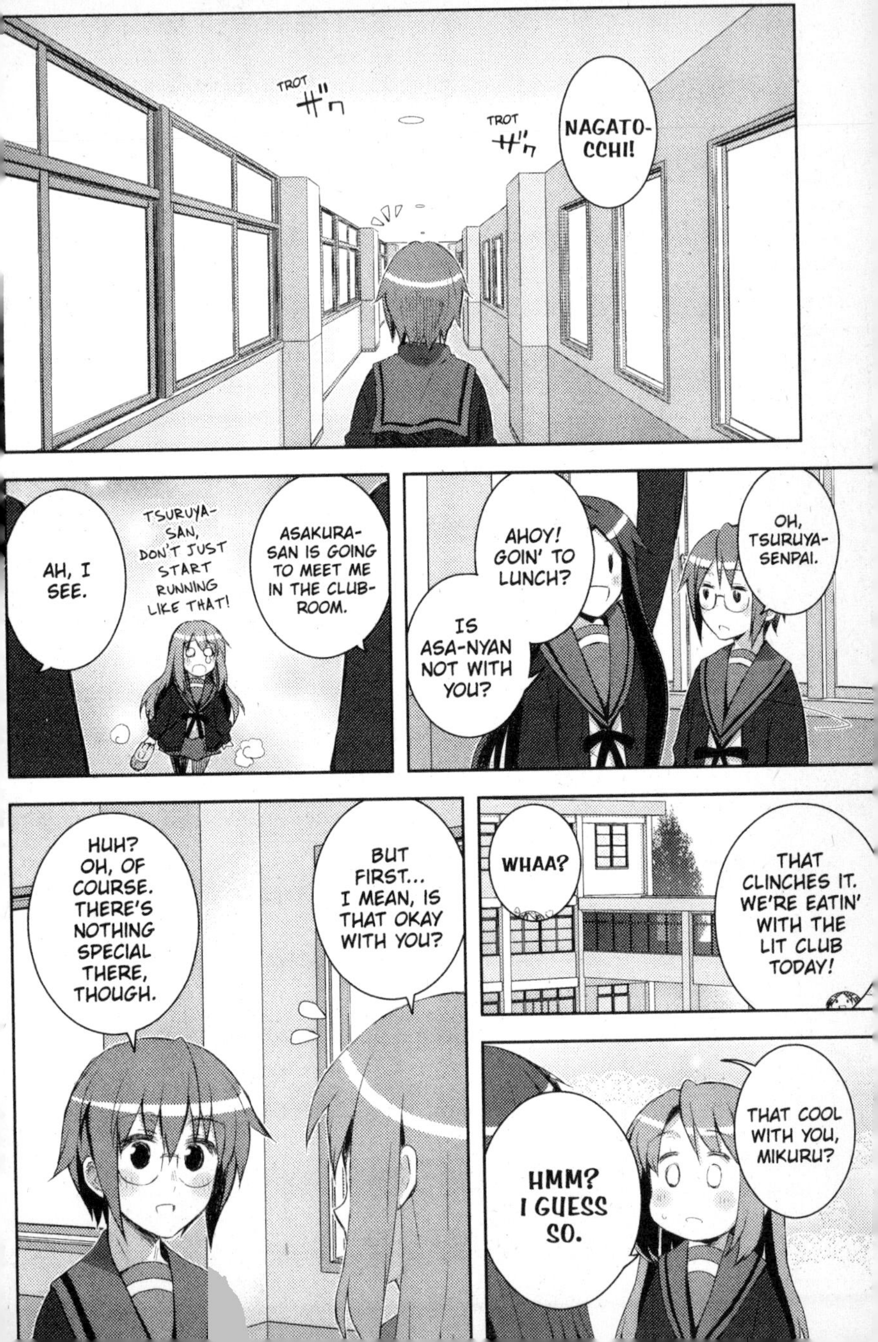
NAGATO-CCHI!
TROT ザッ
TROT ザッ
OH, TSURUYA-SENPAI.
AHOY! GOIN' TO LUNCH?
IS ASA-NYAN NOT WITH YOU?
ASAKURA-SAN IS GOING TO MEET ME IN THE CLUB-ROOM.
TSURUYA-SAN, DON'T JUST START RUNNING LIKE THAT!
AH, I SEE.
THAT CLINCHES IT. WE'RE EATIN' WITH THE LIT CLUB TODAY!
WHAA?
THAT COOL WITH YOU, MIKURU?
HMM? I GUESS SO.
BUT FIRST... I MEAN, IS THAT OKAY WITH YOU?
HUH? OH, OF COURSE. THERE'S NOTHING SPECIAL THERE, THOUGH.

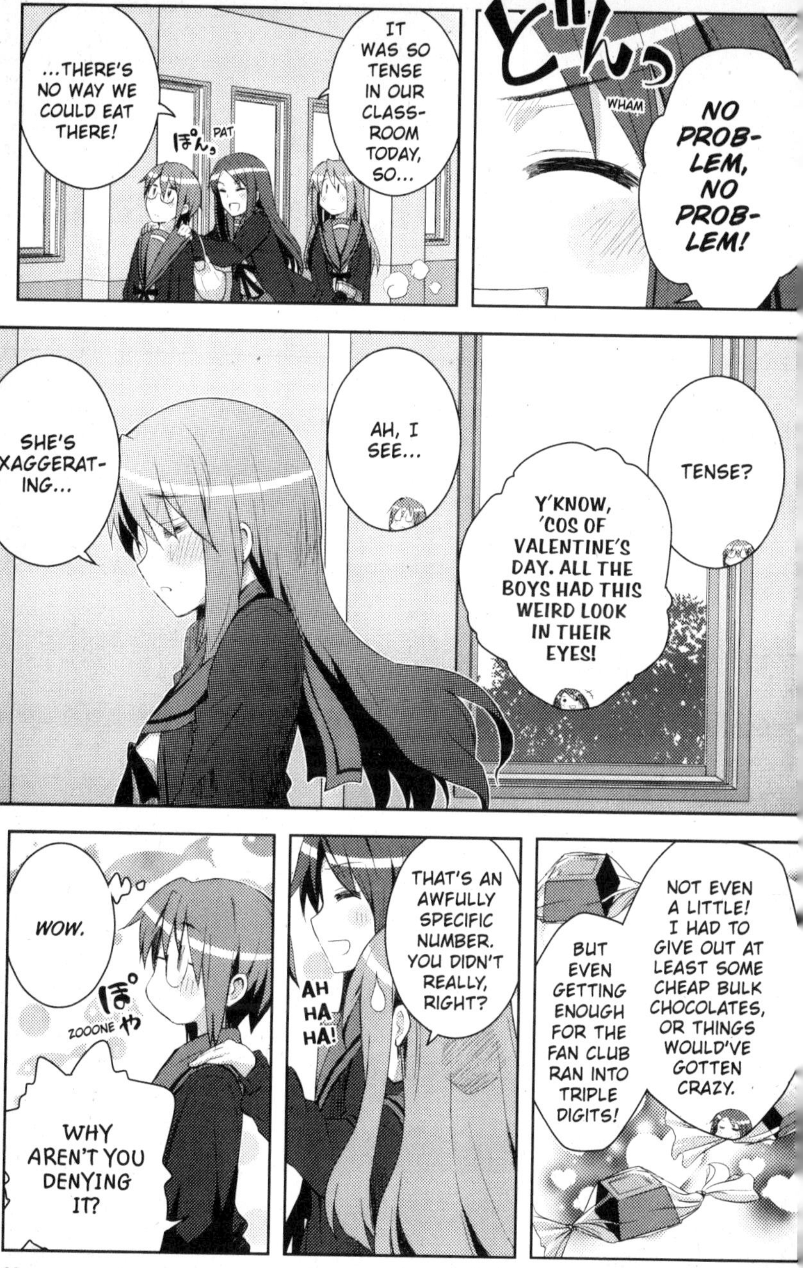
どんっ
WHAM
NO PROBLEM, NO PROBLEM!
IT WAS SO TENSE IN OUR CLASSROOM TODAY, SO...
...THERE'S NO WAY WE COULD EAT THERE!
ぽん
PAT
TENSE?
Y'KNOW, 'COS OF VALENTINE'S DAY. ALL THE BOYS HAD THIS WEIRD LOOK IN THEIR EYES!
AH, I SEE...
SHE'S EXAGGERATING...
NOT EVEN A LITTLE! I HAD TO GIVE OUT AT LEAST SOME CHEAP BULK CHOCOLATES, OR THINGS WOULD'VE GOTTEN CRAZY.
BUT EVEN GETTING ENOUGH FOR THE FAN CLUB RAN INTO TRIPLE DIGITS!
THAT'S AN AWFULLY SPECIFIC NUMBER. YOU DIDN'T REALLY, RIGHT?
AH HA HA!
WOW.
ぽや
ZOOONE
WHY AREN'T YOU DENYING IT?

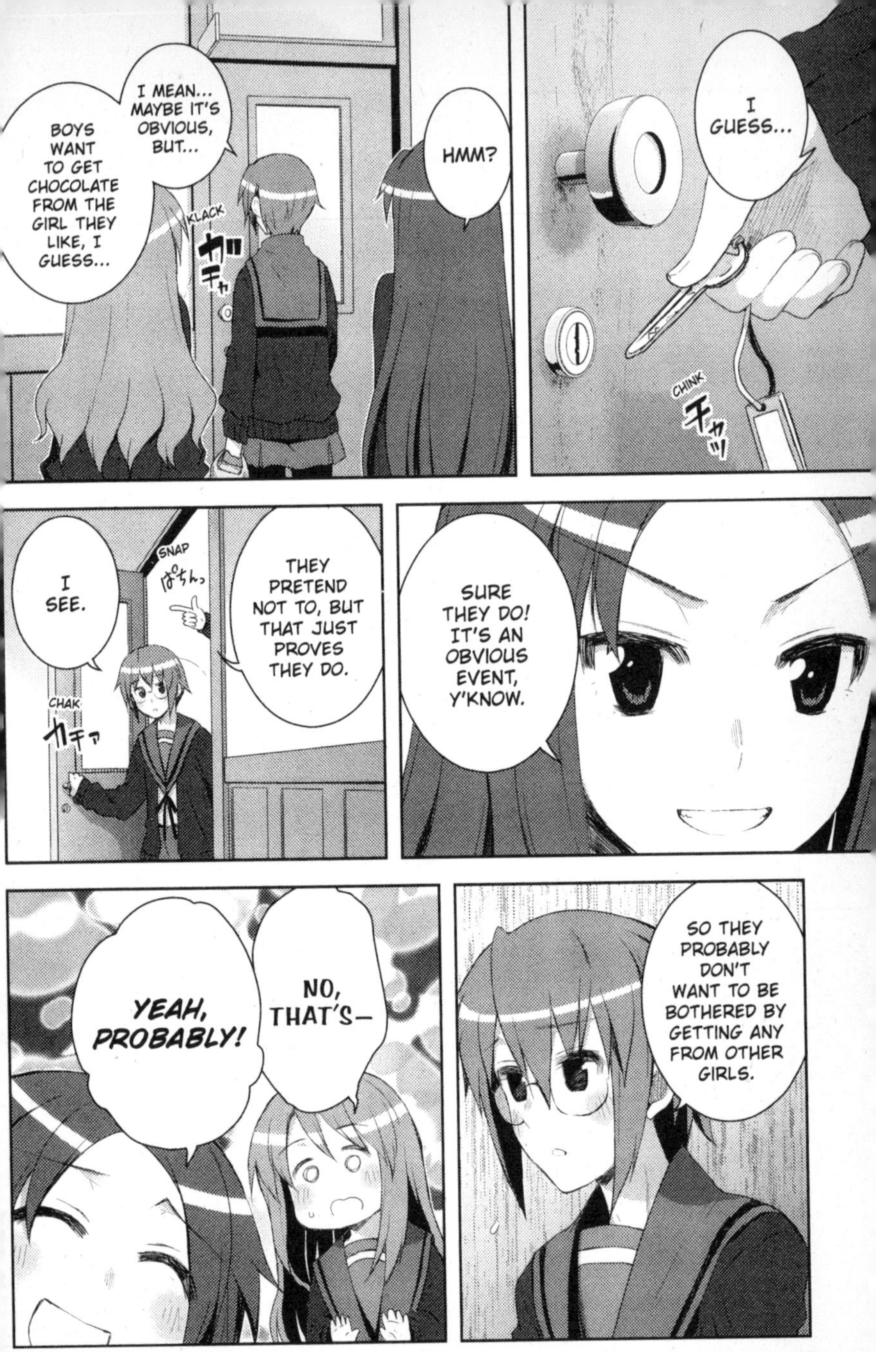
I GUESS...
CHINK
HMM?
I MEAN... MAYBE IT'S OBVIOUS, BUT...
BOYS WANT TO GET CHOCOLATE FROM THE GIRL THEY LIKE, I GUESS...
KLACK
SURE THEY DO! IT'S AN OBVIOUS EVENT, Y'KNOW.
THEY PRETEND NOT TO, BUT THAT JUST PROVES THEY DO.
SNAP
I SEE.
CHAK
SO THEY PROBABLY DON'T WANT TO BE BOTHERED BY GETTING ANY FROM OTHER GIRLS.
NO, THAT'S—
YEAH, PROBABLY!

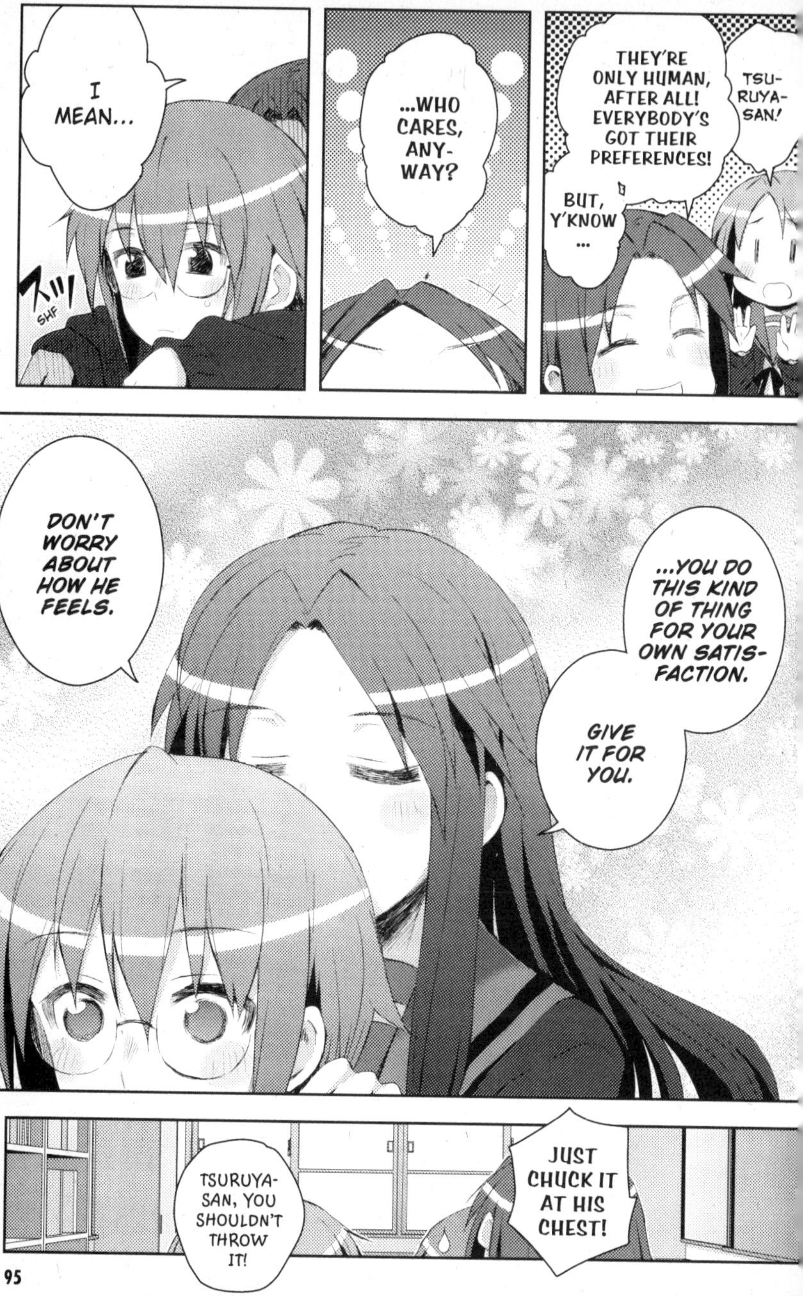
TSU-RUYA-SAN!
THEY'RE ONLY HUMAN, AFTER ALL! EVERYBODY'S GOT THEIR PREFERENCES!
BUT, Y'KNOW ...
...WHO CARES, ANY-WAY?
I MEAN...
スッ
SHF
...YOU DO THIS KIND OF THING FOR YOUR OWN SATIS-FACTION.
GIVE IT FOR YOU.
DON'T WORRY ABOUT HOW HE FEELS.
JUST CHUCK IT AT HIS CHEST!
TSURUYA-SAN, YOU SHOULDN'T THROW IT!

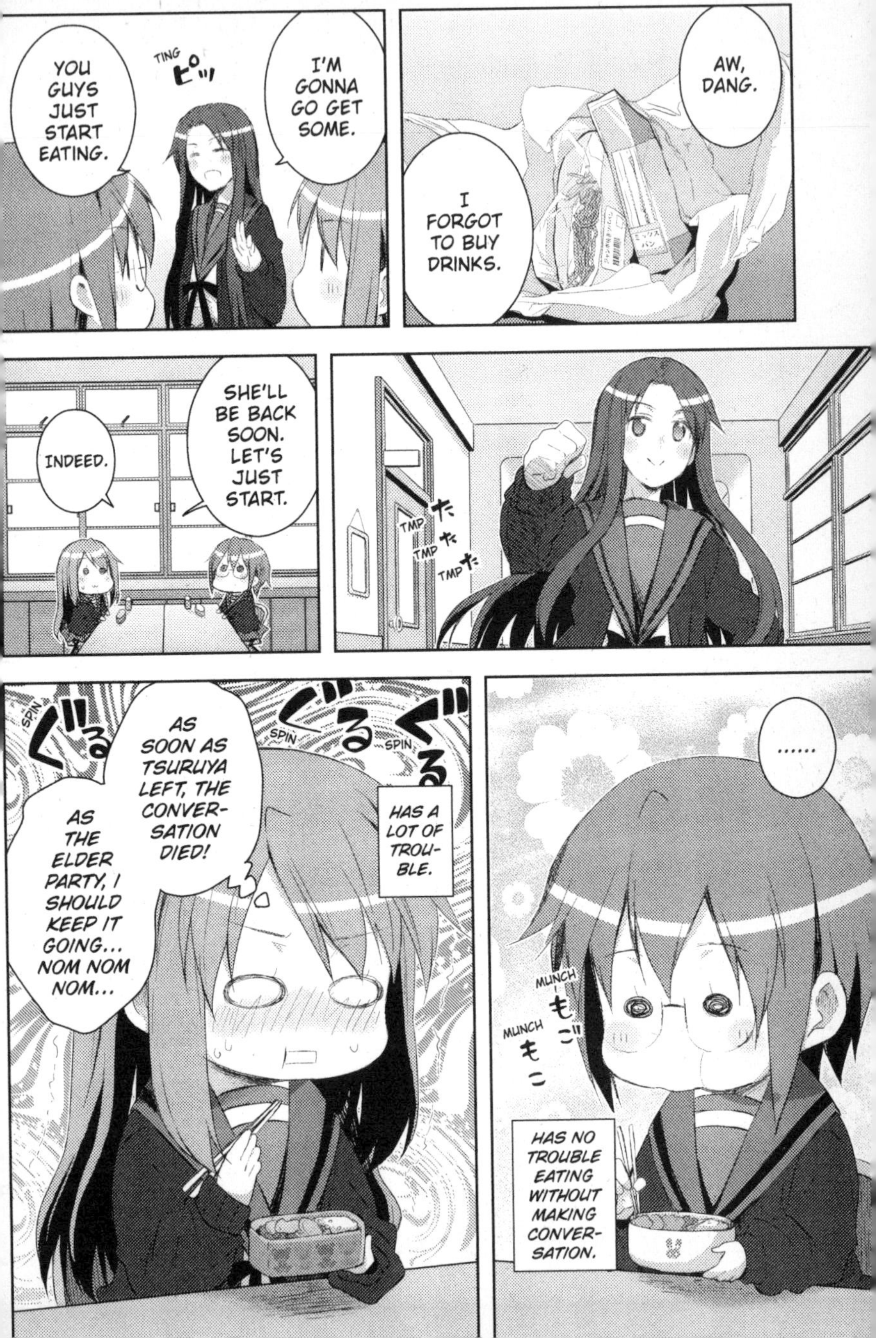
AW, DANG.
I FORGOT TO BUY DRINKS.
I'M GONNA GO GET SOME.
TING ピッ
YOU GUYS JUST START EATING.
TMP た
TMP た
TMP た
SHE'LL BE BACK SOON. LET'S JUST START.
INDEED.
......
MUNCH もご
MUNCH もこ
HAS NO TROUBLE EATING WITHOUT MAKING CONVERSATION.
SPIN ぐる
SPIN ぐる
SPIN ぐる
HAS A LOT OF TROUBLE.
AS SOON AS TSURUYA LEFT, THE CONVERSATION DIED!
AS THE ELDER PARTY, I SHOULD KEEP IT GOING... NOM NOM NOM...

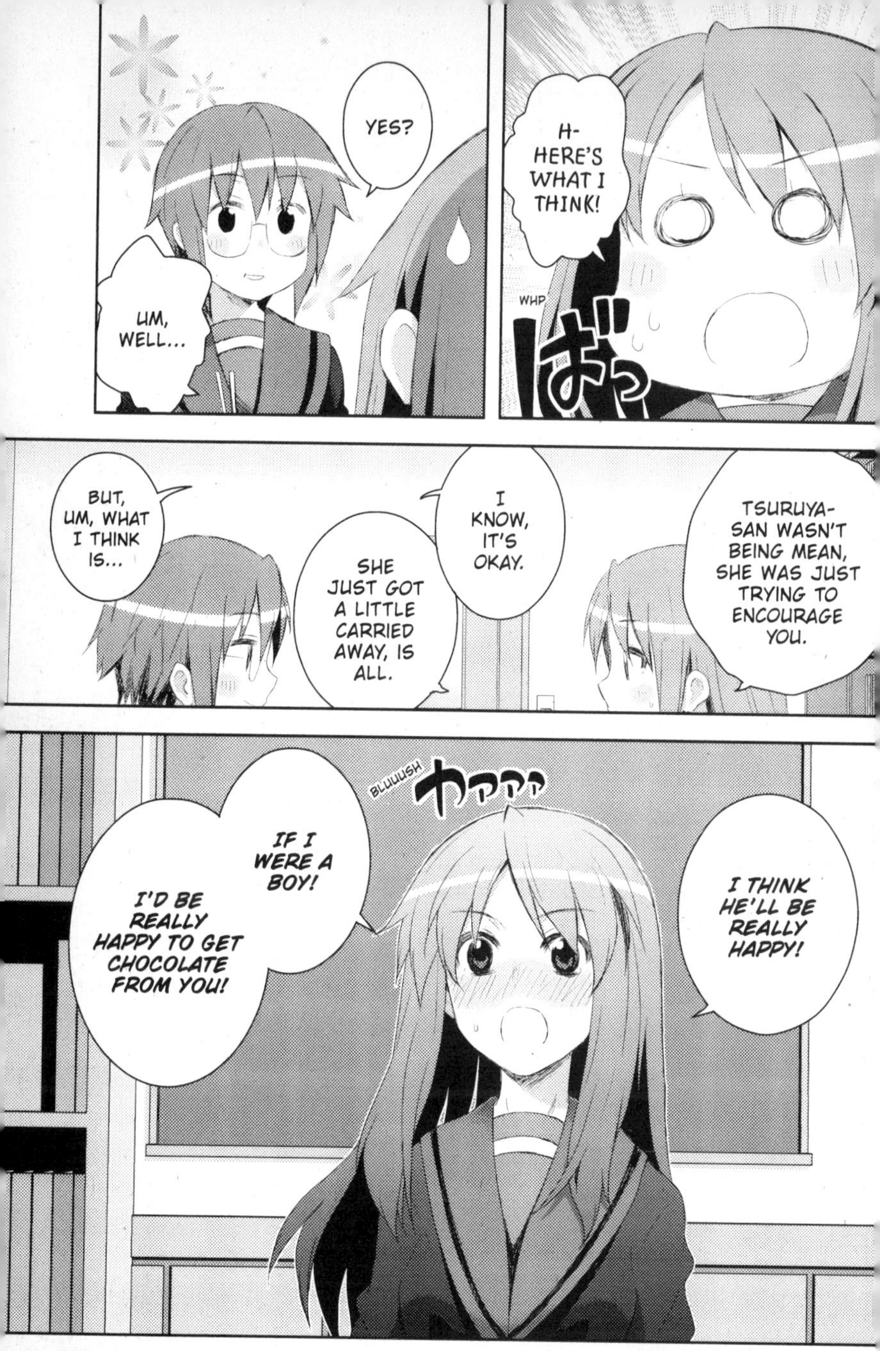
H-
HERE'S
WHAT I
THINK!
WHP
ばっ
YES?
UM,
WELL...
TSURUYA-
SAN WASN'T
BEING MEAN,
SHE WAS JUST
TRYING TO
ENCOURAGE
YOU.
I
KNOW,
IT'S
OKAY.
SHE
JUST GOT
A LITTLE
CARRIED
AWAY, IS
ALL.
BUT,
UM, WHAT
I THINK
IS...
BLUUUSH
カァァァ
I THINK
HE'LL BE
REALLY
HAPPY!
IF I
WERE A
BOY!
I'D BE
REALLY
HAPPY TO GET
CHOCOLATE
FROM YOU!

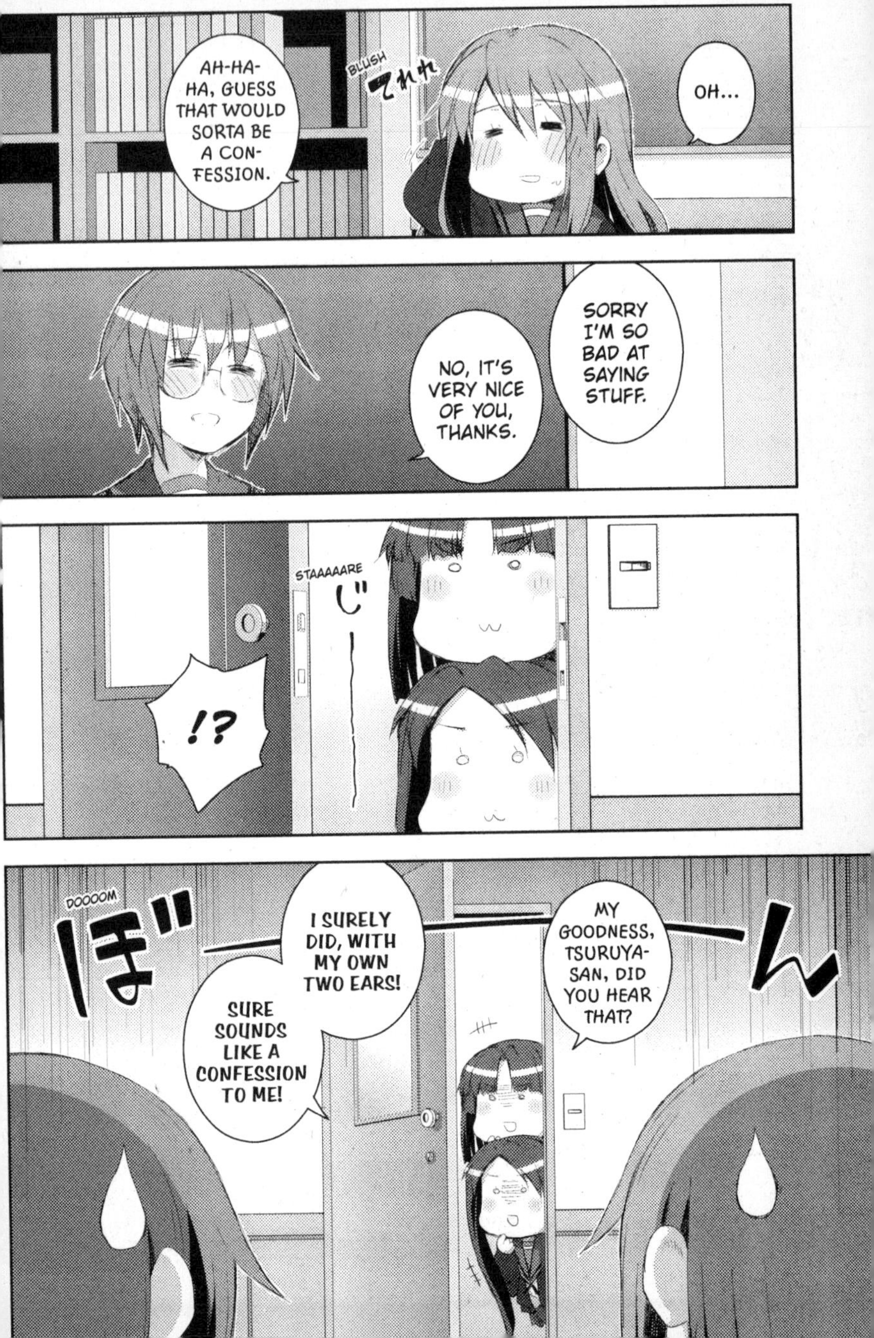
OH...
BLUSH
てれれ
AH-HA-HA, GUESS THAT WOULD SORTA BE A CON-FESSION.
SORRY I'M SO BAD AT SAYING STUFF.
NO, IT'S VERY NICE OF YOU, THANKS.
STAAAAARE
じー
!?
DOOOOM
ぼーん
MY GOODNESS, TSURUYA-SAN, DID YOU HEAR THAT?
I SURELY DID, WITH MY OWN TWO EARS!
SURE SOUNDS LIKE A CONFESSION TO ME!

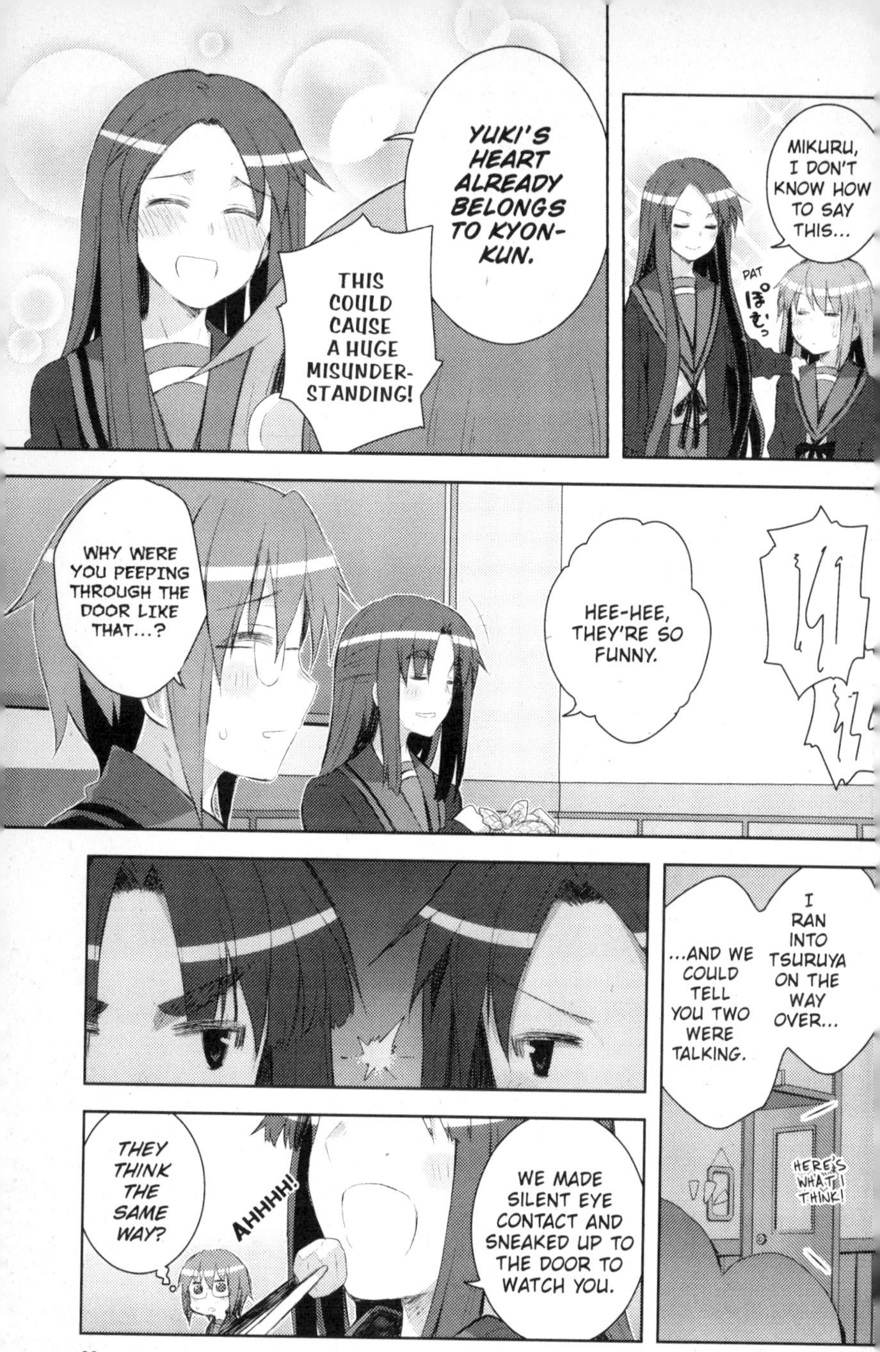
MIKURU, I DON'T KNOW HOW TO SAY THIS...
PAT
ぽむっ
YUKI'S HEART ALREADY BELONGS TO KYON-KUN.
THIS COULD CAUSE A HUGE MISUNDERSTANDING!
HEE-HEE, THEY'RE SO FUNNY.
WHY WERE YOU PEEPING THROUGH THE DOOR LIKE THAT...?
I RAN INTO TSURUYA ON THE WAY OVER...
...AND WE COULD TELL YOU TWO WERE TALKING.
HERE'S WHAT I THINK!
WE MADE SILENT EYE CONTACT AND SNEAKED UP TO THE DOOR TO WATCH YOU.
AHHHH!
THEY THINK THE SAME WAY?

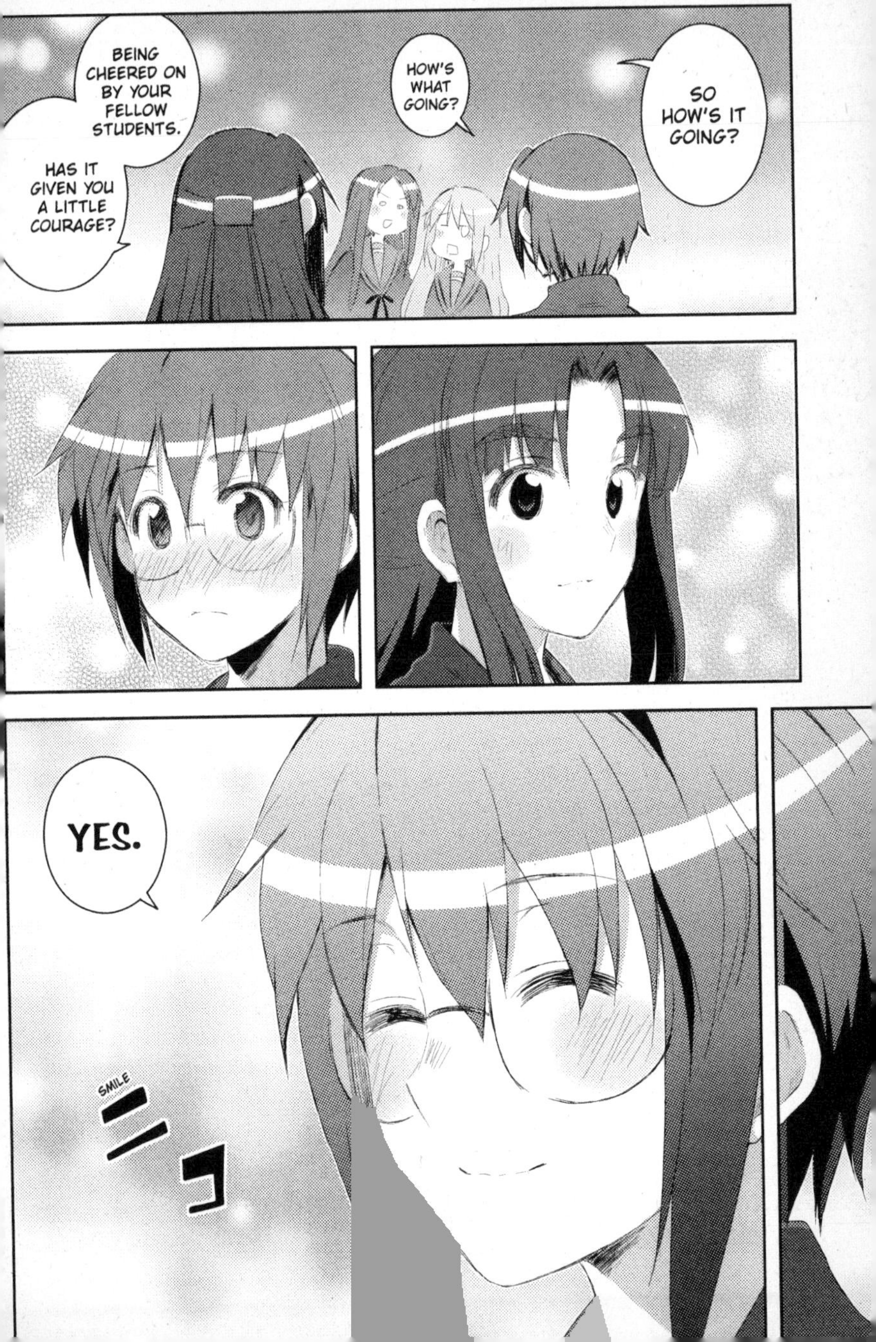
SO HOW'S IT GOING?
HOW'S WHAT GOING?
BEING CHEERED ON BY YOUR FELLOW STUDENTS.
HAS IT GIVEN YOU A LITTLE COURAGE?
YES.
SMILE
ニコ

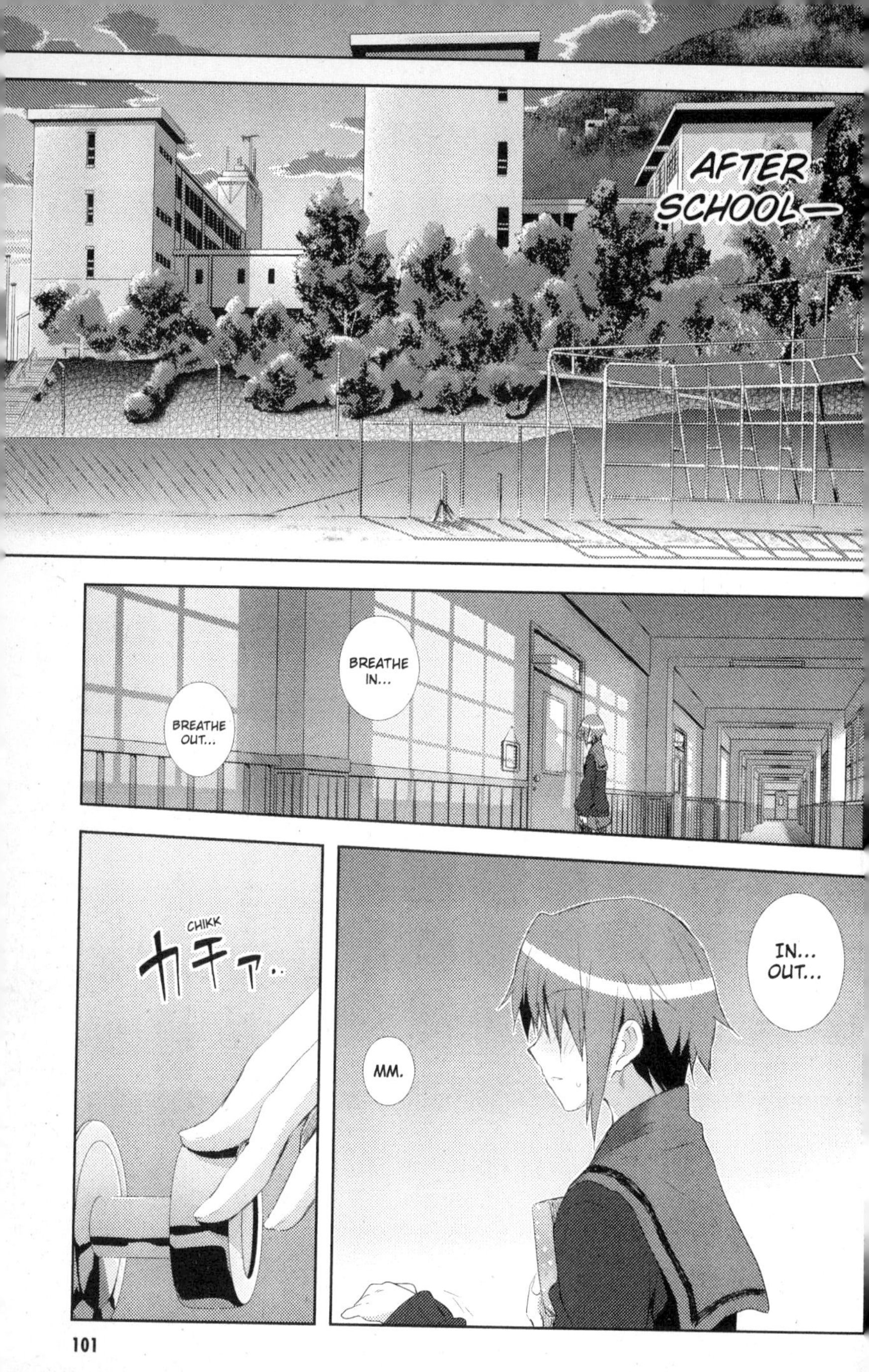
AFTER SCHOOL—
BREATHE IN...
BREATHE OUT...
IN... OUT...
MM.
CHIKK
カチャ..

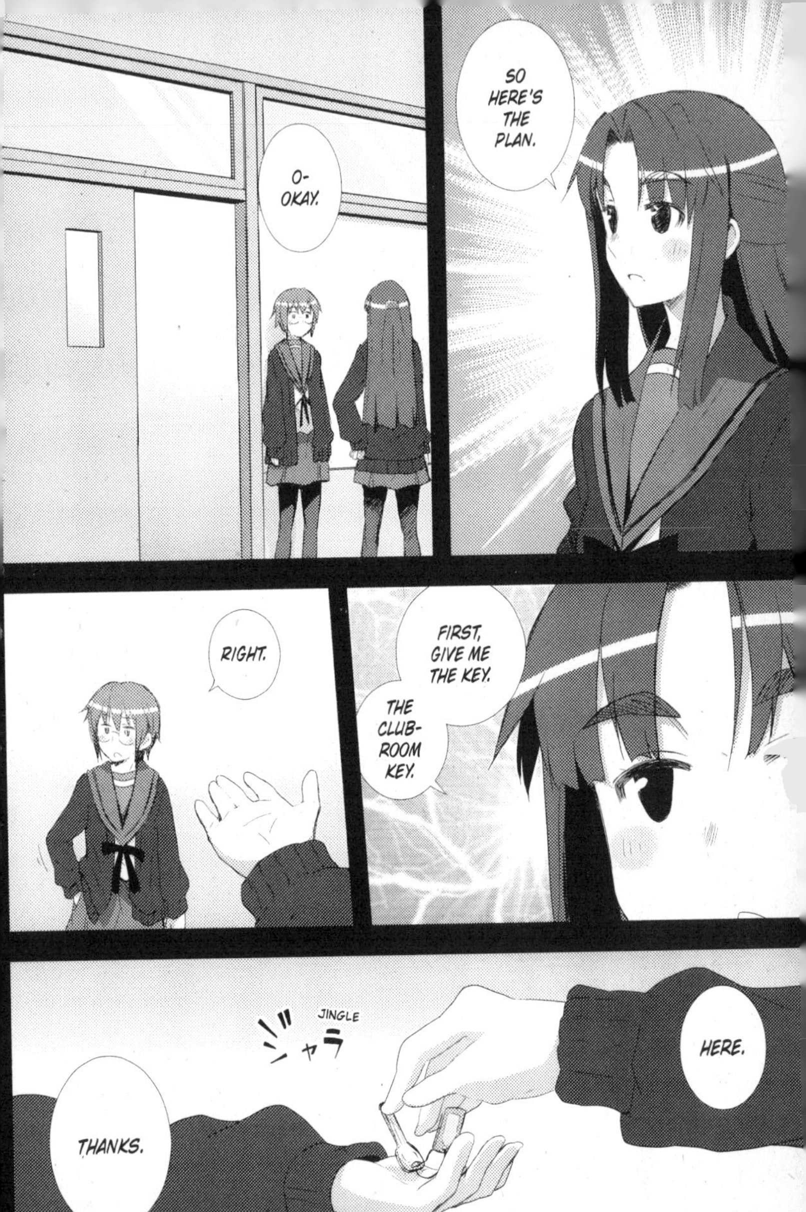
SO HERE'S THE PLAN.
O-OKAY.
FIRST, GIVE ME THE KEY.
THE CLUB-ROOM KEY.
RIGHT.
HERE.
ジャラ JINGLE
THANKS.

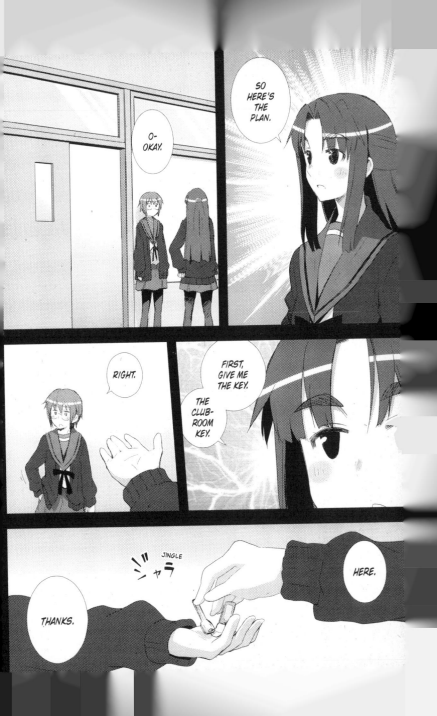

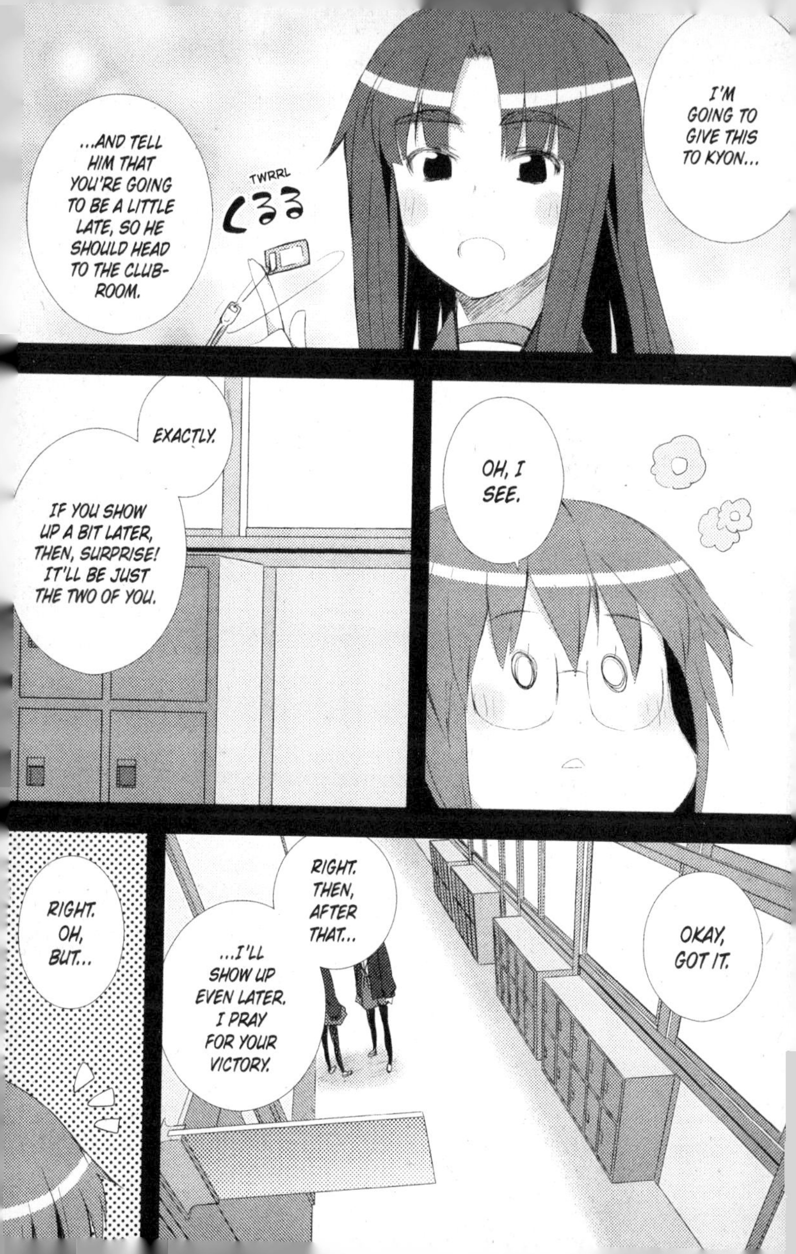
I'M GOING TO GIVE THIS TO KYON...
TWRRL
くるる
...AND TELL HIM THAT YOU'RE GOING TO BE A LITTLE LATE, SO HE SHOULD HEAD TO THE CLUB-ROOM.
OH, I SEE.
EXACTLY.
IF YOU SHOW UP A BIT LATER, THEN, SURPRISE! IT'LL BE JUST THE TWO OF YOU.
OKAY, GOT IT.
RIGHT. THEN, AFTER THAT...
...I'LL SHOW UP EVEN LATER. I PRAY FOR YOUR VICTORY.
RIGHT. OH, BUT...

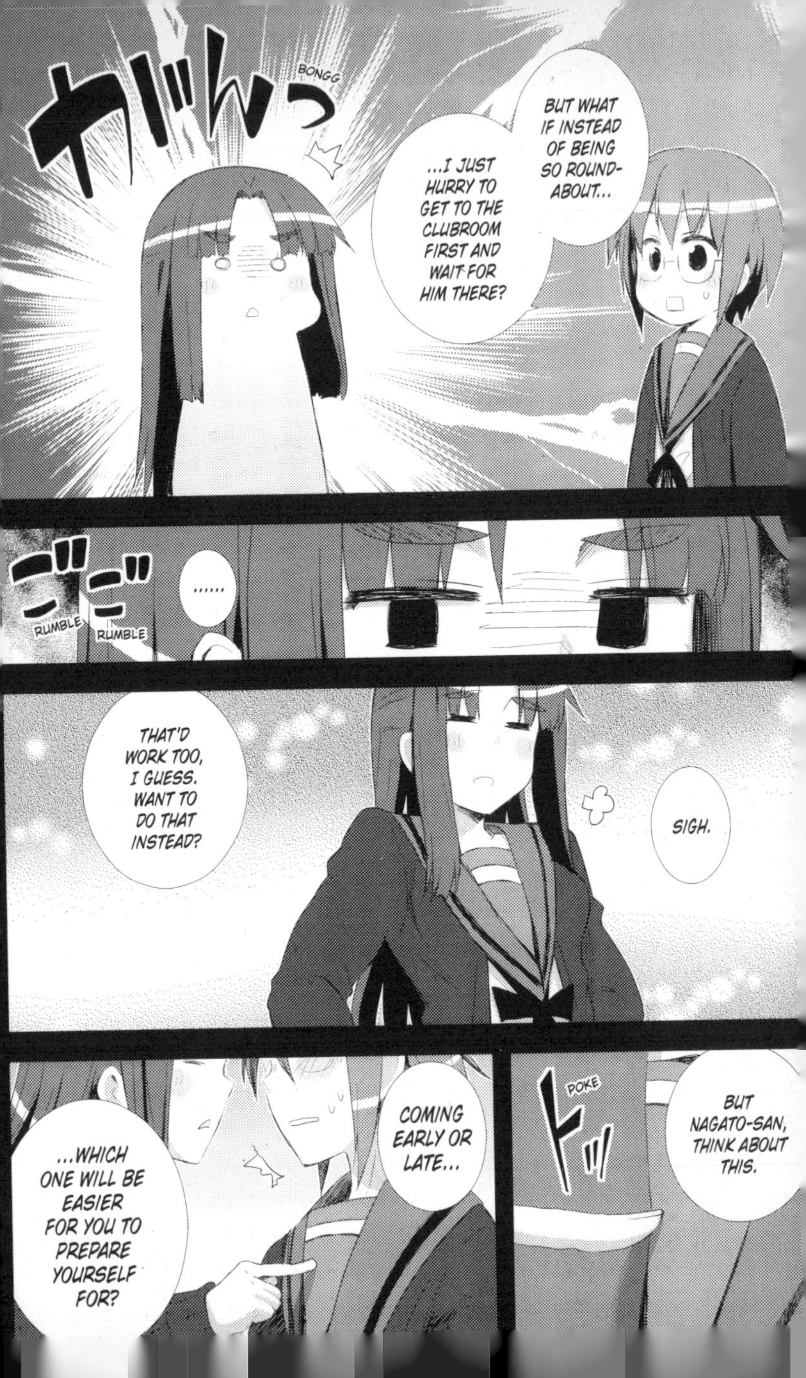
BUT WHAT IF INSTEAD OF BEING SO ROUND-ABOUT...
...I JUST HURRY TO GET TO THE CLUBROOM FIRST AND WAIT FOR HIM THERE?
BONGG
......
RUMBLE RUMBLE
SIGH.
THAT'D WORK TOO, I GUESS. WANT TO DO THAT INSTEAD?
BUT NAGATO-SAN, THINK ABOUT THIS.
POKE
COMING EARLY OR LATE...
...WHICH ONE WILL BE EASIER FOR YOU TO PREPARE YOURSELF FOR?

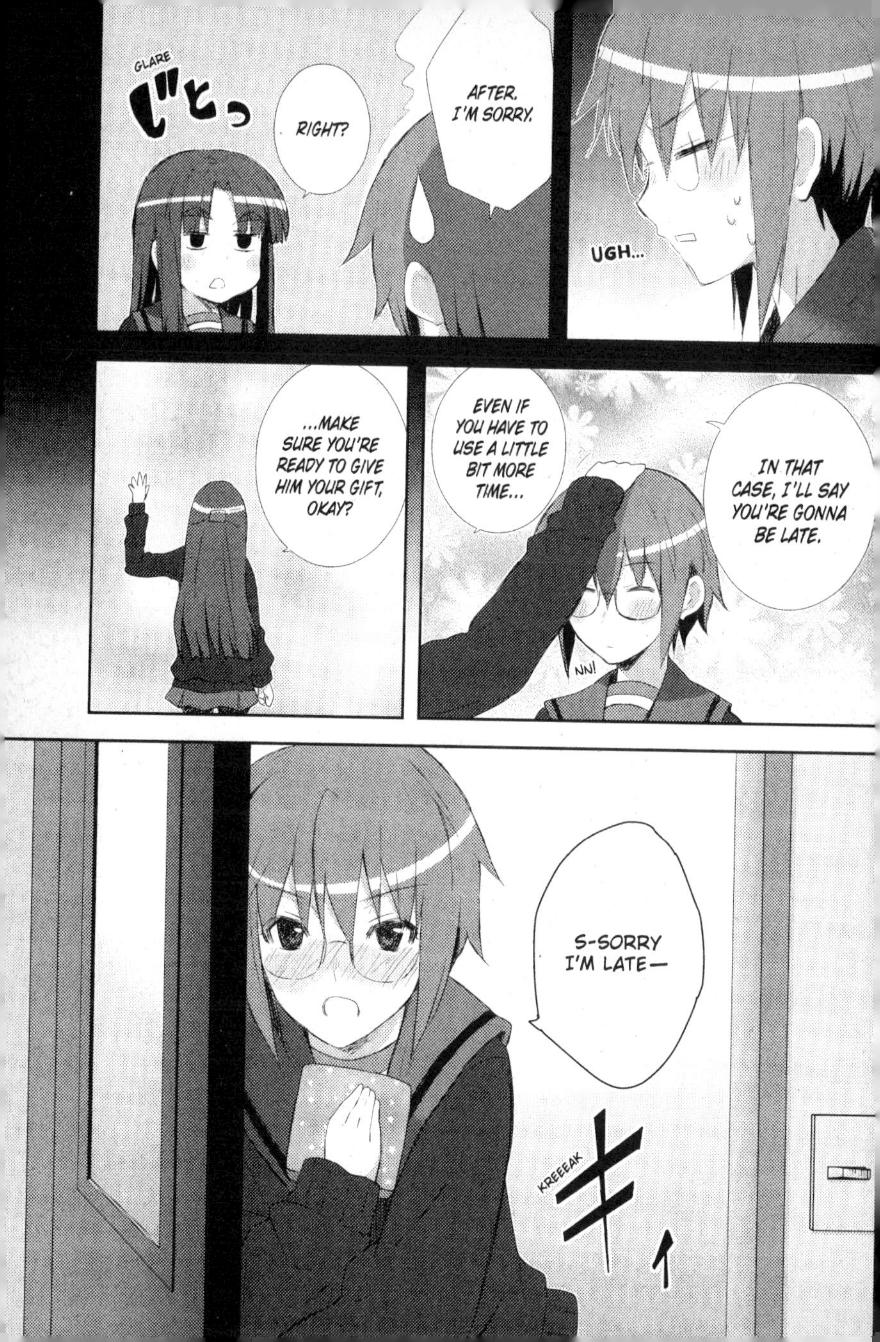
UGH...
AFTER. I'M SORRY.
RIGHT?
GLARE
じとっ
IN THAT CASE, I'LL SAY YOU'RE GONNA BE LATE.
EVEN IF YOU HAVE TO USE A LITTLE BIT MORE TIME...
NN!
...MAKE SURE YOU'RE READY TO GIVE HIM YOUR GIFT, OKAY?
S-SORRY I'M LATE—
KREEEAK
キィ

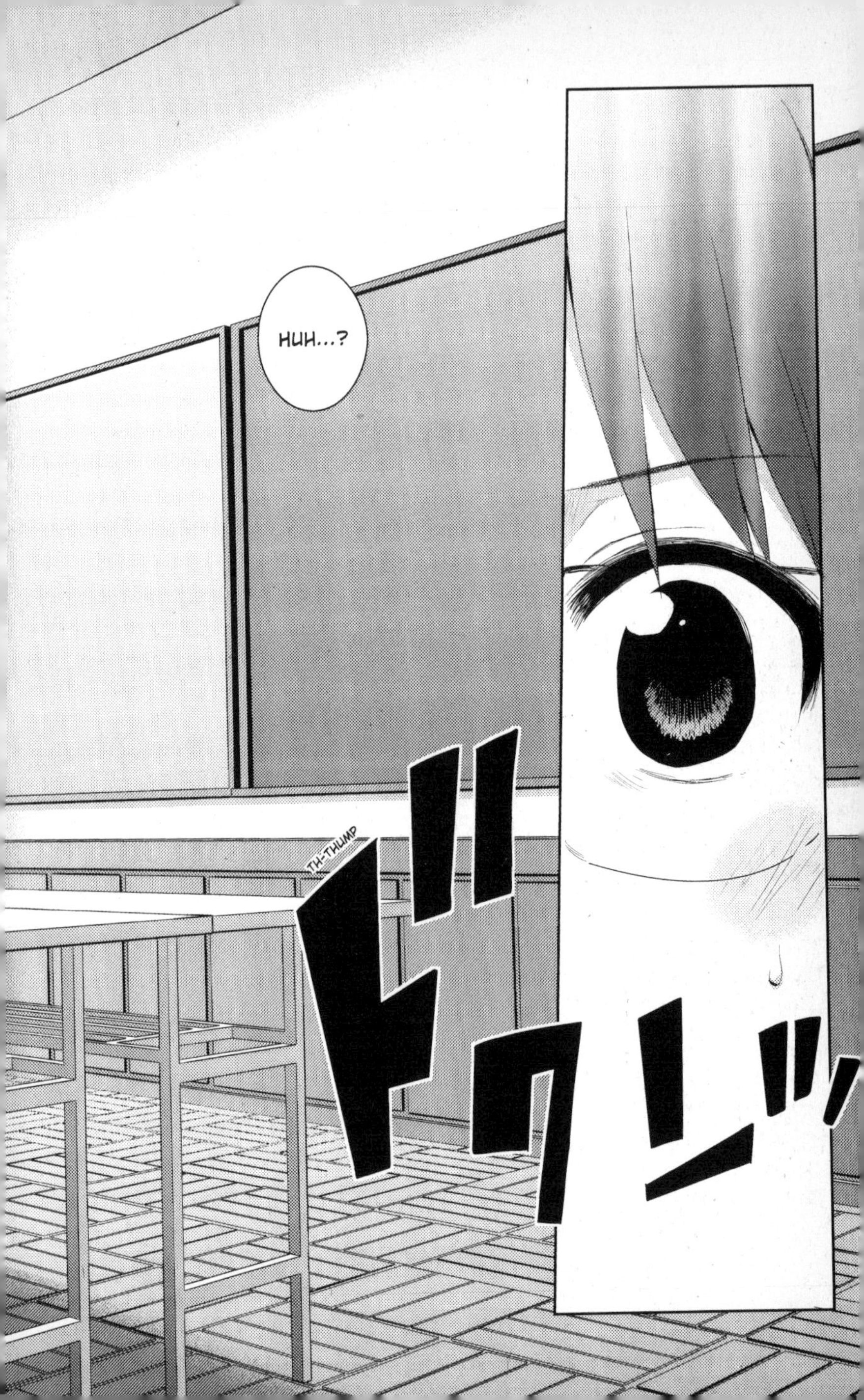
HUH...?
TH-THUMP
ドクン

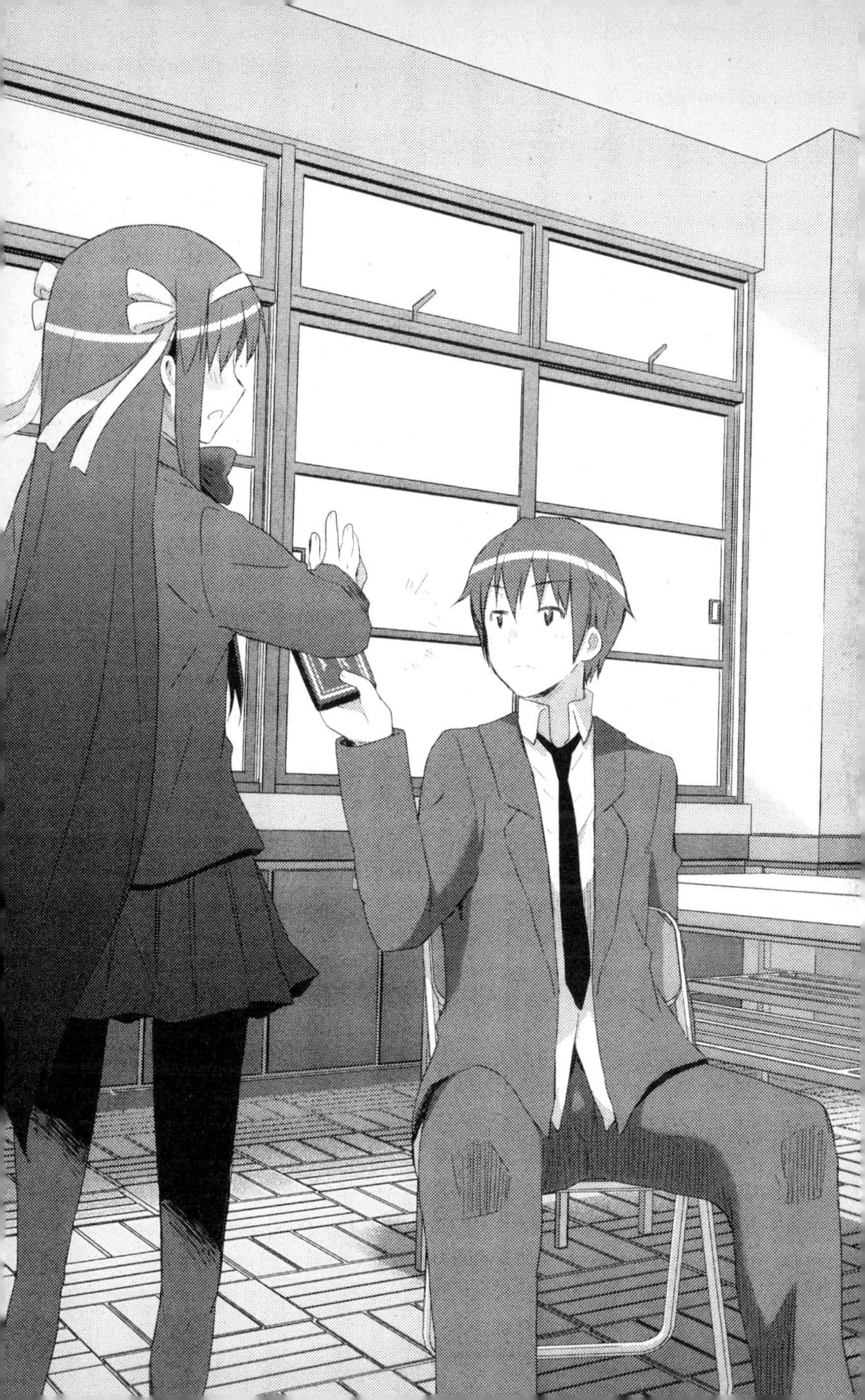

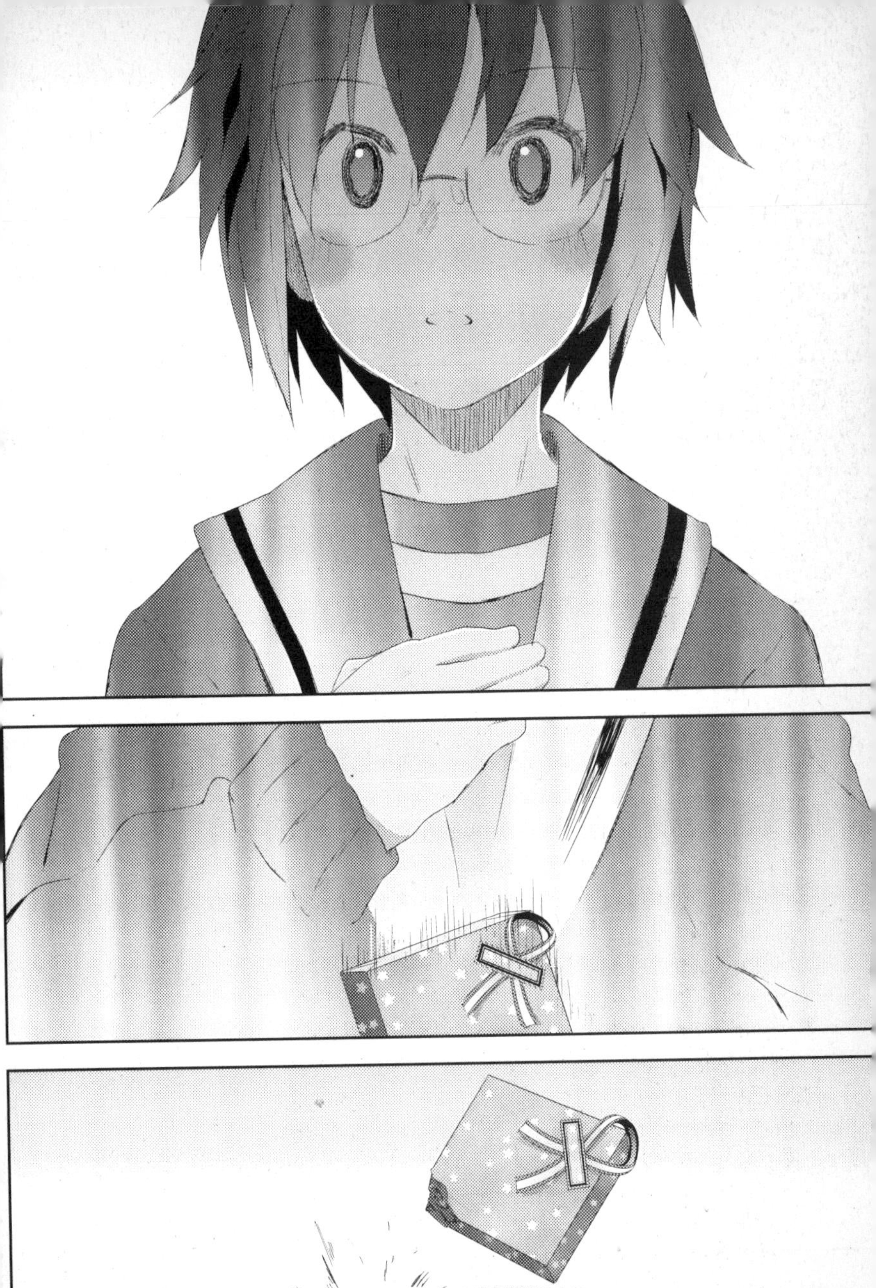

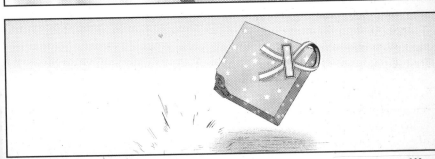

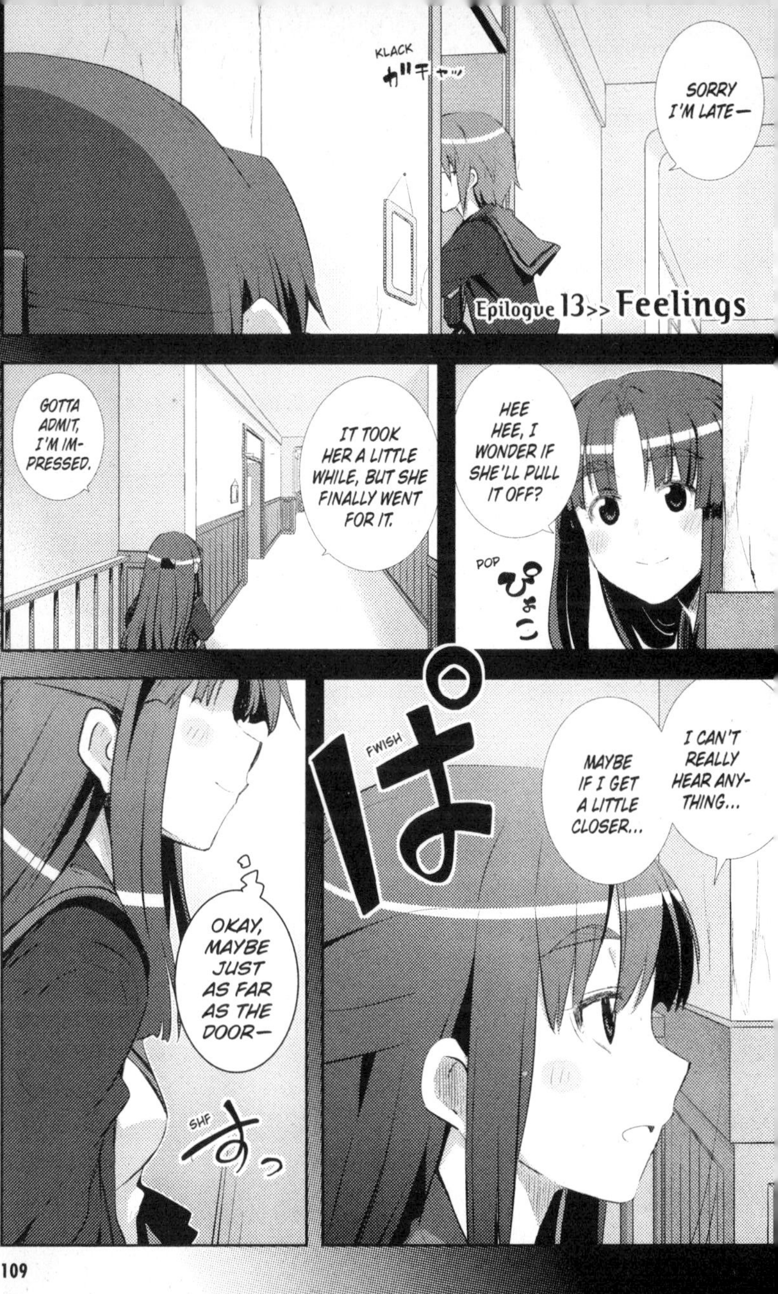
KLACK
ガチャッ
SORRY I'M LATE—
Epilogue 13>> Feelings
HEE HEE, I WONDER IF SHE'LL PULL IT OFF?
POP
ぴょこ
IT TOOK HER A LITTLE WHILE, BUT SHE FINALLY WENT FOR IT.
GOTTA ADMIT, I'M IMPRESSED.
I CAN'T REALLY HEAR ANYTHING...
MAYBE IF I GET A LITTLE CLOSER...
FWISH
ぱ
OKAY, MAYBE JUST AS FAR AS THE DOOR—
SHF
すっ

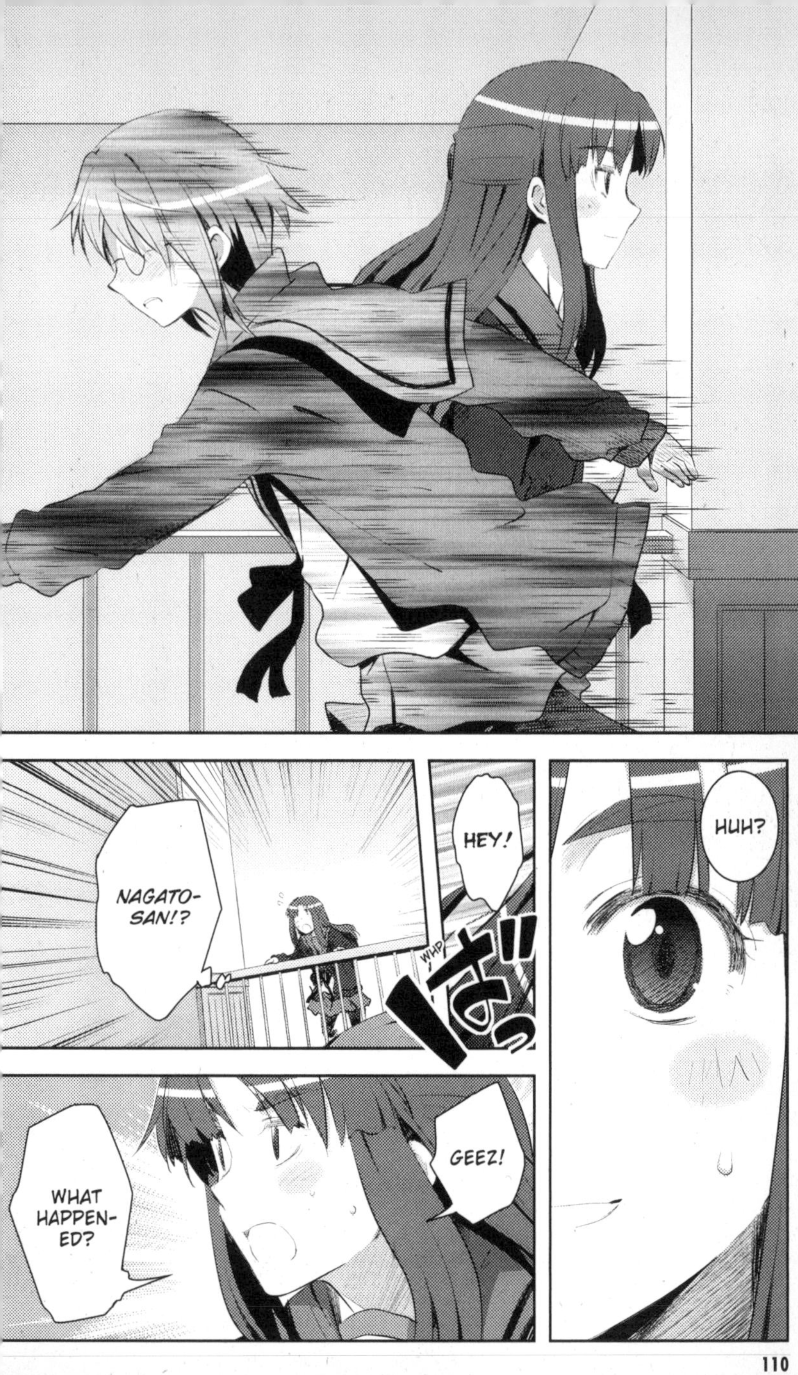
HUH?
HEY!
WHAP
NAGATO-SAN!?
GEEZ!
WHAT HAPPEN-ED?

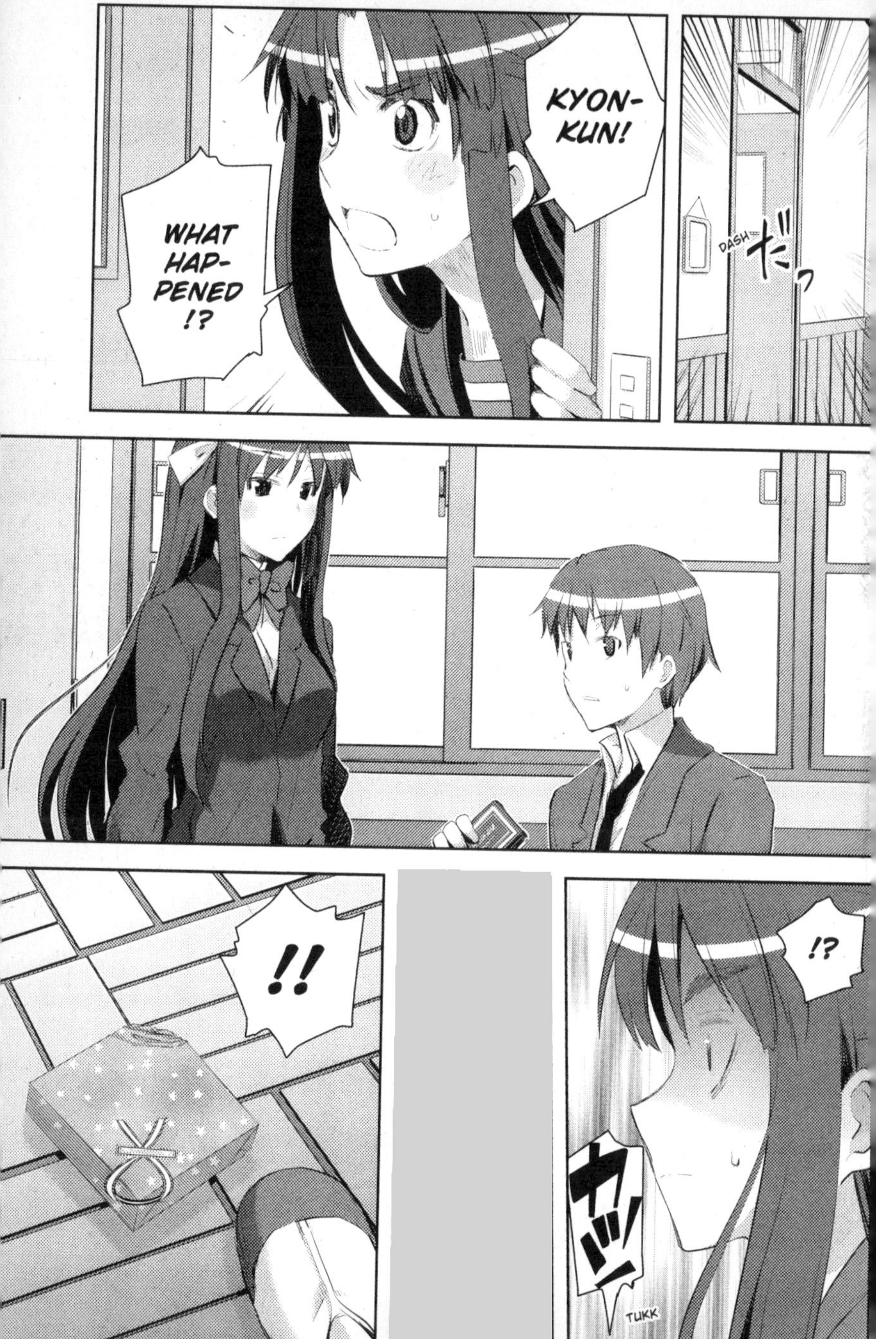
DASH
だっ
KYON-KUN!
WHAT HAP-PENED !?
!?
TUKK
!!

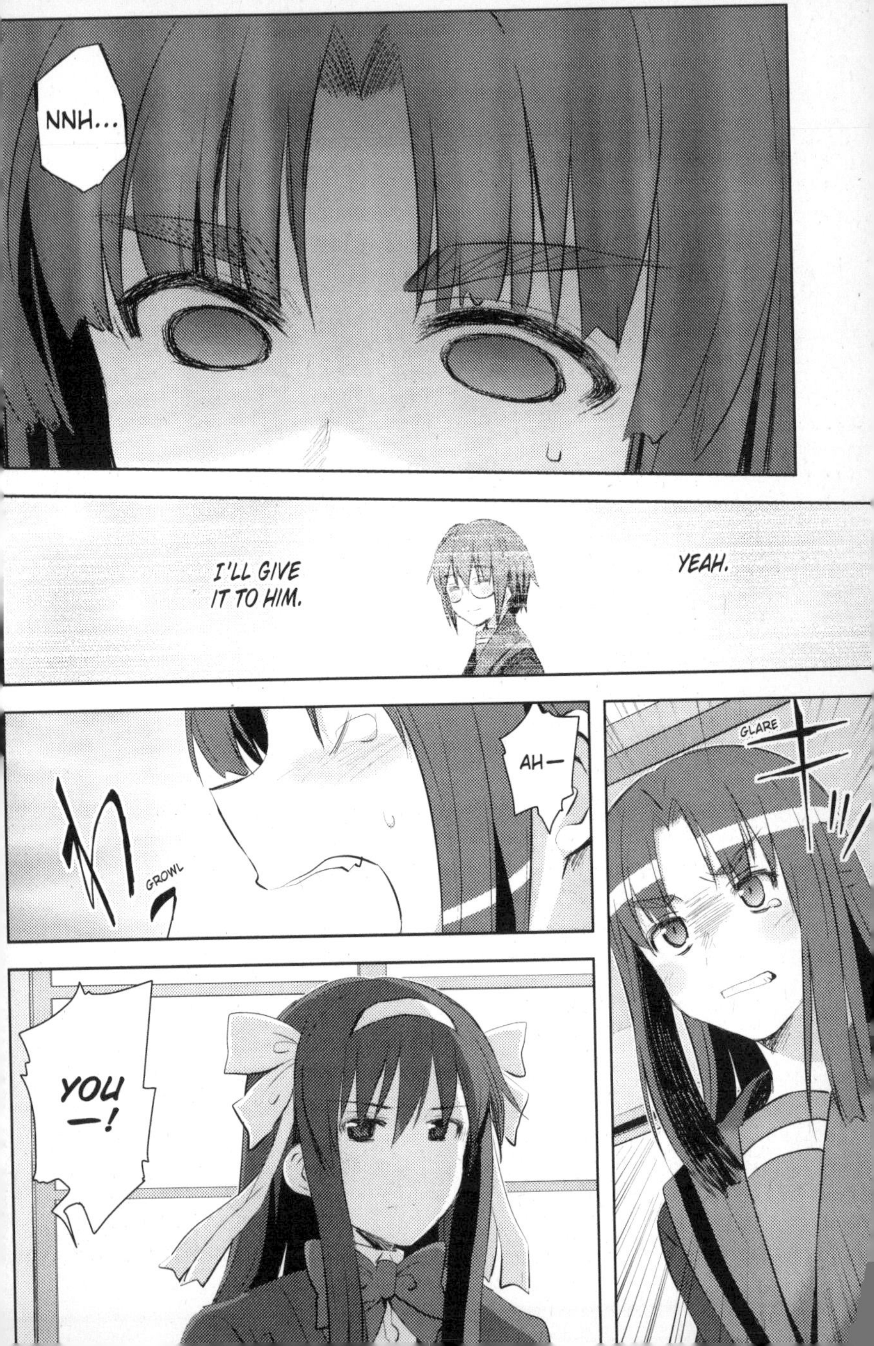
NNH...
YEAH.
I'LL GIVE IT TO HIM.
GLARE
AH—
GROWL
YOU—!

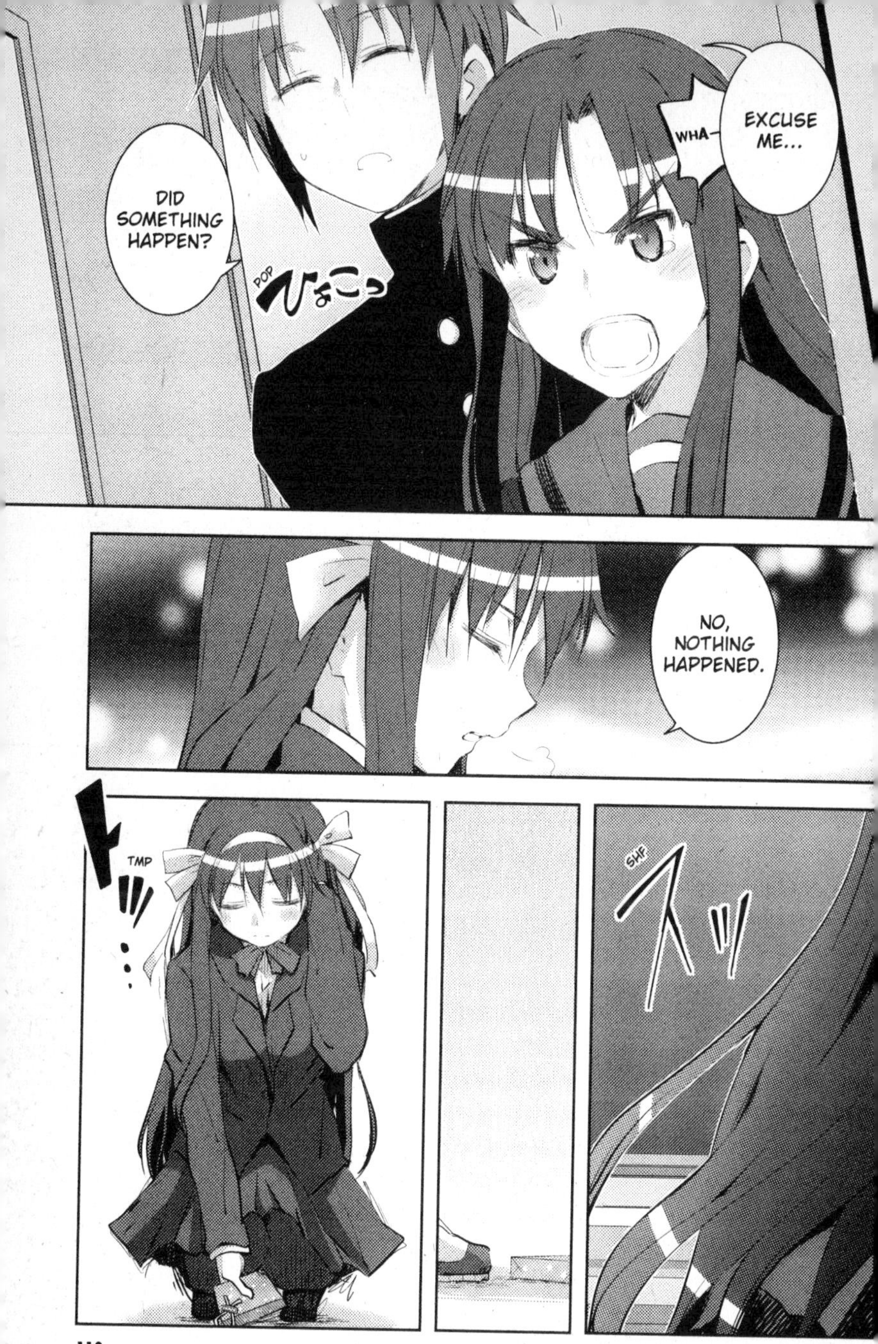
EXCUSE ME...
WHA—
DID SOMETHING HAPPEN?
POP
NO, NOTHING HAPPENED.
SHF
TMP

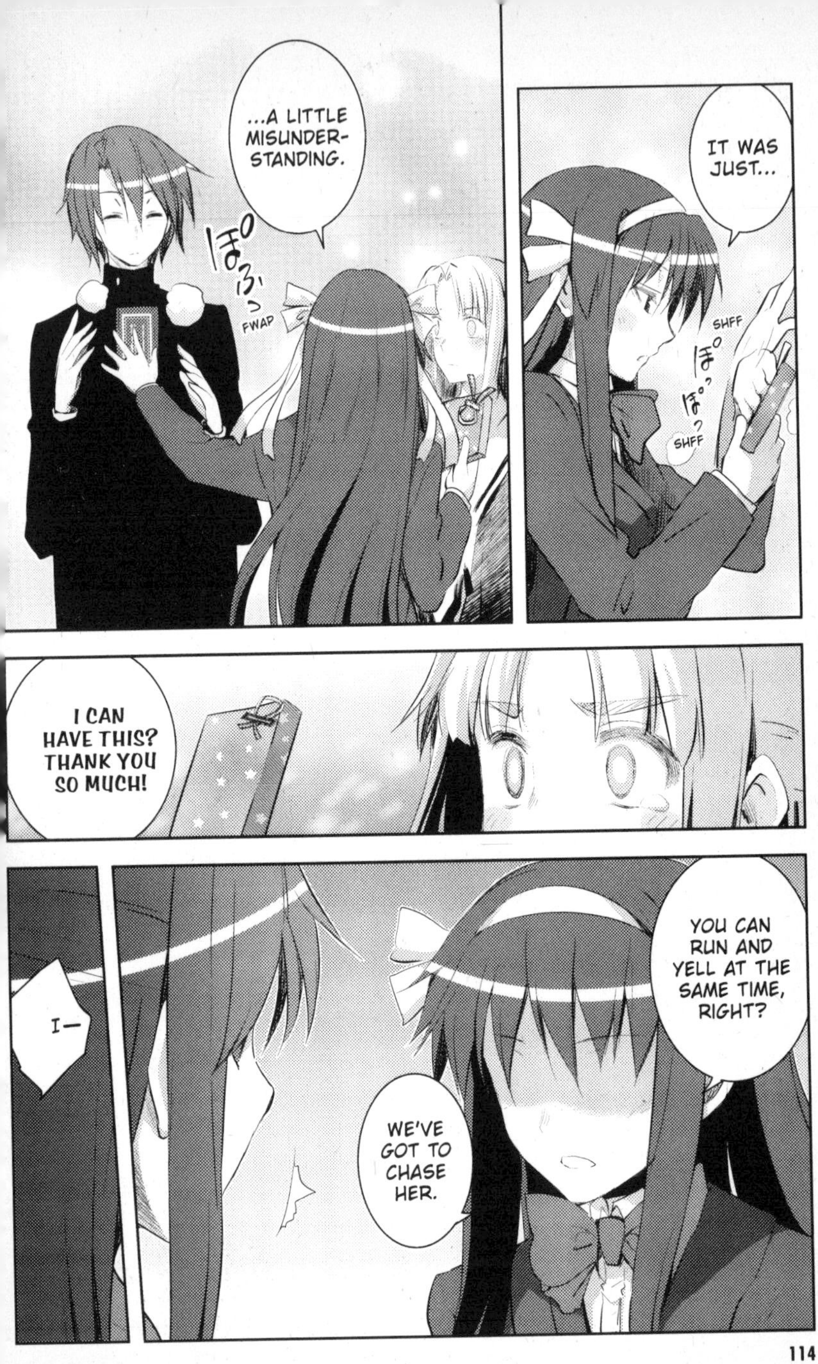
IT WAS JUST...
SHFF
ぽっ
ぽっ
SHFF
...A LITTLE MISUNDER-STANDING.
ぽふっ
FWAP
I CAN HAVE THIS? THANK YOU SO MUCH!
YOU CAN RUN AND YELL AT THE SAME TIME, RIGHT?
WE'VE GOT TO CHASE HER.
I—

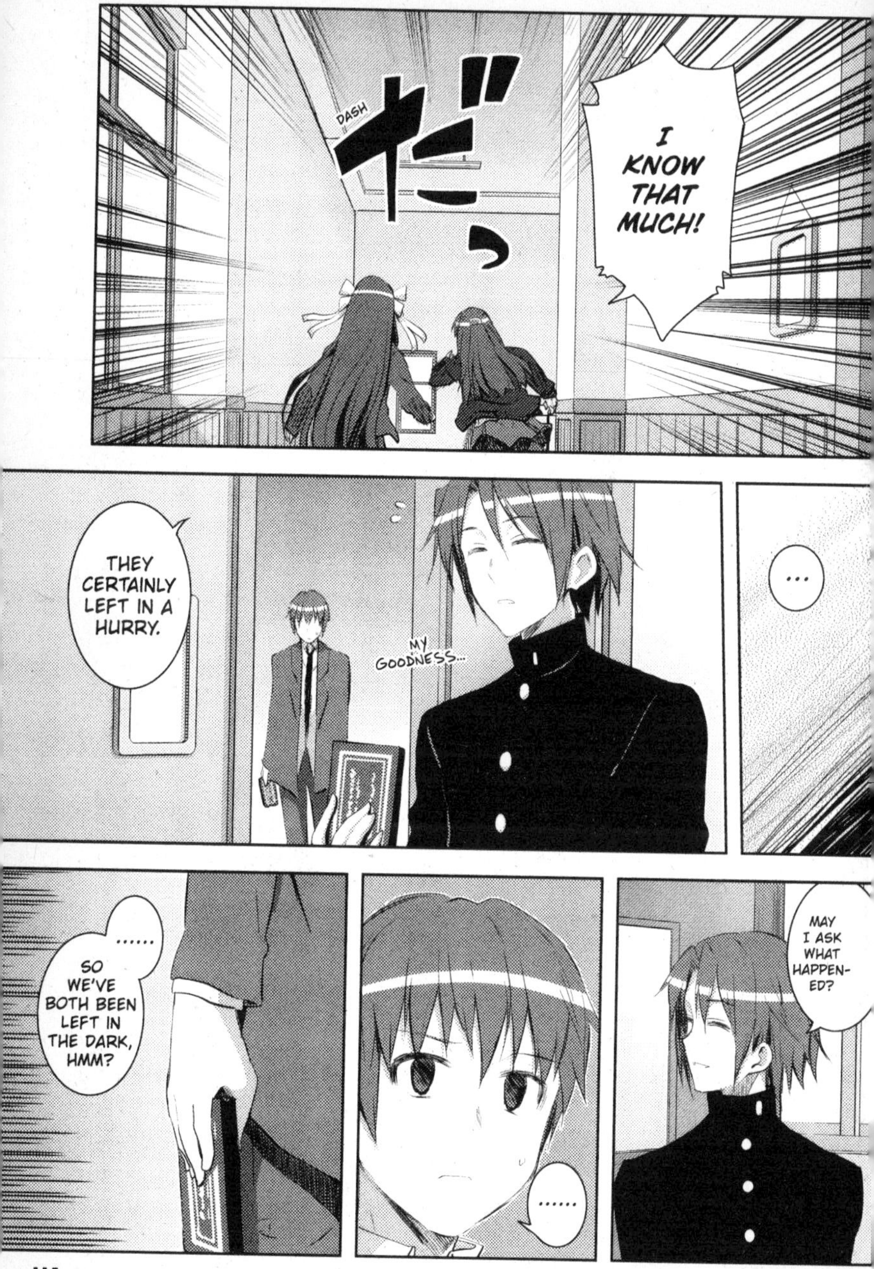
DASH
I KNOW THAT MUCH!
...
MY GOODNESS...
THEY CERTAINLY LEFT IN A HURRY.
MAY I ASK WHAT HAPPEN-ED?
......
......
SO WE'VE BOTH BEEN LEFT IN THE DARK, HMM?

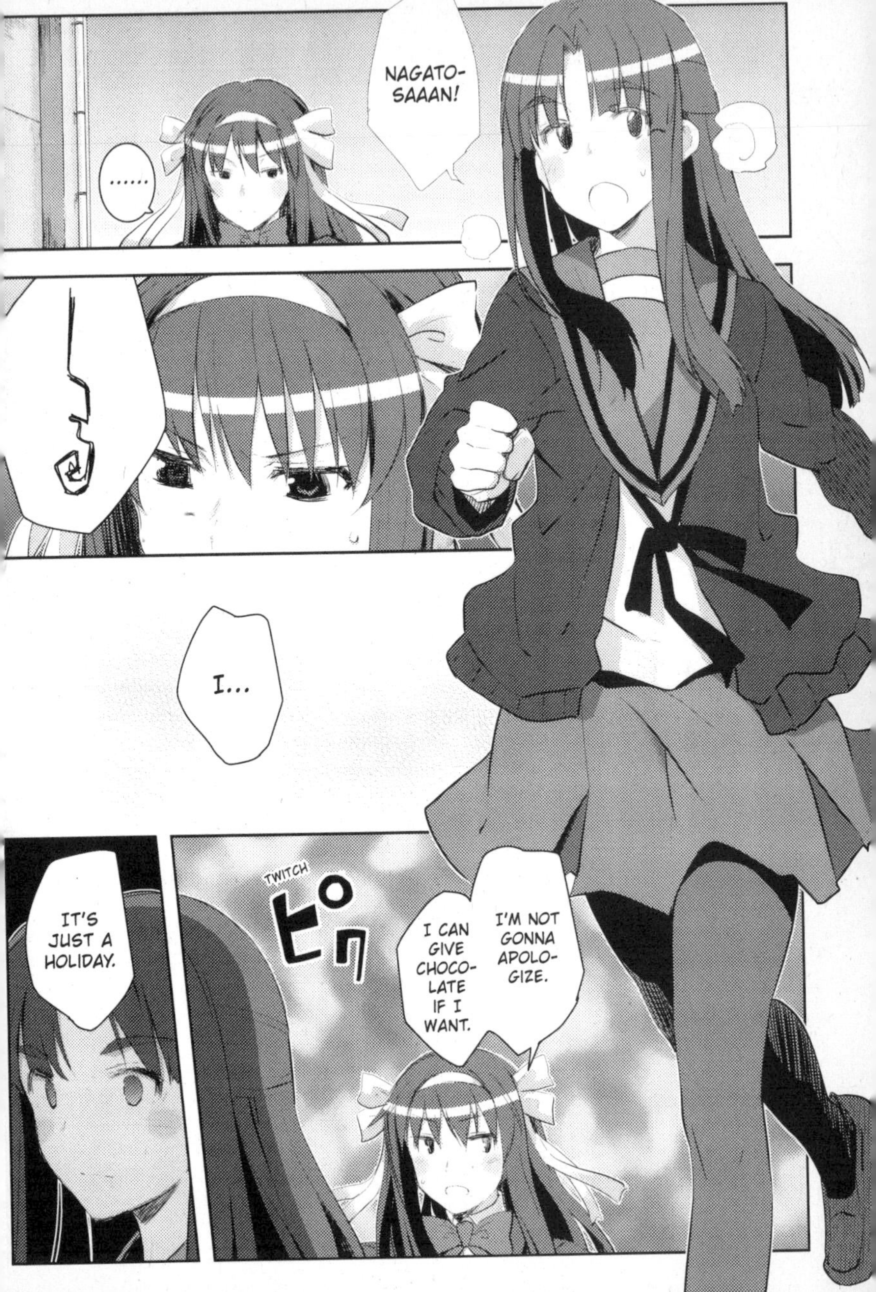
NAGATO-SAAAN!
......
I...
I'M NOT GONNA APOLOGIZE.
I CAN GIVE CHOCOLATE IF I WANT.
TWITCH
IT'S JUST A HOLIDAY.

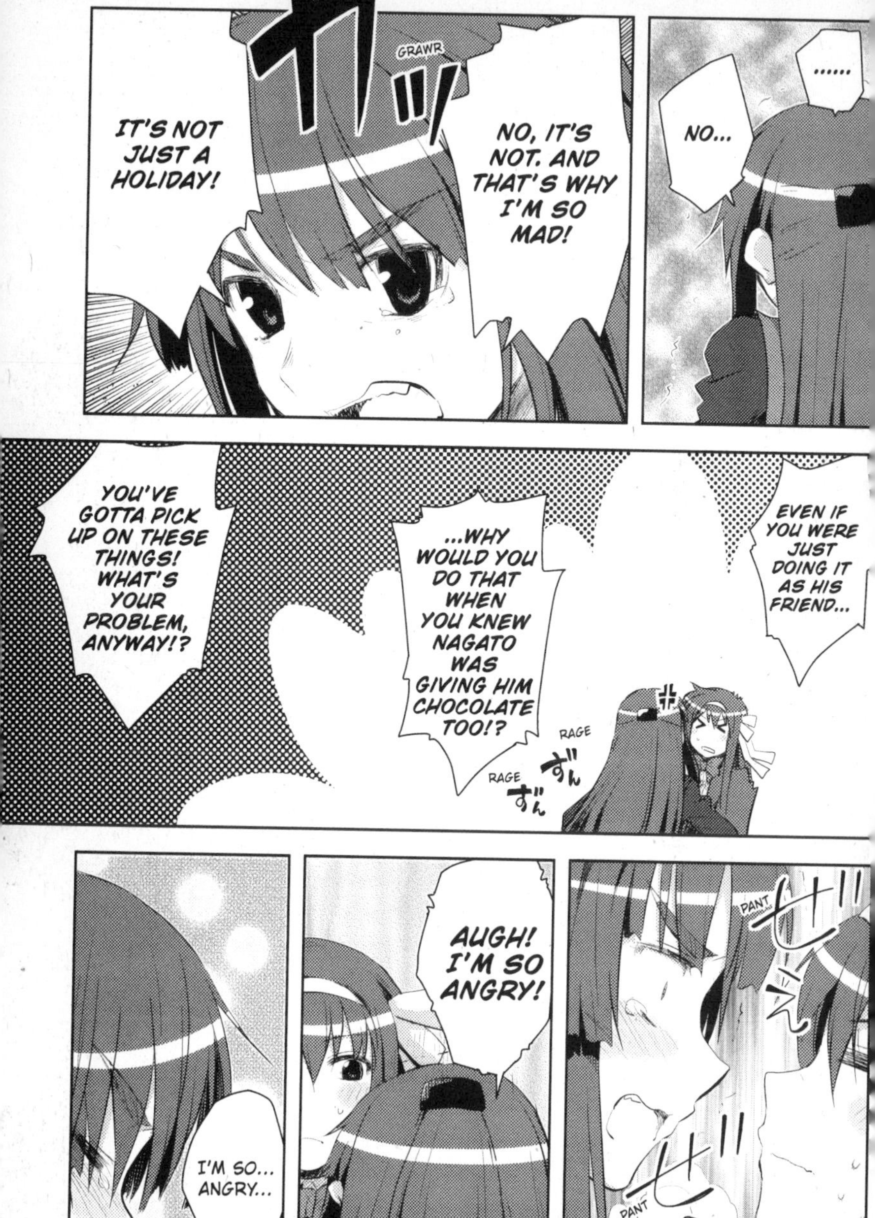

......
NO...
GRAWR
NO, IT'S NOT. AND THAT'S WHY I'M SO MAD!
IT'S NOT JUST A HOLIDAY!
EVEN IF YOU WERE JUST DOING IT AS HIS FRIEND...
...WHY WOULD YOU DO THAT WHEN YOU KNEW NAGATO WAS GIVING HIM CHOCOLATE TOO!?
RAGE
RAGE
YOU'VE GOTTA PICK UP ON THESE THINGS! WHAT'S YOUR PROBLEM, ANYWAY!?
PANT
PANT
AUGH! I'M SO ANGRY!
I'M SO... ANGRY...

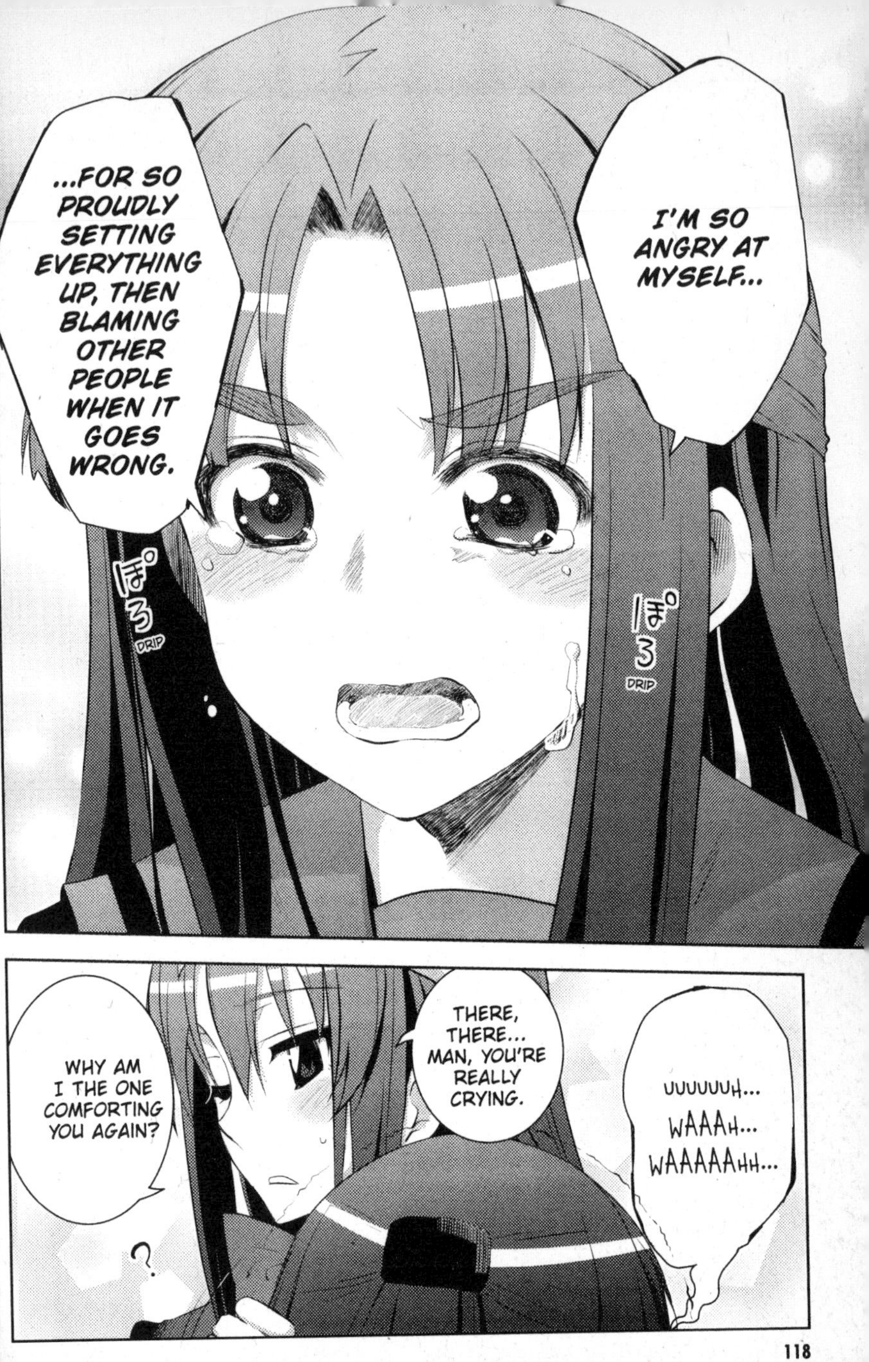
I'M SO ANGRY AT MYSELF...
...FOR SO PROUDLY SETTING EVERYTHING UP, THEN BLAMING OTHER PEOPLE WHEN IT GOES WRONG.
ぽろ
DRIP
ぽろ
DRIP
UUUUUUH... WAAAH... WAAAAAHH...
THERE, THERE... MAN, YOU'RE REALLY CRYING.
WHY AM I THE ONE COMFORTING YOU AGAIN?
?

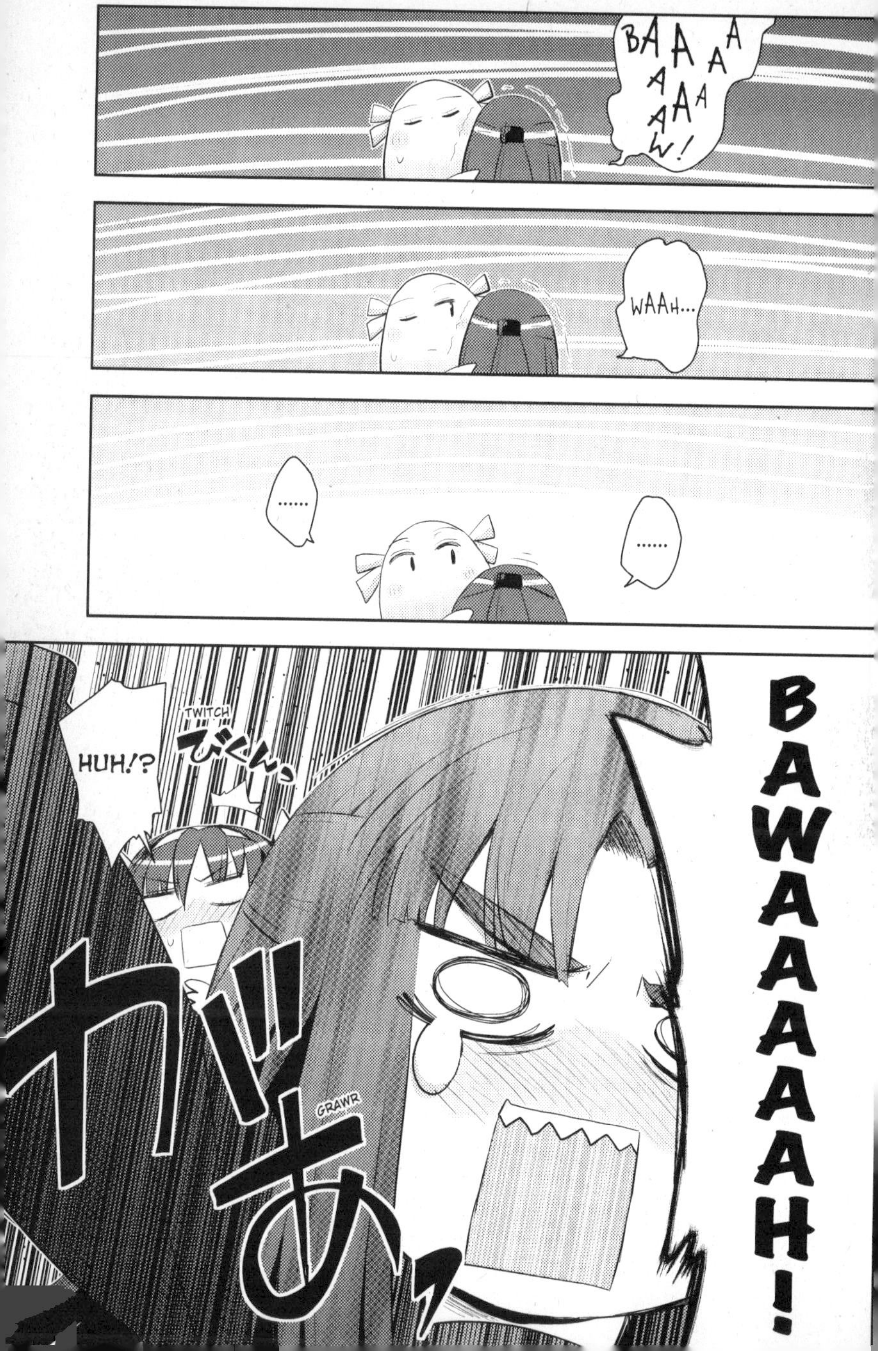
BAAAAAAAAAW!
WAAH...
......
......
BAWAAAAAAAH!
TWITCH
びくんっ
HUH!?
GRAWR
ガあっ

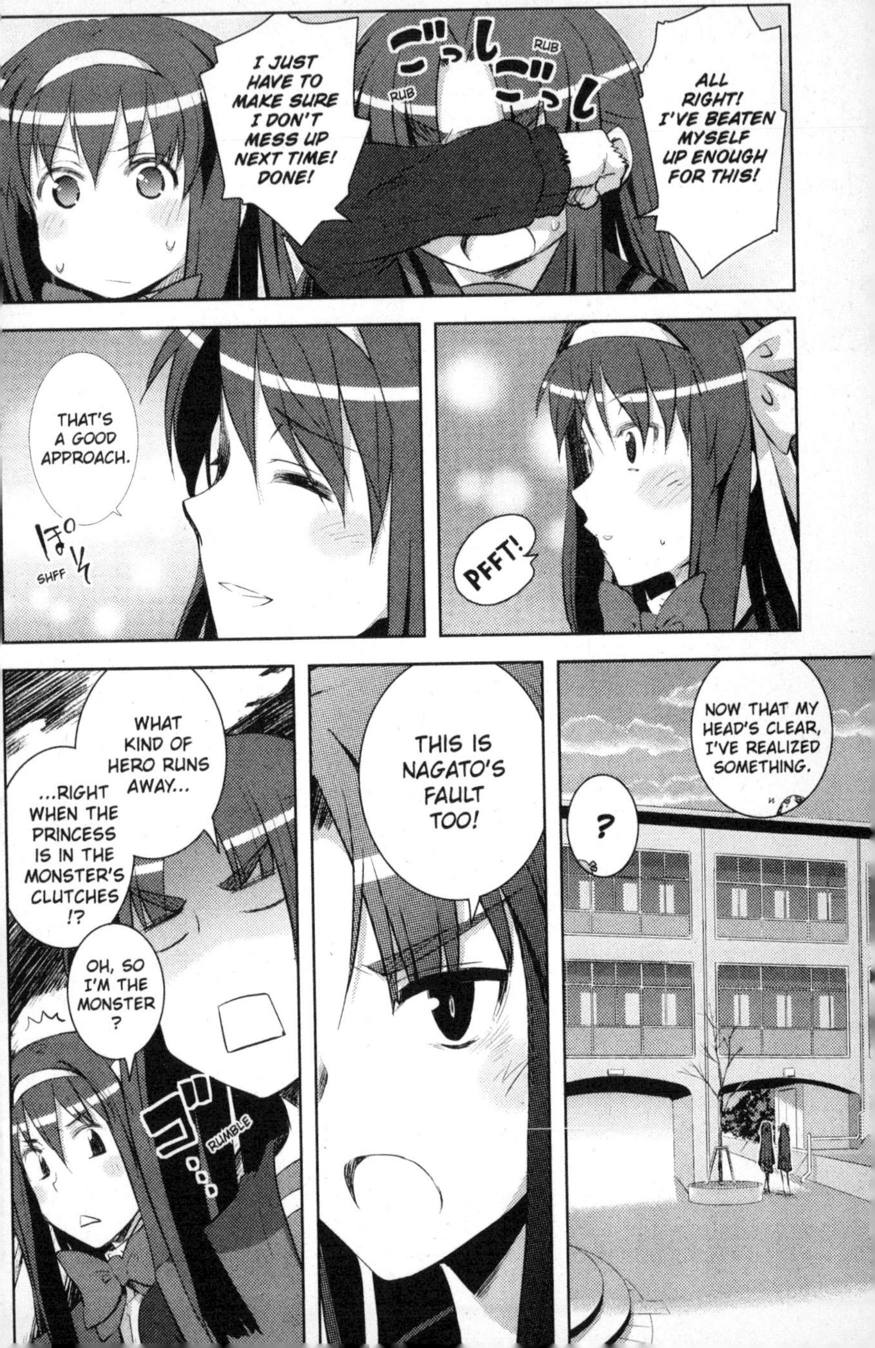
ALL RIGHT! I'VE BEATEN MYSELF UP ENOUGH FOR THIS!
RUB
RUB
I JUST HAVE TO MAKE SURE I DON'T MESS UP NEXT TIME! DONE!
PFFT!
THAT'S A GOOD APPROACH.
SHFF
NOW THAT MY HEAD'S CLEAR, I'VE REALIZED SOMETHING.
?
THIS IS NAGATO'S FAULT TOO!
WHAT KIND OF HERO RUNS AWAY...
...RIGHT WHEN THE PRINCESS IS IN THE MONSTER'S CLUTCHES!?
OH, SO I'M THE MONSTER?
RUMBLE

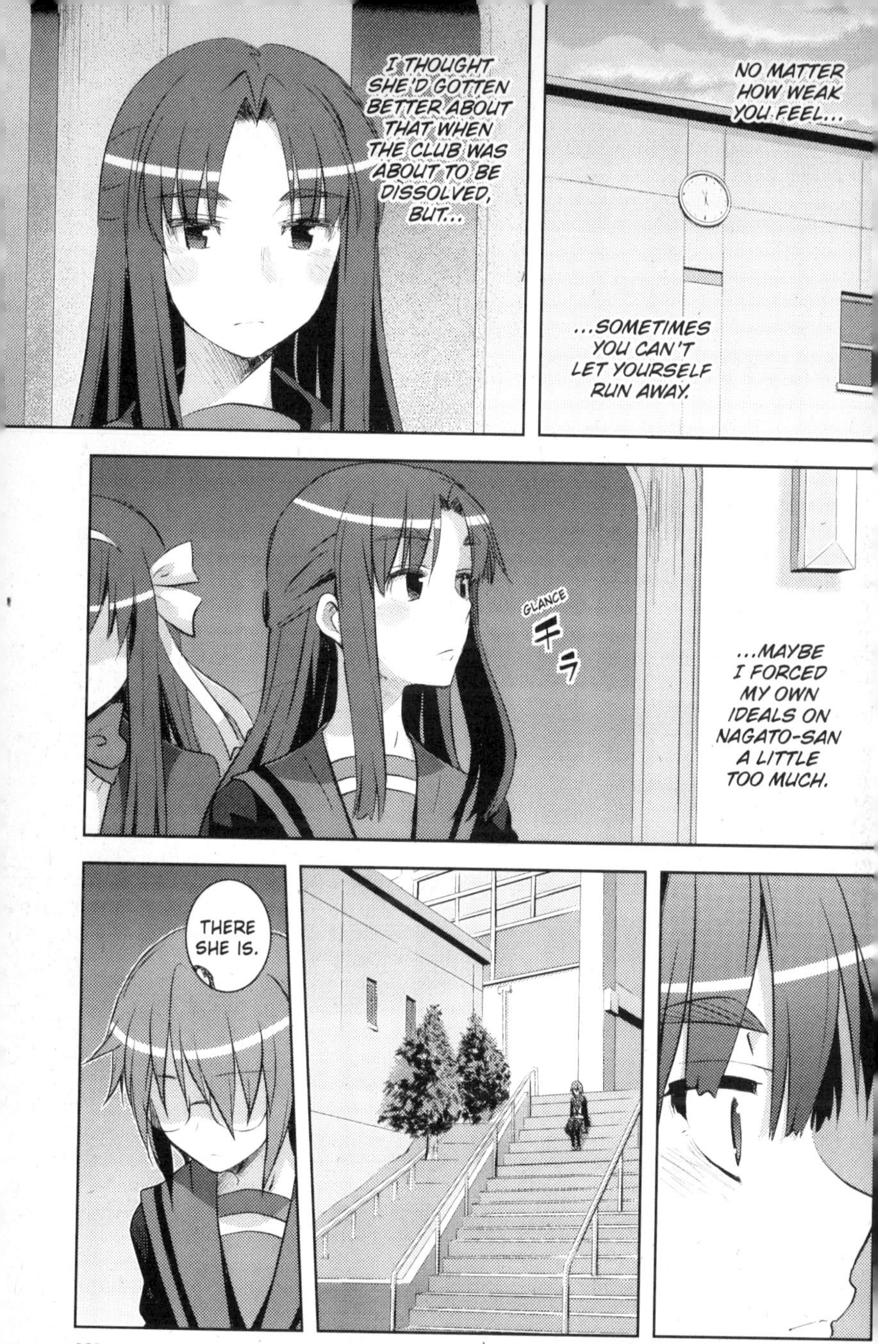
NO MATTER HOW WEAK YOU FEEL...
...SOMETIMES YOU CAN'T LET YOURSELF RUN AWAY.
I THOUGHT SHE'D GOTTEN BETTER ABOUT THAT WHEN THE CLUB WAS ABOUT TO BE DISSOLVED, BUT...
...MAYBE I FORCED MY OWN IDEALS ON NAGATO-SAN A LITTLE TOO MUCH.
GLANCE
チラ
THERE SHE IS.

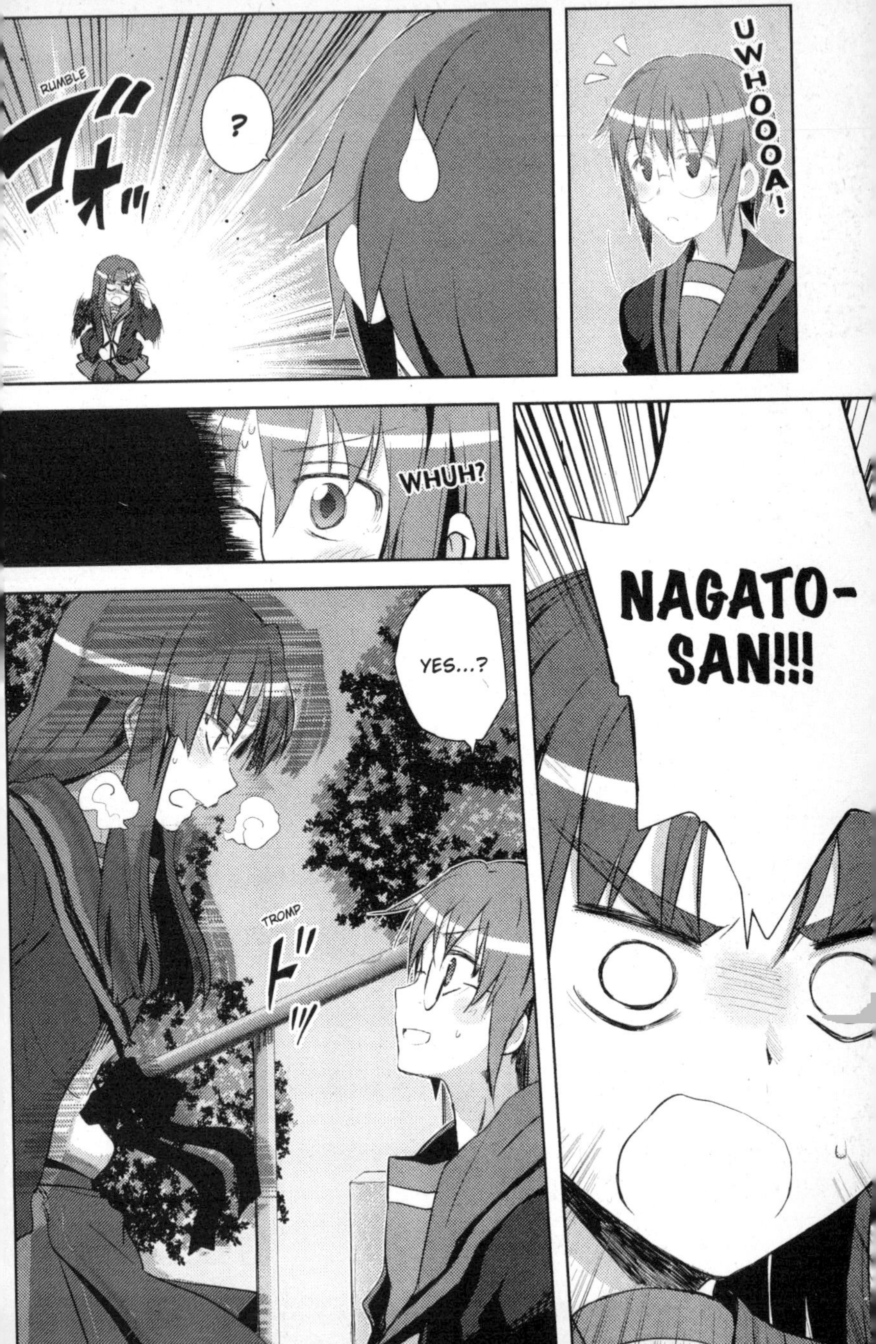
UWHOOOA!
RUMBLE
?
NAGATO-SAN!!!
WHUH?
YES...?
TROMP

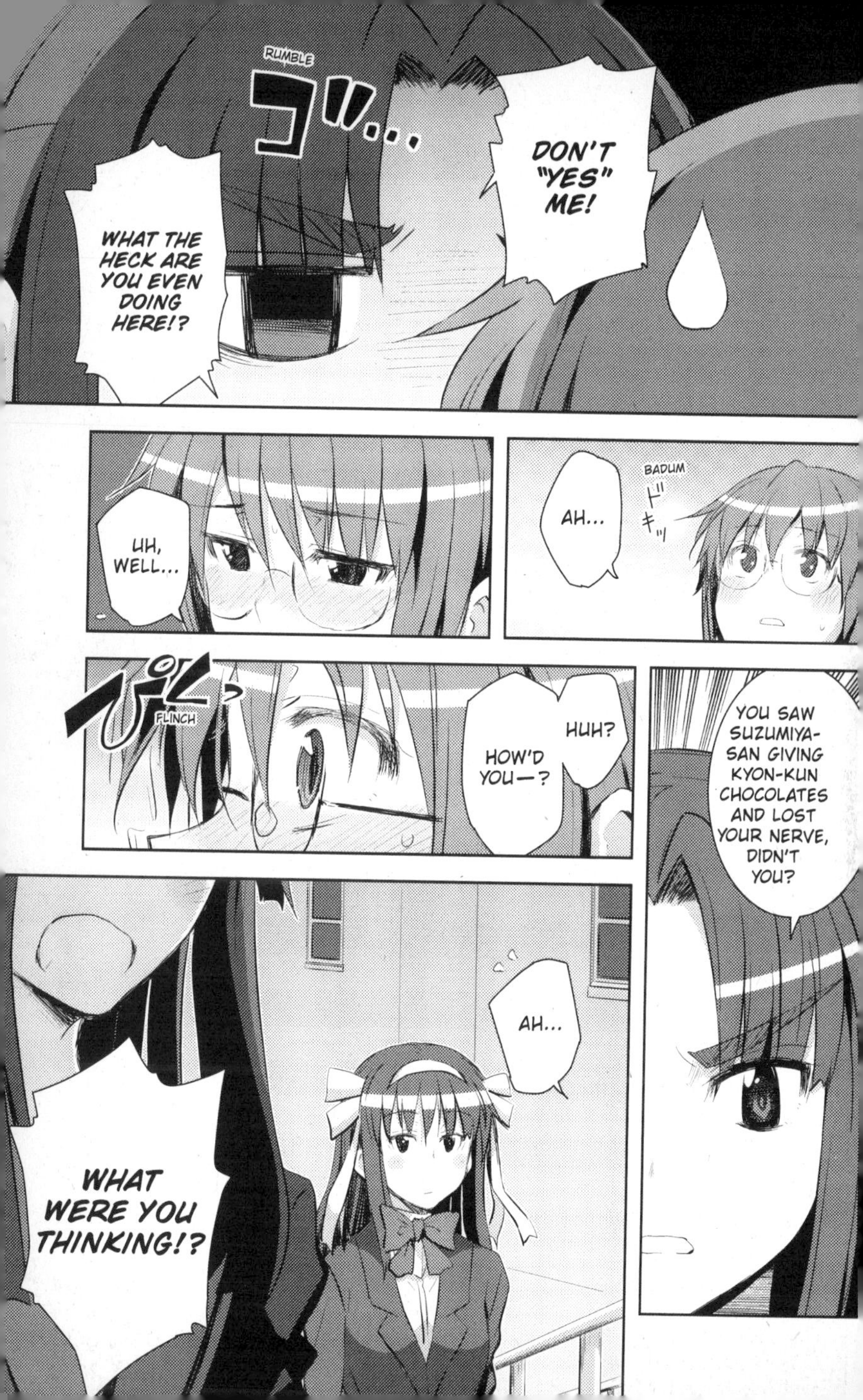
DON'T "YES" ME!
RUMBLE
WHAT THE HECK ARE YOU EVEN DOING HERE!?
AH...
BADUM
UH, WELL...
YOU SAW SUZUMIYA-SAN GIVING KYON-KUN CHOCOLATES AND LOST YOUR NERVE, DIDN'T YOU?
HUH?
HOW'D YOU—?
FLINCH
AH...
WHAT WERE YOU THINKING!?

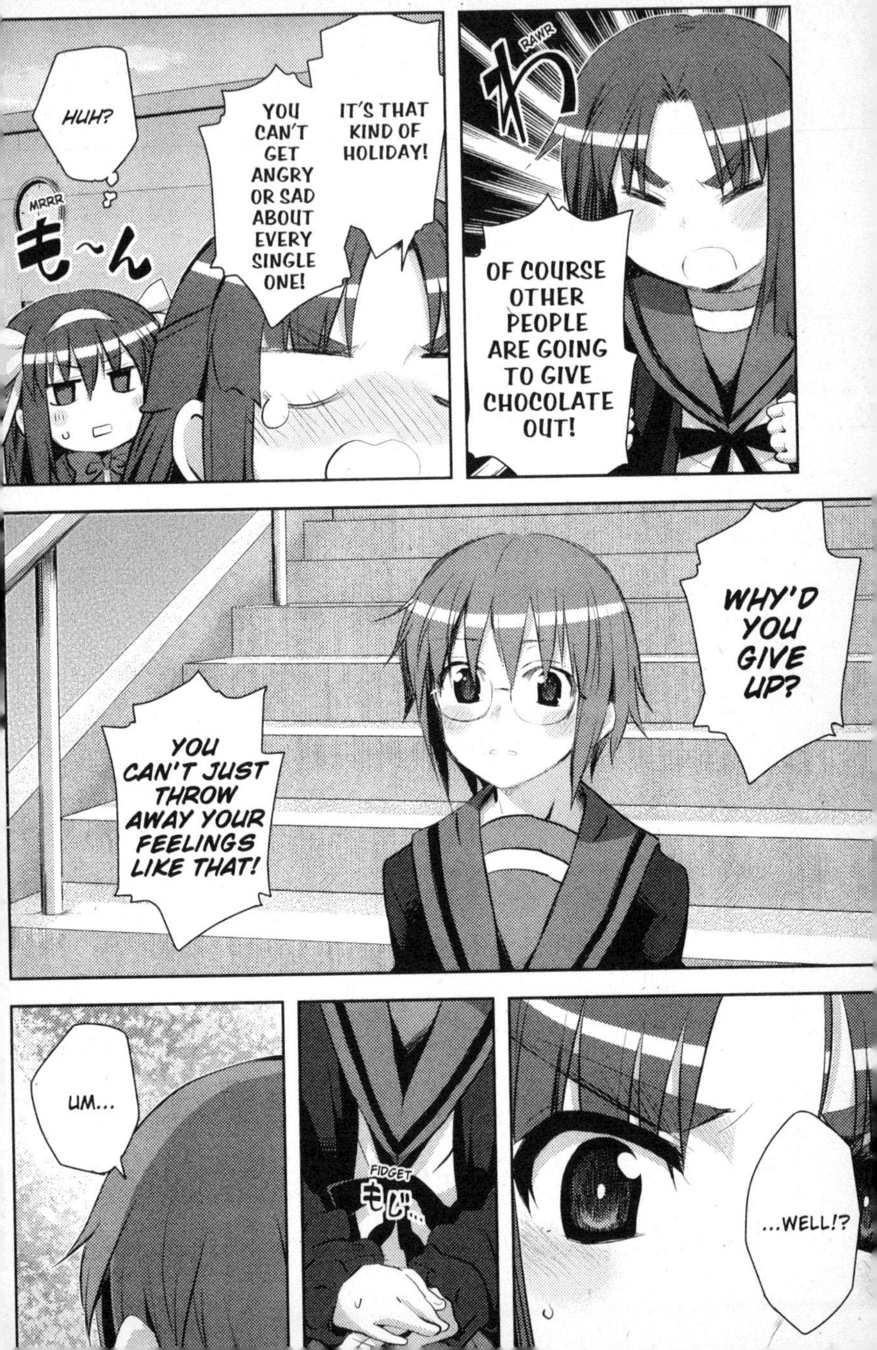

RAWR
わ
OF COURSE OTHER PEOPLE ARE GOING TO GIVE CHOCOLATE OUT!
IT'S THAT KIND OF HOLIDAY!
YOU CAN'T GET ANGRY OR SAD ABOUT EVERY SINGLE ONE!
HUH?
MRRR
も~ん
WHY'D YOU GIVE UP?
YOU CAN'T JUST THROW AWAY YOUR FEELINGS LIKE THAT!
...WELL!?
FIDGET
もじ…
UM...

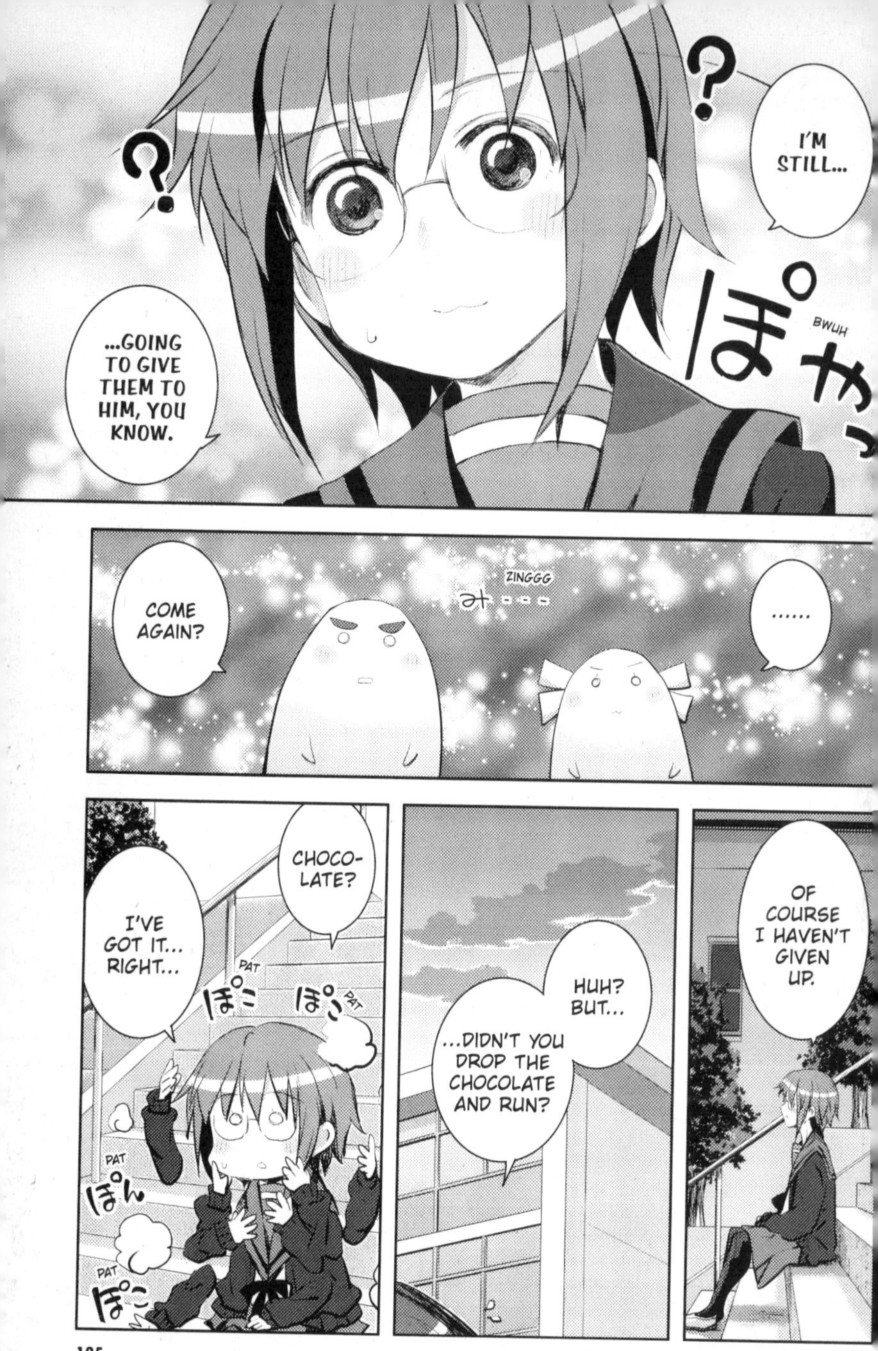
I'M STILL...
ぽやっ
BWUH
...GOING TO GIVE THEM TO HIM, YOU KNOW.
......
みーーー
ZINGGG
COME AGAIN?
OF COURSE I HAVEN'T GIVEN UP.
HUH? BUT...
...DIDN'T YOU DROP THE CHOCOLATE AND RUN?
CHOCO-LATE?
ぽこ
PAT
ぽこ
PAT
I'VE GOT IT... RIGHT...
ぽん
PAT
ぽこ
PAT

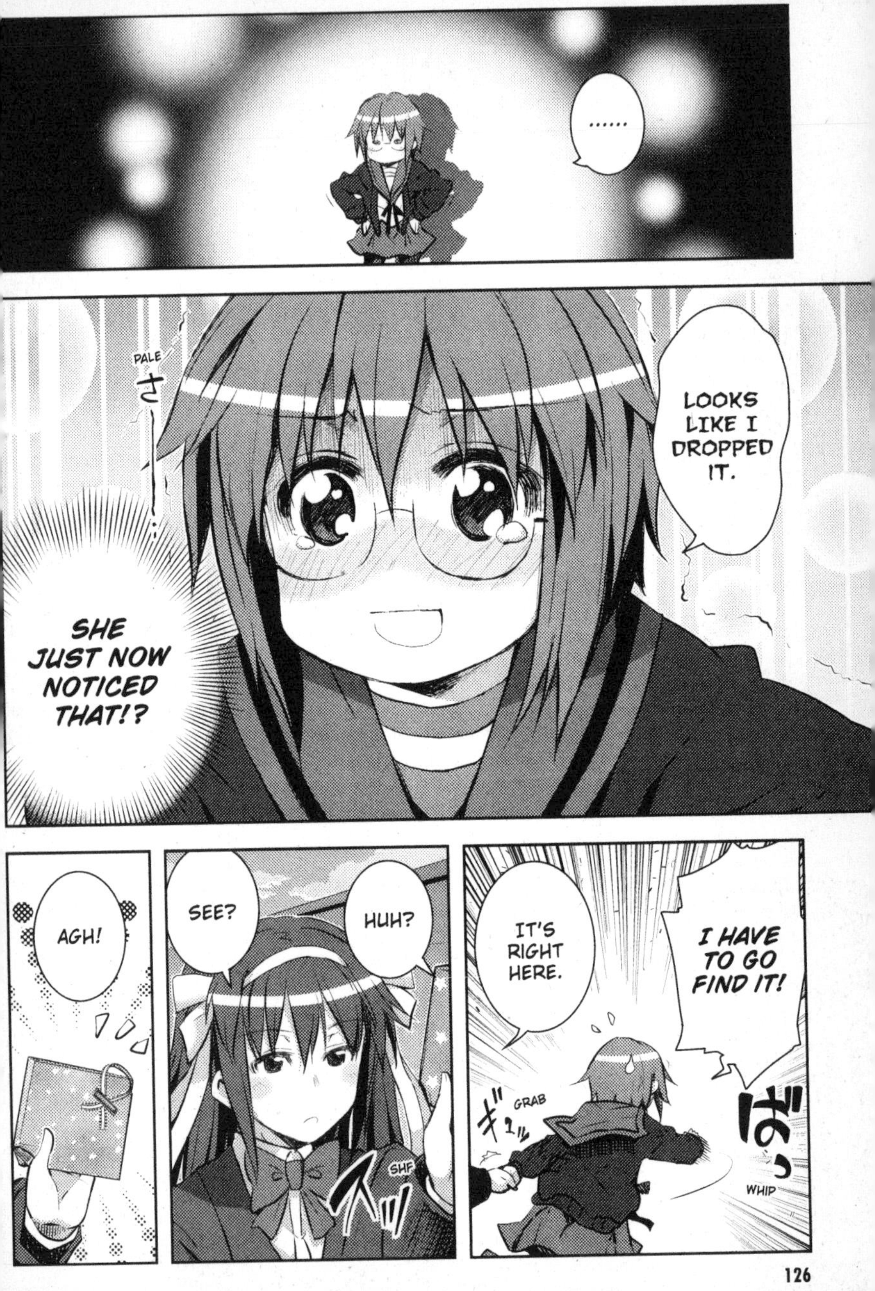
......
LOOKS LIKE I DROPPED IT.
PALE
SHE JUST NOW NOTICED THAT!?
I HAVE TO GO FIND IT!
ばっ
WHIP
IT'S RIGHT HERE.
GRAB
HUH?
SEE?
SHF
AGH!

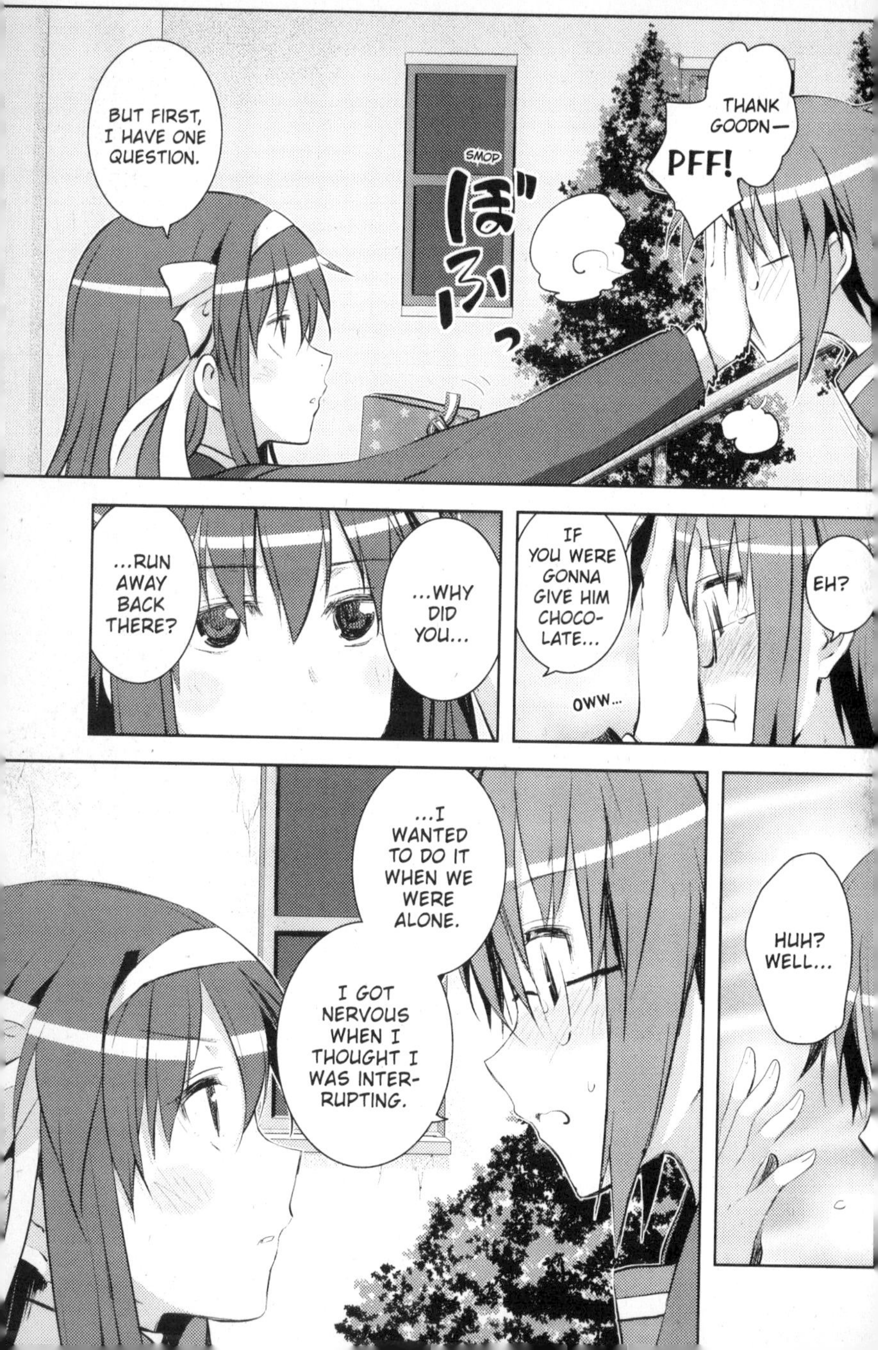
THANK GOODN— PFF!
SMOP
BUT FIRST, I HAVE ONE QUESTION.
EH?
IF YOU WERE GONNA GIVE HIM CHOCO-LATE...
OWW...
...WHY DID YOU...
...RUN AWAY BACK THERE?
HUH? WELL...
...I WANTED TO DO IT WHEN WE WERE ALONE.
I GOT NERVOUS WHEN I THOUGHT I WAS INTER-RUPTING.

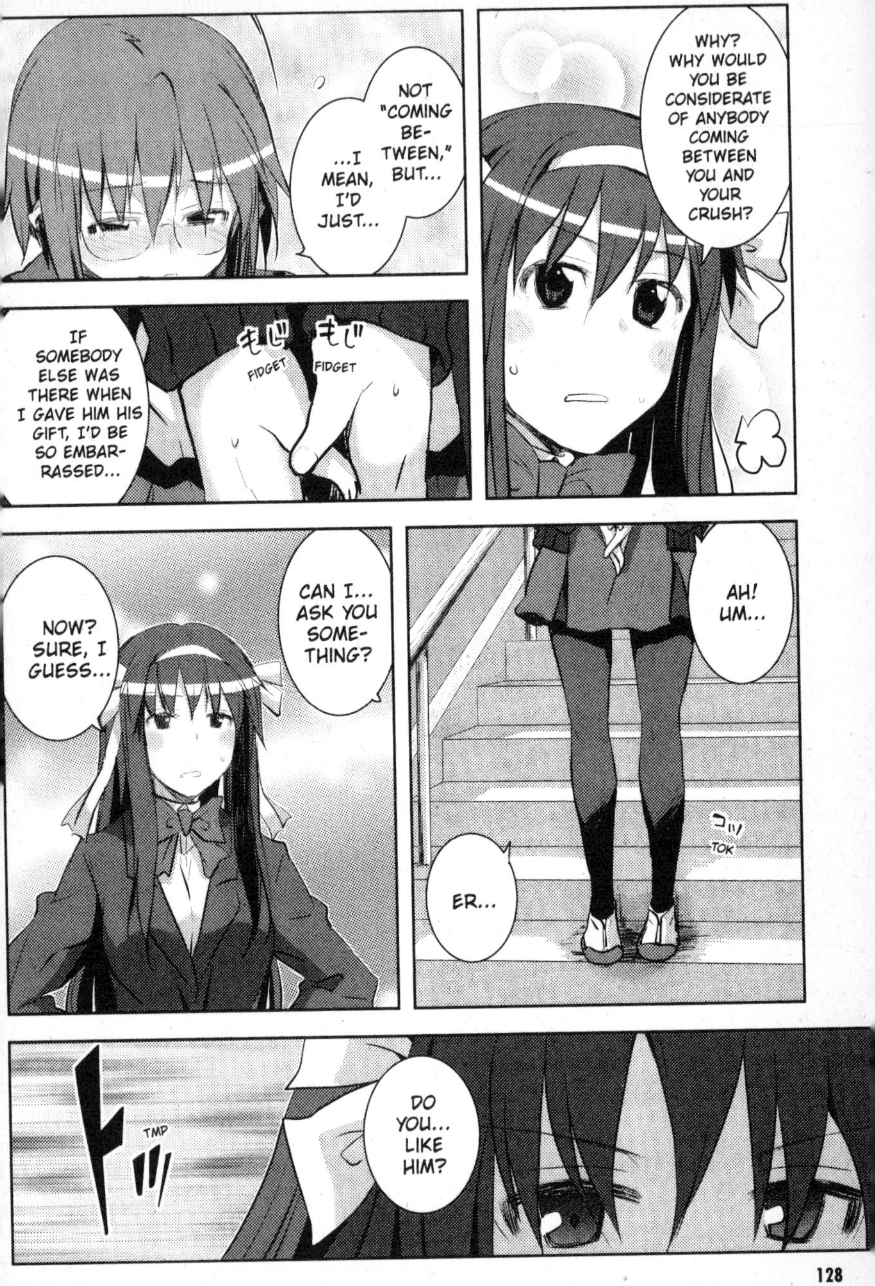
WHY? WHY WOULD YOU BE CONSIDERATE OF ANYBODY COMING BETWEEN YOU AND YOUR CRUSH?
NOT "COMING BE-TWEEN," BUT...
...I MEAN, I'D JUST...
FIDGET
FIDGET
IF SOMEBODY ELSE WAS THERE WHEN I GAVE HIM HIS GIFT, I'D BE SO EMBAR-RASSED...
AH! UM...
TOK
ER...
CAN I... ASK YOU SOME-THING?
NOW? SURE, I GUESS...
DO YOU... LIKE HIM?
TMP

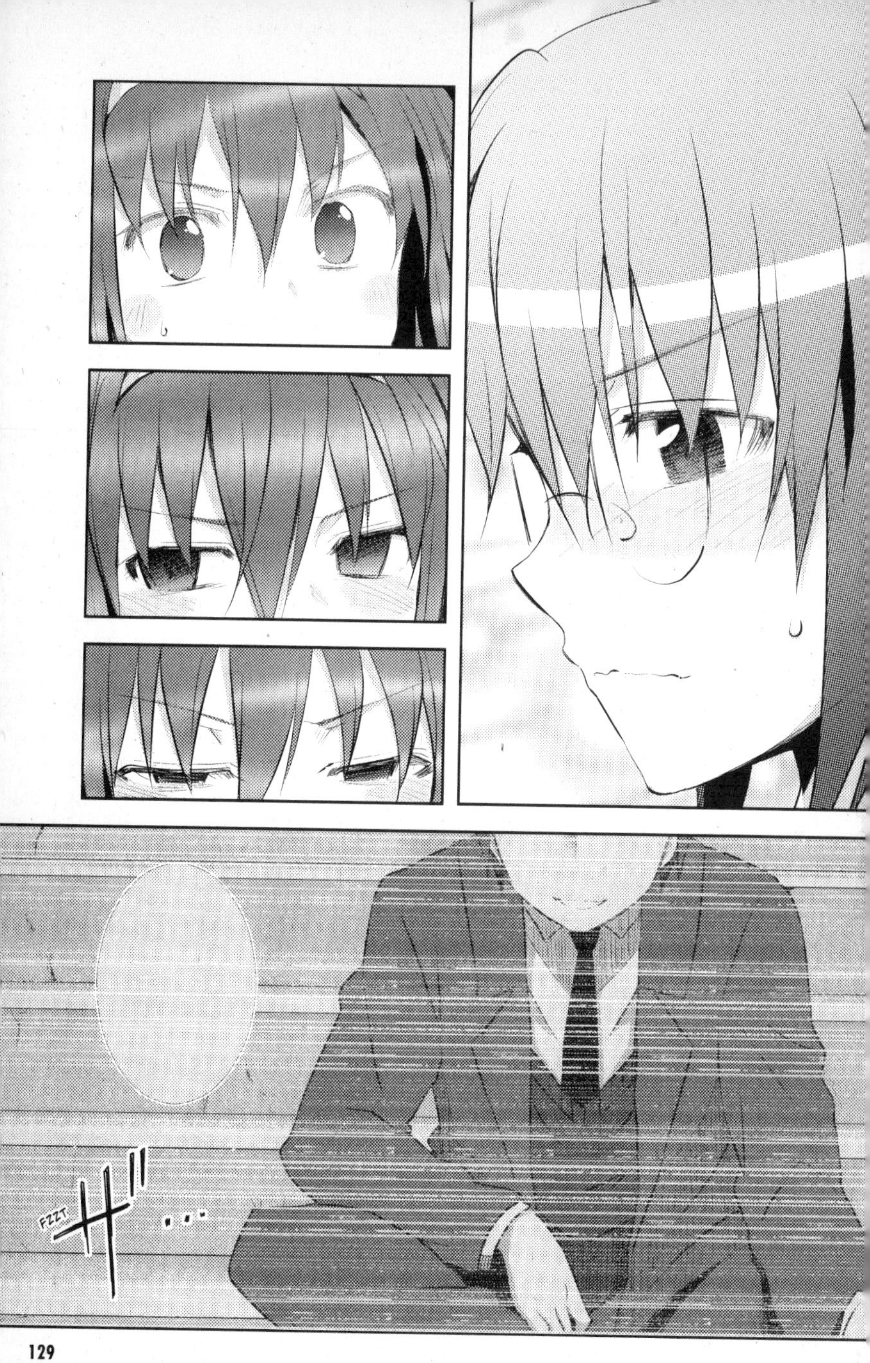
FZZT
...

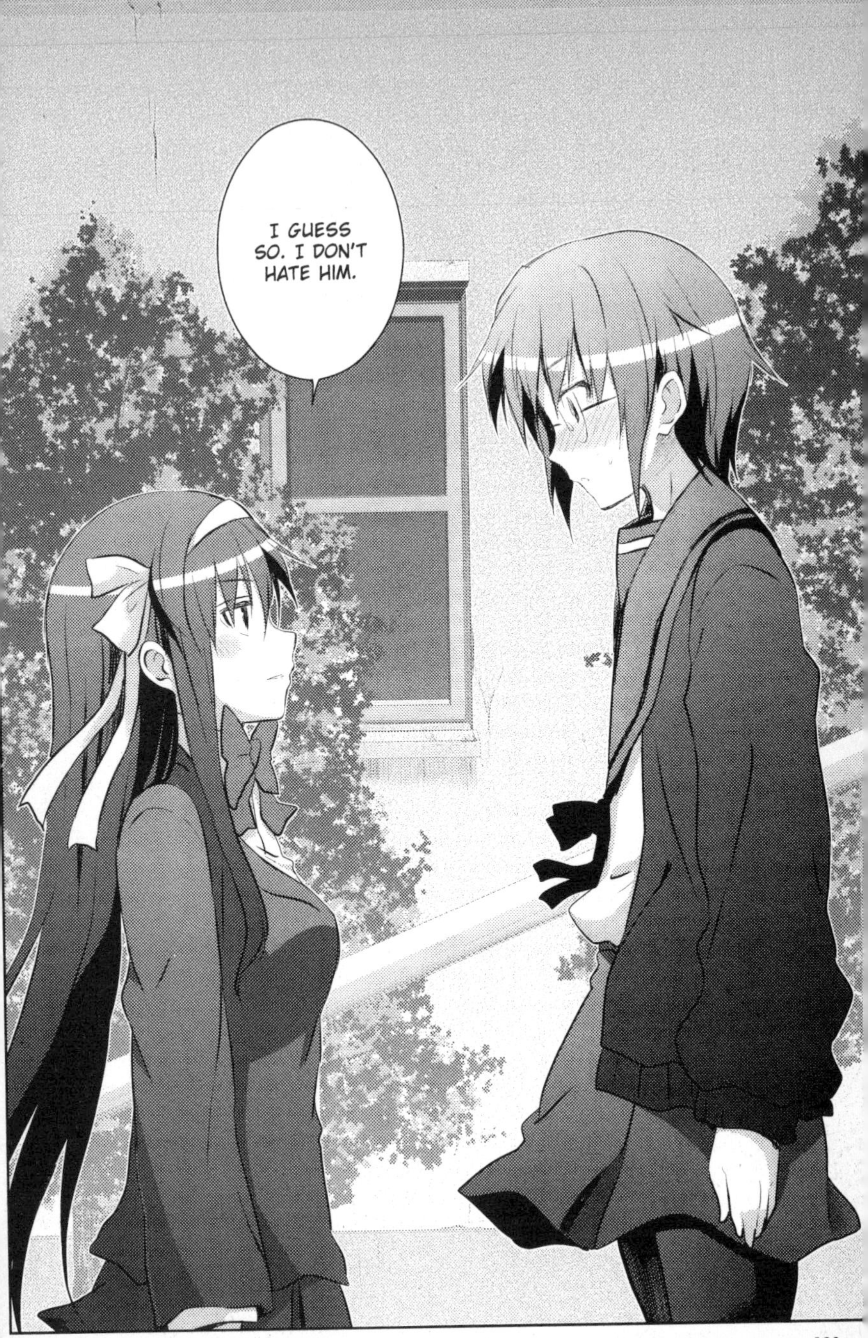
I GUESS SO. I DON'T HATE HIM.

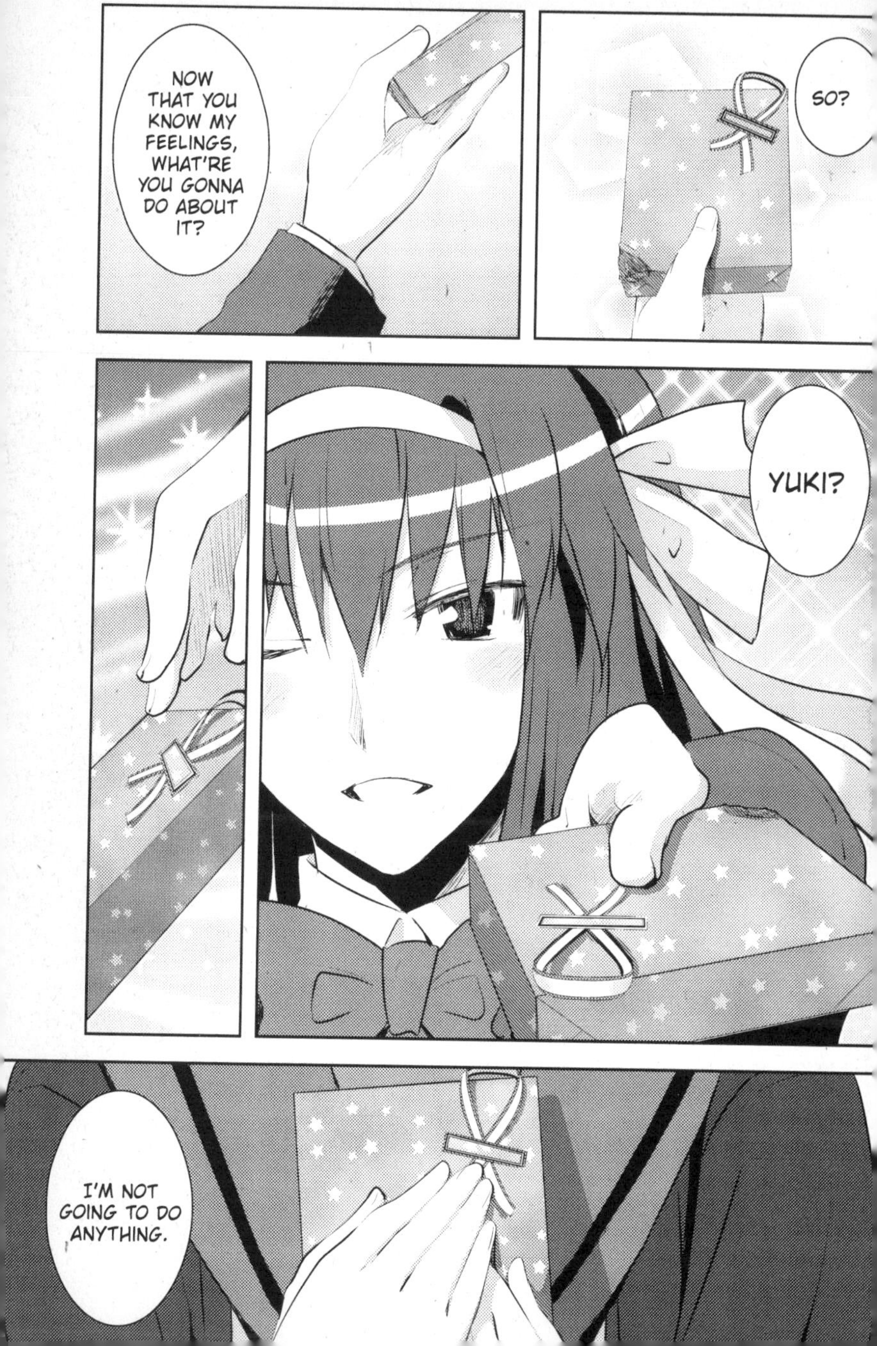
SO?
NOW THAT YOU KNOW MY FEELINGS, WHAT'RE YOU GONNA DO ABOUT IT?
YUKI?
I'M NOT GOING TO DO ANYTHING.

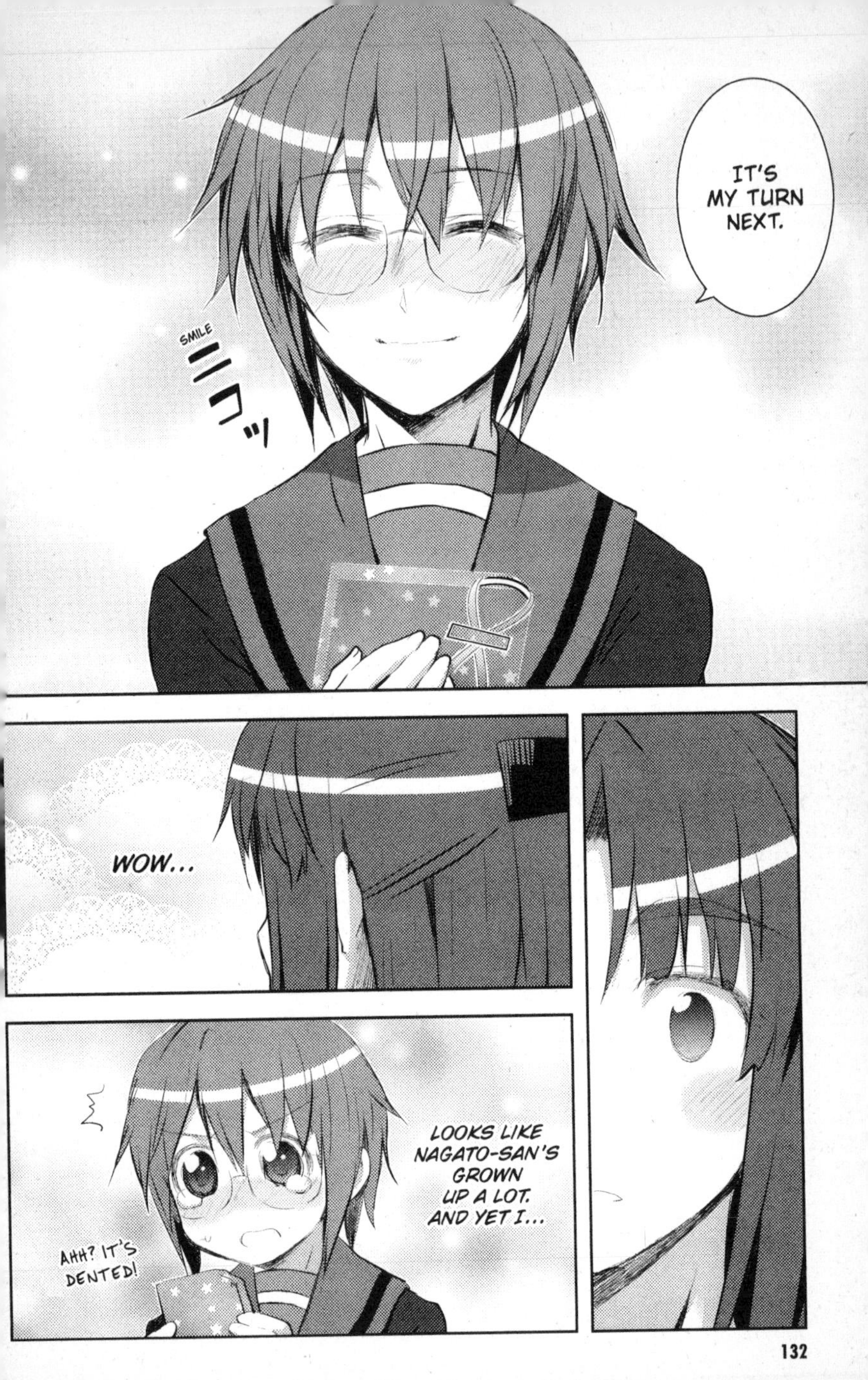
IT'S MY TURN NEXT.
SMILE
ニコッ
WOW...
LOOKS LIKE NAGATO-SAN'S GROWN UP A LOT. AND YET I...
AHH? IT'S DENTED!

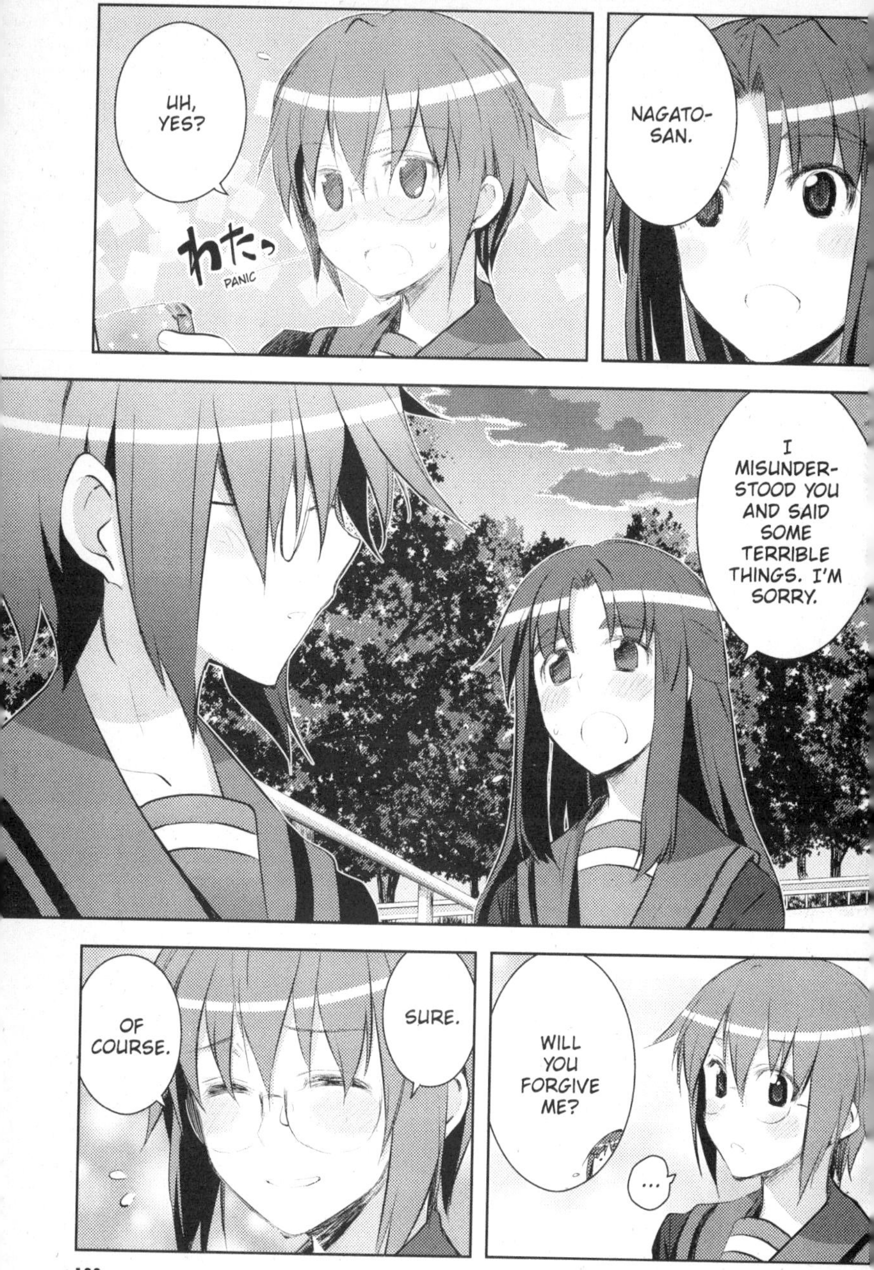
NAGATO-SAN.
UH, YES?
わたっ
PANIC
I MISUNDERSTOOD YOU AND SAID SOME TERRIBLE THINGS. I'M SORRY.
WILL YOU FORGIVE ME?
...
SURE.
OF COURSE.

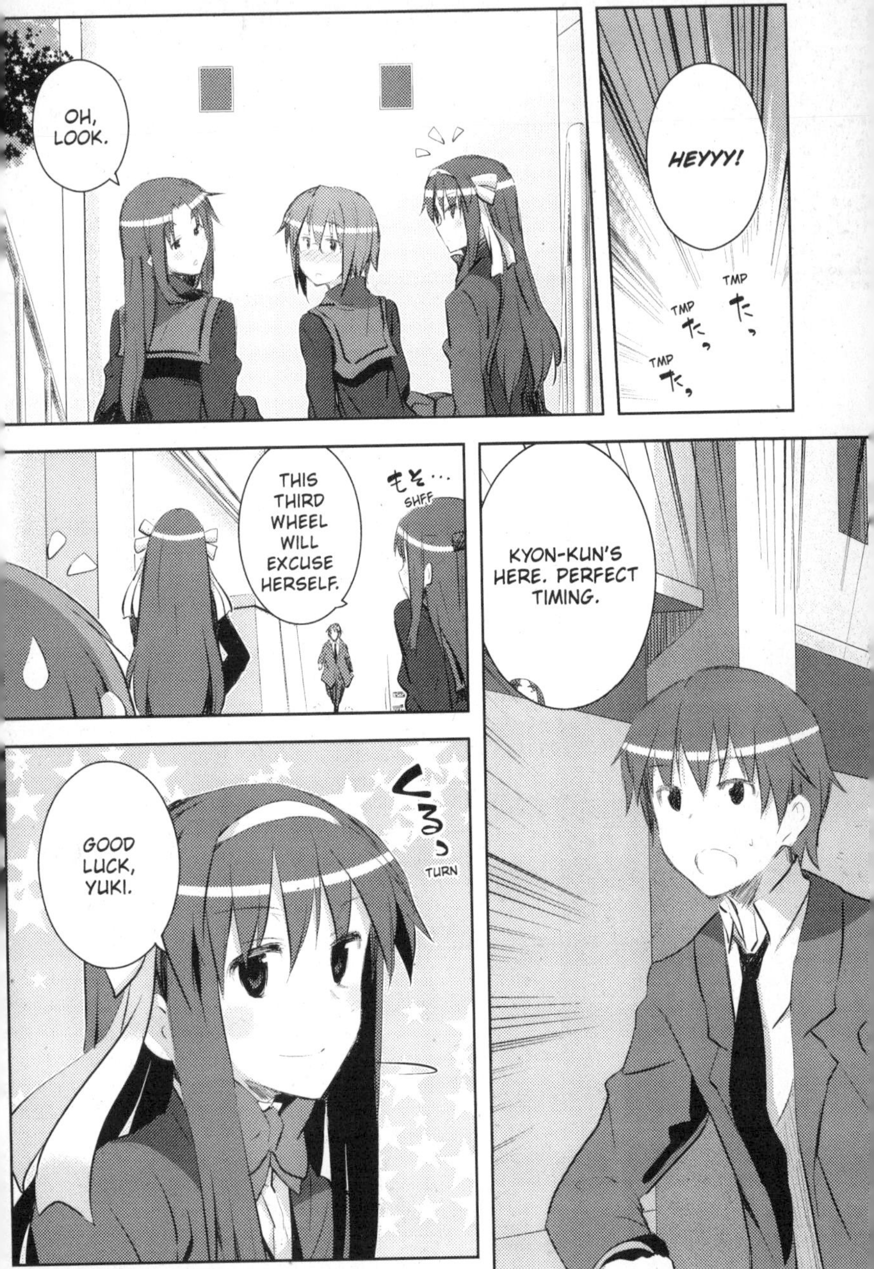
HEYYY!
TMP たっ
TMP たっ
TMP たっ
OH, LOOK.
KYON-KUN'S HERE. PERFECT TIMING.
もそ… SHFF
THIS THIRD WHEEL WILL EXCUSE HERSELF.
くるっ TURN
GOOD LUCK, YUKI.

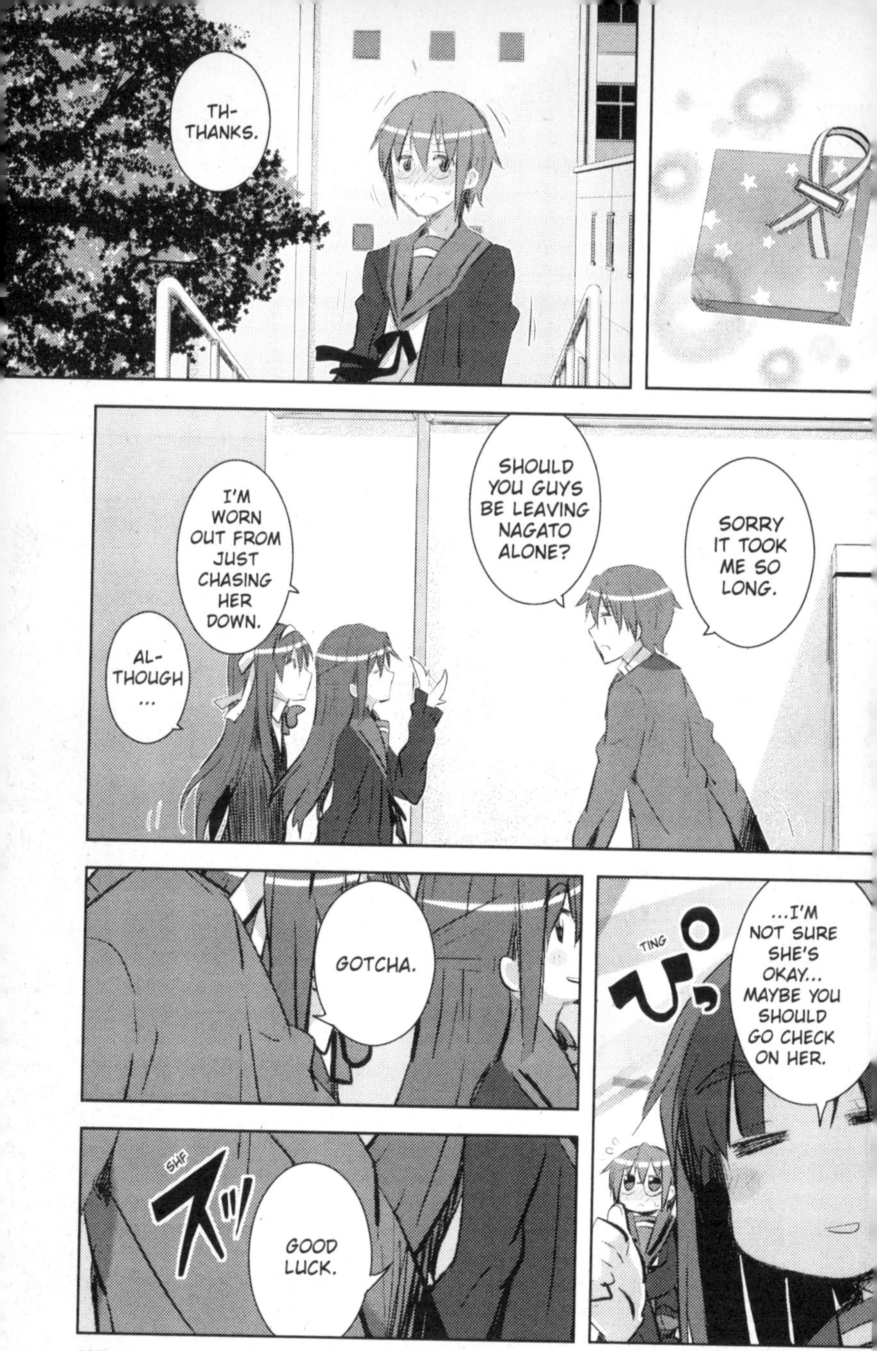
TH- THANKS.
SORRY IT TOOK ME SO LONG.
SHOULD YOU GUYS BE LEAVING NAGATO ALONE?
I'M WORN OUT FROM JUST CHASING HER DOWN.
AL- THOUGH...
TING
...I'M NOT SURE SHE'S OKAY... MAYBE YOU SHOULD GO CHECK ON HER.
GOTCHA.
SHF
GOOD LUCK.

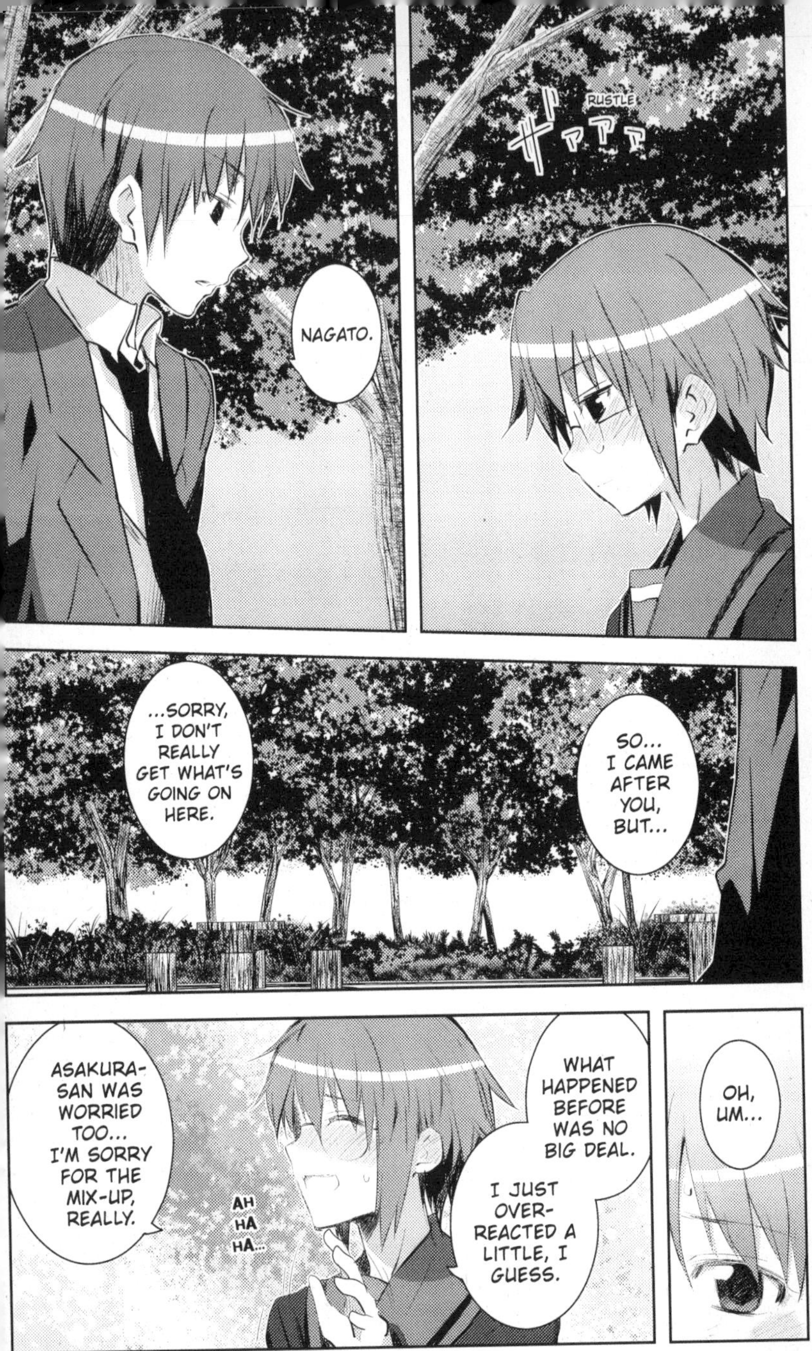
RUSTLE
ザァァァ
NAGATO.
SO... I CAME AFTER YOU, BUT...
...SORRY, I DON'T REALLY GET WHAT'S GOING ON HERE.
OH, UM...
WHAT HAPPENED BEFORE WAS NO BIG DEAL.
I JUST OVER-REACTED A LITTLE, I GUESS.
AH HA HA...
ASAKURA-SAN WAS WORRIED TOO... I'M SORRY FOR THE MIX-UP, REALLY.

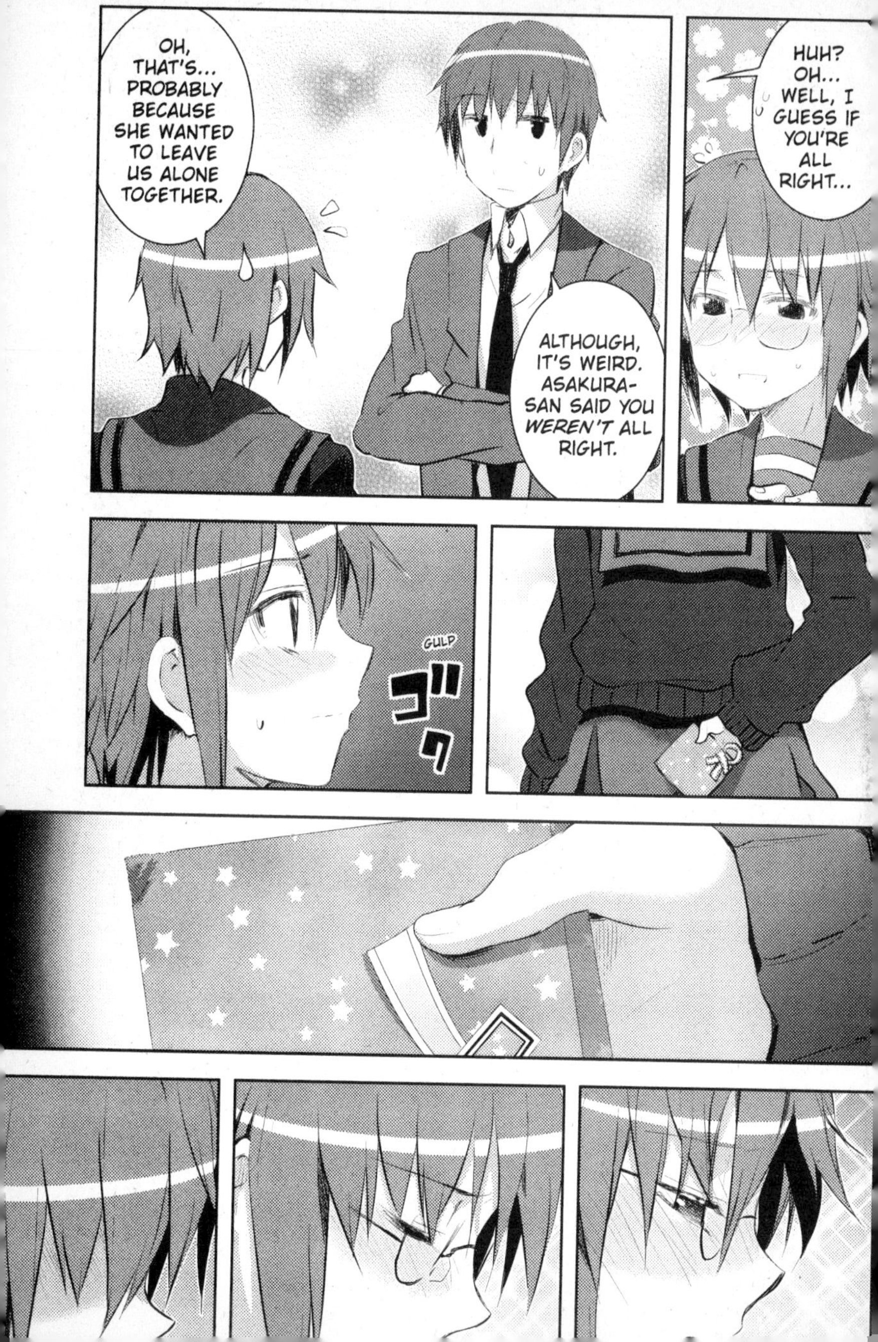
HUH? OH... WELL, I GUESS IF YOU'RE ALL RIGHT...
ALTHOUGH, IT'S WEIRD. ASAKURA-SAN SAID YOU *WEREN'T* ALL RIGHT.
OH, THAT'S... PROBABLY BECAUSE SHE WANTED TO LEAVE US ALONE TOGETHER.
GULP
ゴク

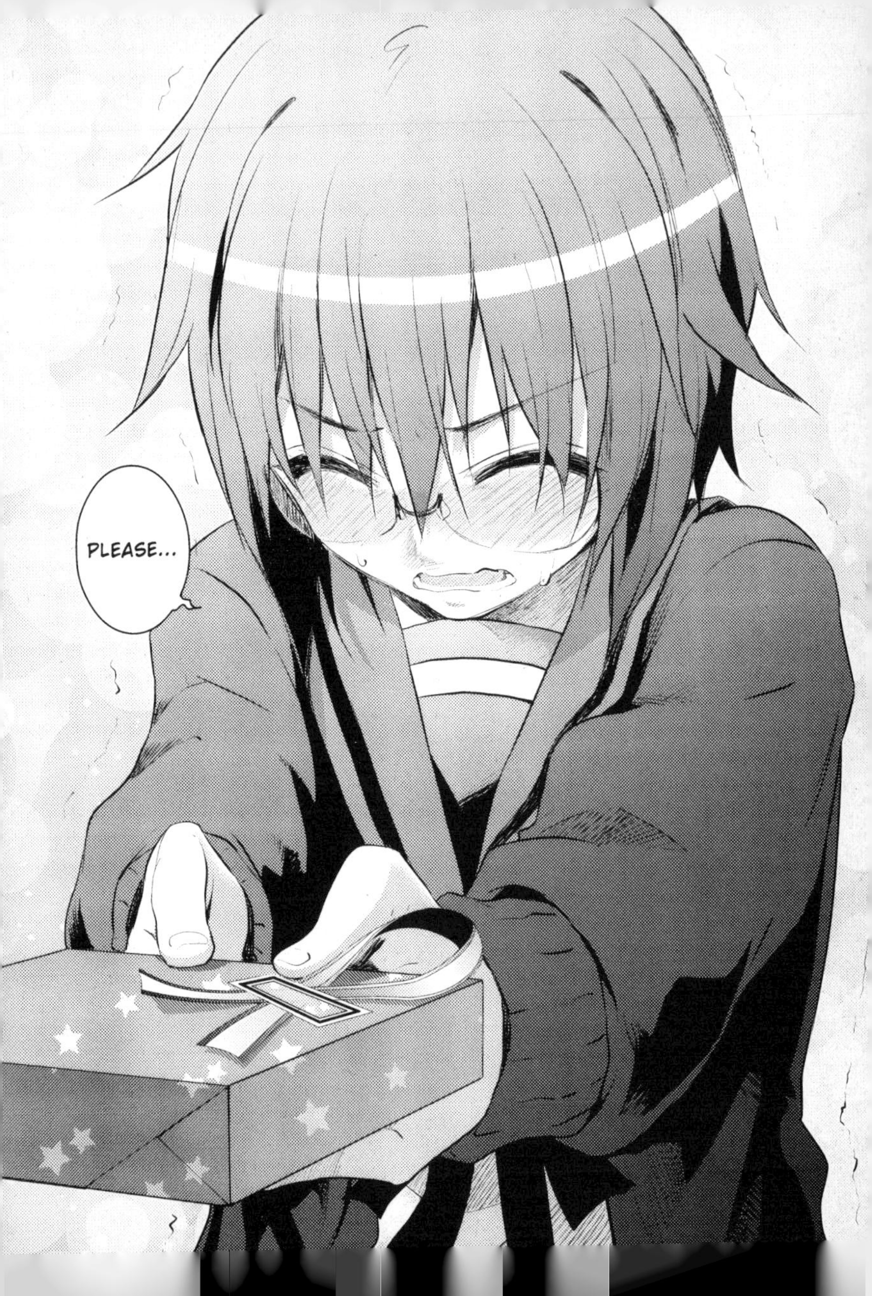
PLEASE...

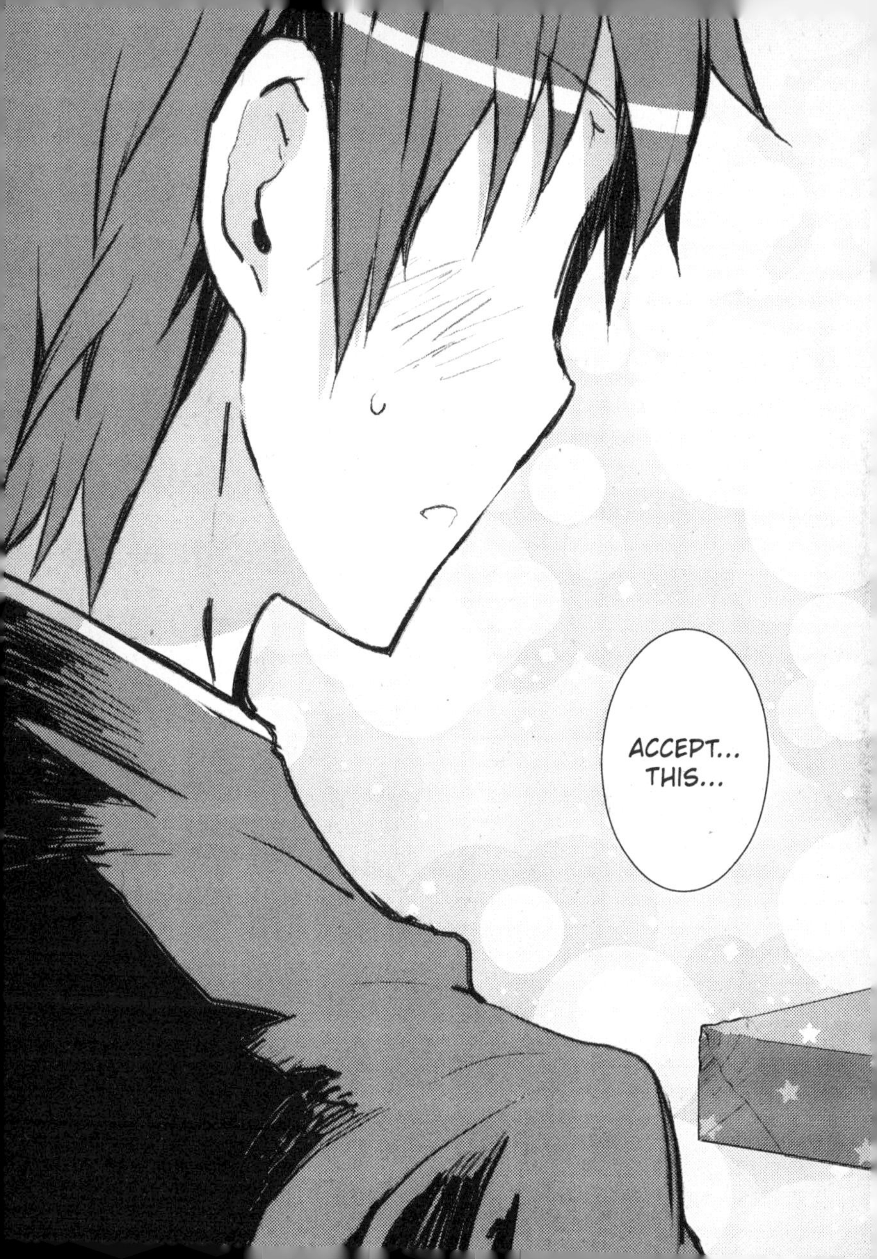
ACCEPT... THIS...

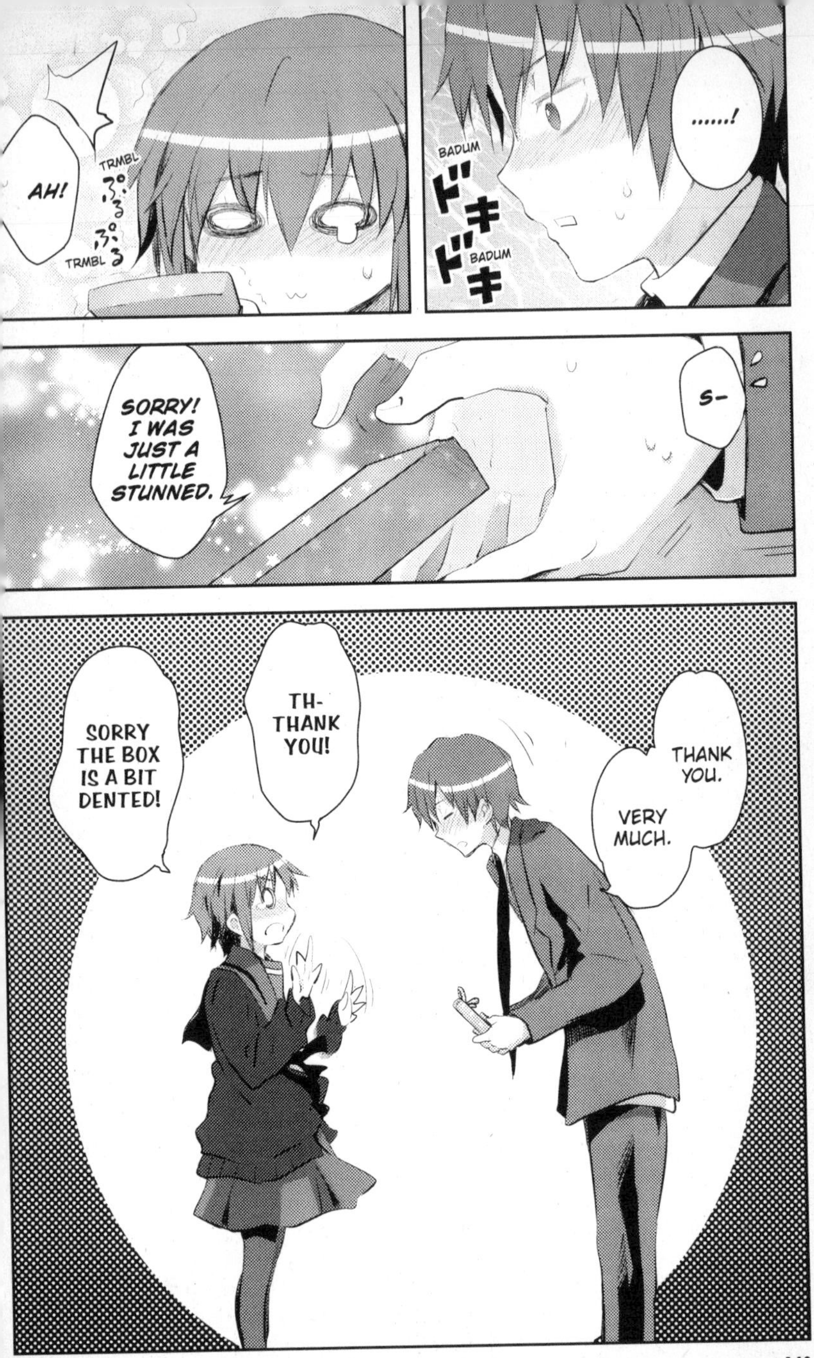
......!
BADUM
ドキ
BADUM
ドキ
AH!
TRMBL
ぷる
TRMBL
ぷる
S-
SORRY! I WAS JUST A LITTLE STUNNED.
THANK YOU.
VERY MUCH.
TH- THANK YOU!
SORRY THE BOX IS A BIT DENTED!

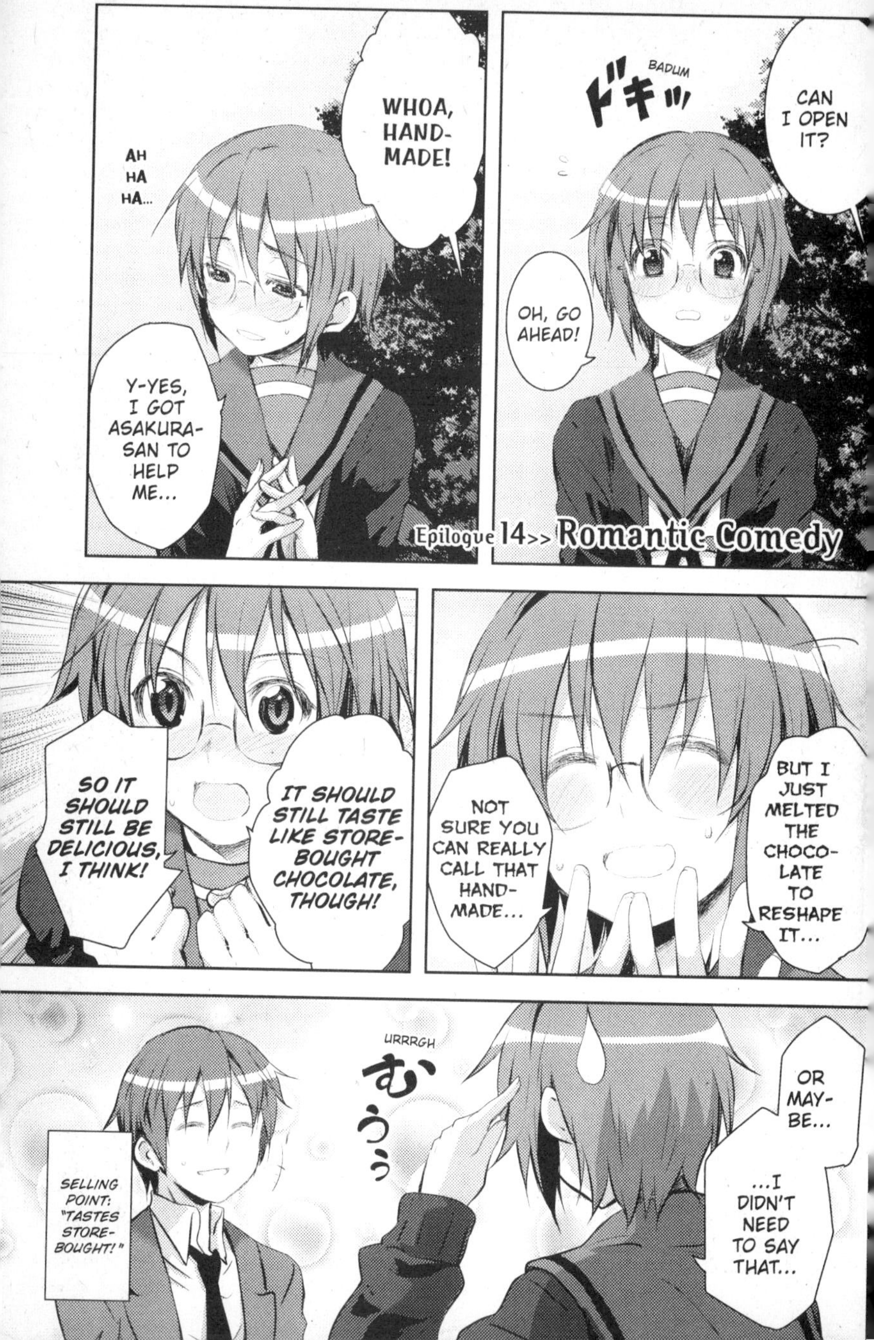
CAN I OPEN IT?
BADUM
ドキッ
OH, GO AHEAD!
Epilogue 14>> Romantic Comedy
WHOA, HAND-MADE!
AH HA HA...
Y-YES, I GOT ASAKURA-SAN TO HELP ME...
BUT I JUST MELTED THE CHOCOLATE TO RESHAPE IT...
NOT SURE YOU CAN REALLY CALL THAT HAND-MADE...
IT SHOULD STILL TASTE LIKE STORE-BOUGHT CHOCOLATE, THOUGH!
SO IT SHOULD STILL BE DELICIOUS, I THINK!
OR MAY-BE...
...I DIDN'T NEED TO SAY THAT...
URRRGH
むうぅ
SELLING POINT: "TASTES STORE-BOUGHT!"

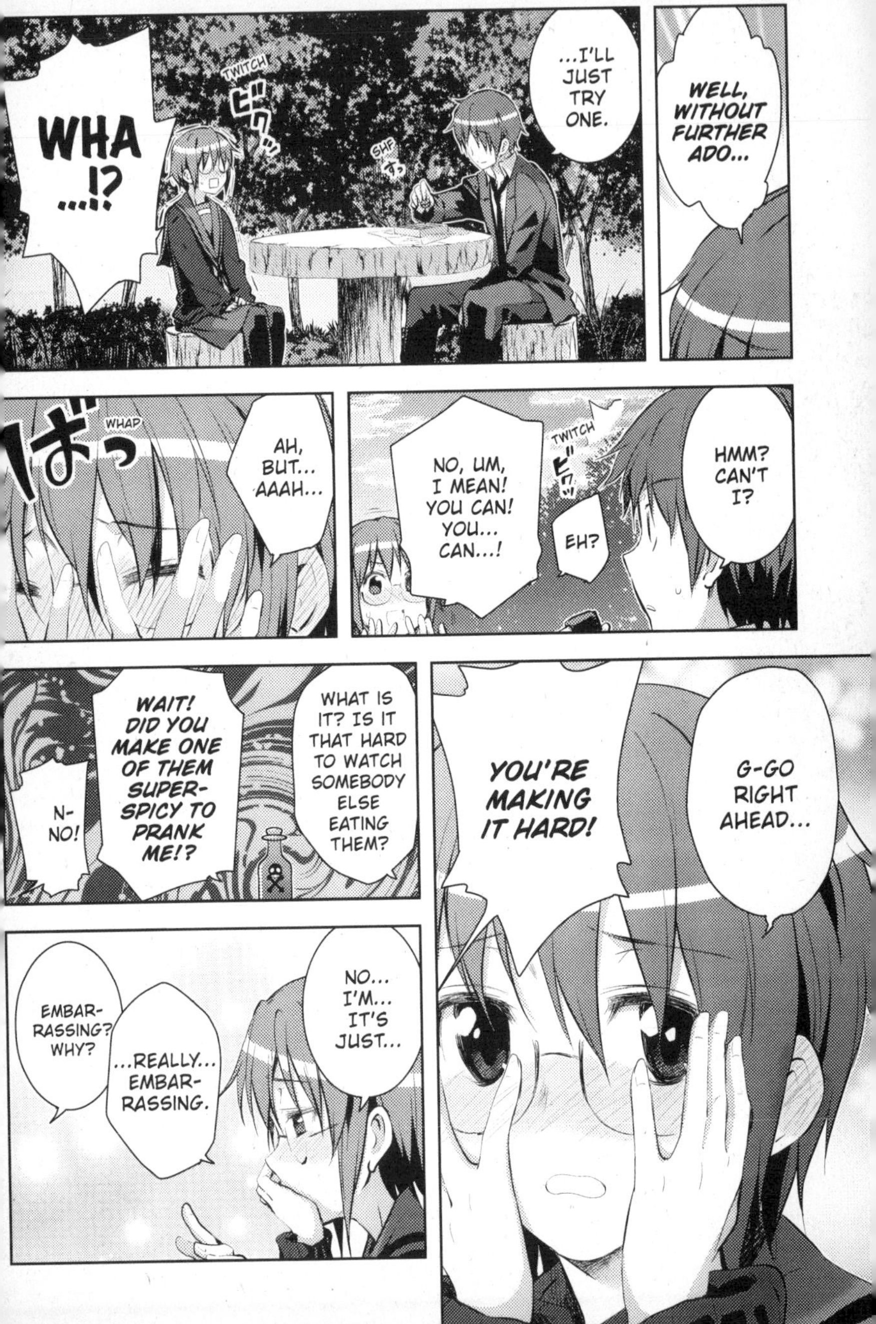
WELL, WITHOUT FURTHER ADO...
...I'LL JUST TRY ONE.
SHF
す
TWITCH
ビクッ
WHA ...!?
HMM? CAN'T I?
EH?
TWITCH
ビクッ
NO, UM, I MEAN! YOU CAN! YOU... CAN...!
AH, BUT... AAAH...
WHAP
ぱっ
G-GO RIGHT AHEAD...
YOU'RE MAKING IT HARD!
WHAT IS IT? IS IT THAT HARD TO WATCH SOMEBODY ELSE EATING THEM?
WAIT! DID YOU MAKE ONE OF THEM SUPER-SPICY TO PRANK ME!?
N-NO!
NO... I'M... IT'S JUST...
...REALLY... EMBARRASSING.
EMBARRASSING? WHY?

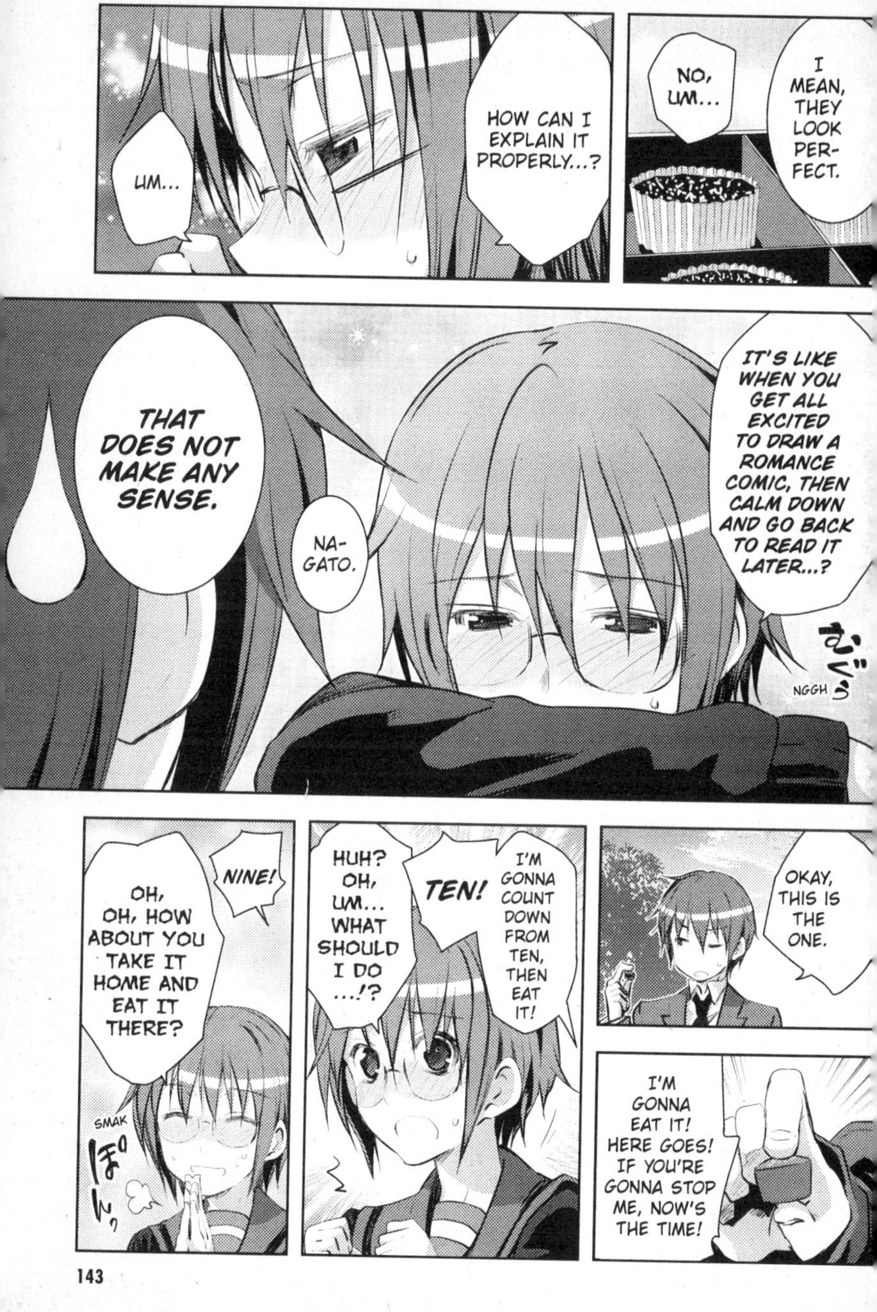
I MEAN, THEY LOOK PER-FECT.
NO, UM...
HOW CAN I EXPLAIN IT PROPERLY...?
UM...
IT'S LIKE WHEN YOU GET ALL EXCITED TO DRAW A ROMANCE COMIC, THEN CALM DOWN AND GO BACK TO READ IT LATER...?
NGGH
NA-GATO.
THAT DOES NOT MAKE ANY SENSE.
OKAY, THIS IS THE ONE.
I'M GONNA EAT IT! HERE GOES! IF YOU'RE GONNA STOP ME, NOW'S THE TIME!
I'M GONNA COUNT DOWN FROM TEN, THEN EAT IT!
TEN!
HUH? OH, UM... WHAT SHOULD I DO ...!?
NINE!
OH, OH, HOW ABOUT YOU TAKE IT HOME AND EAT IT THERE?
SMAK

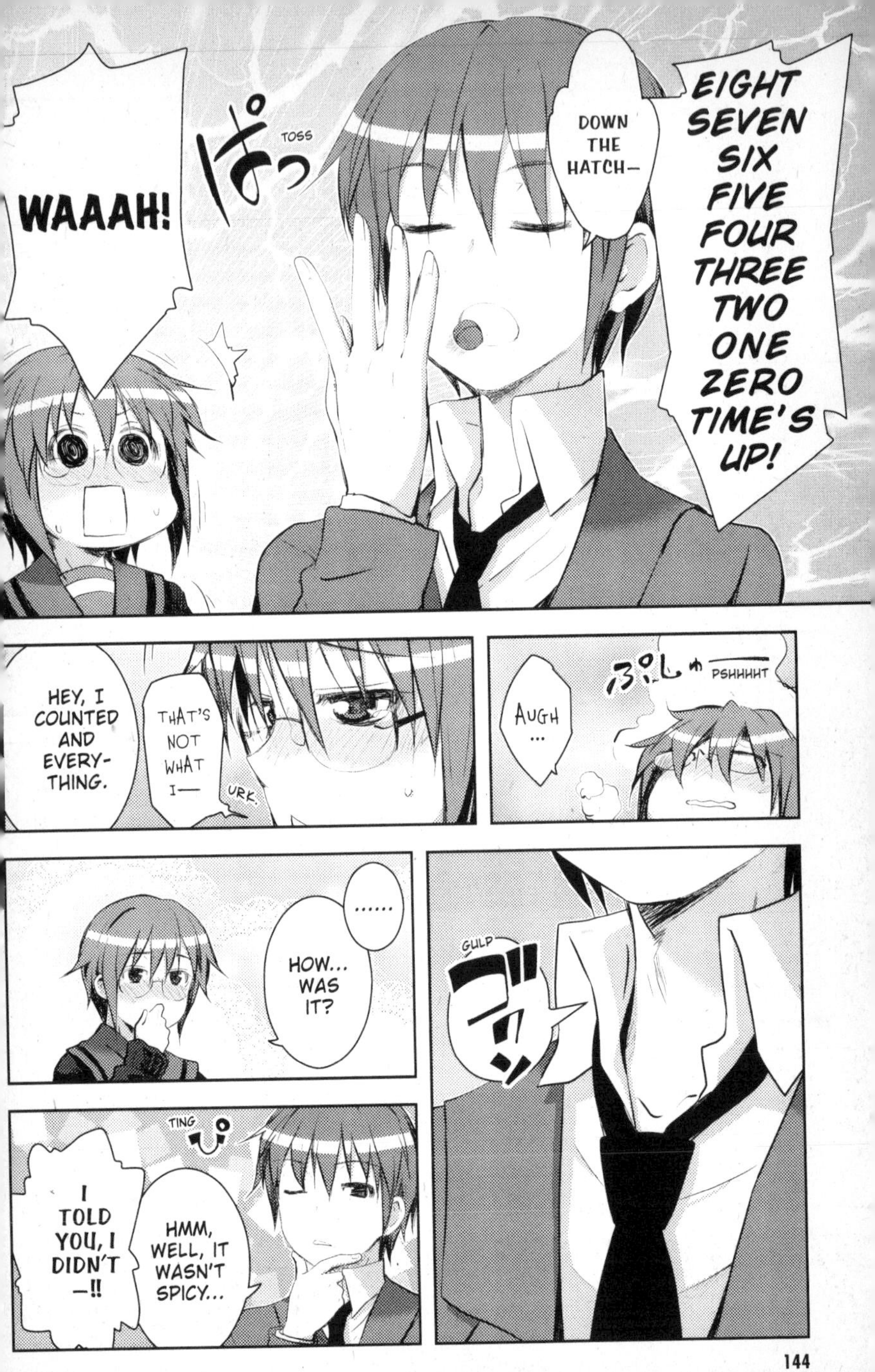
EIGHT SEVEN SIX FIVE FOUR THREE TWO ONE ZERO TIME'S UP!
DOWN THE HATCH—
ぱっ
TOSS
WAAAH!
ぷしゅ
PSHHHHT
AUGH ...
THAT'S NOT WHAT I—
URK.
HEY, I COUNTED AND EVERYTHING.
GULP
......
HOW... WAS IT?
TING
HMM, WELL, IT WASN'T SPICY...
I TOLD YOU, I DIDN'T —!!

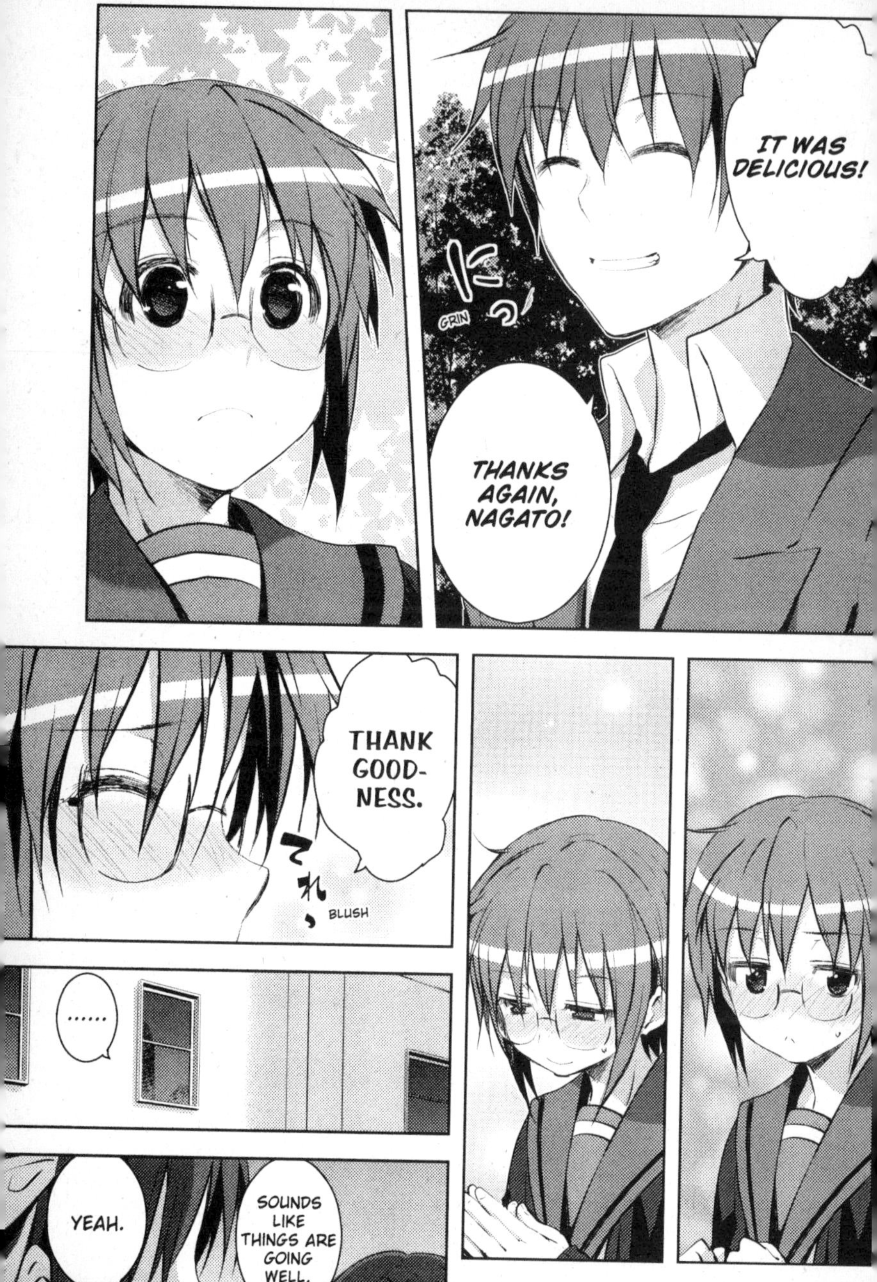
IT WAS DELICIOUS!
にっ
GRIN
THANKS AGAIN, NAGATO!
THANK GOOD-NESS.
てれ
BLUSH
......
SOUNDS LIKE THINGS ARE GOING WELL.
YEAH.

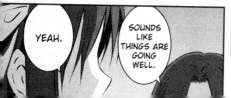

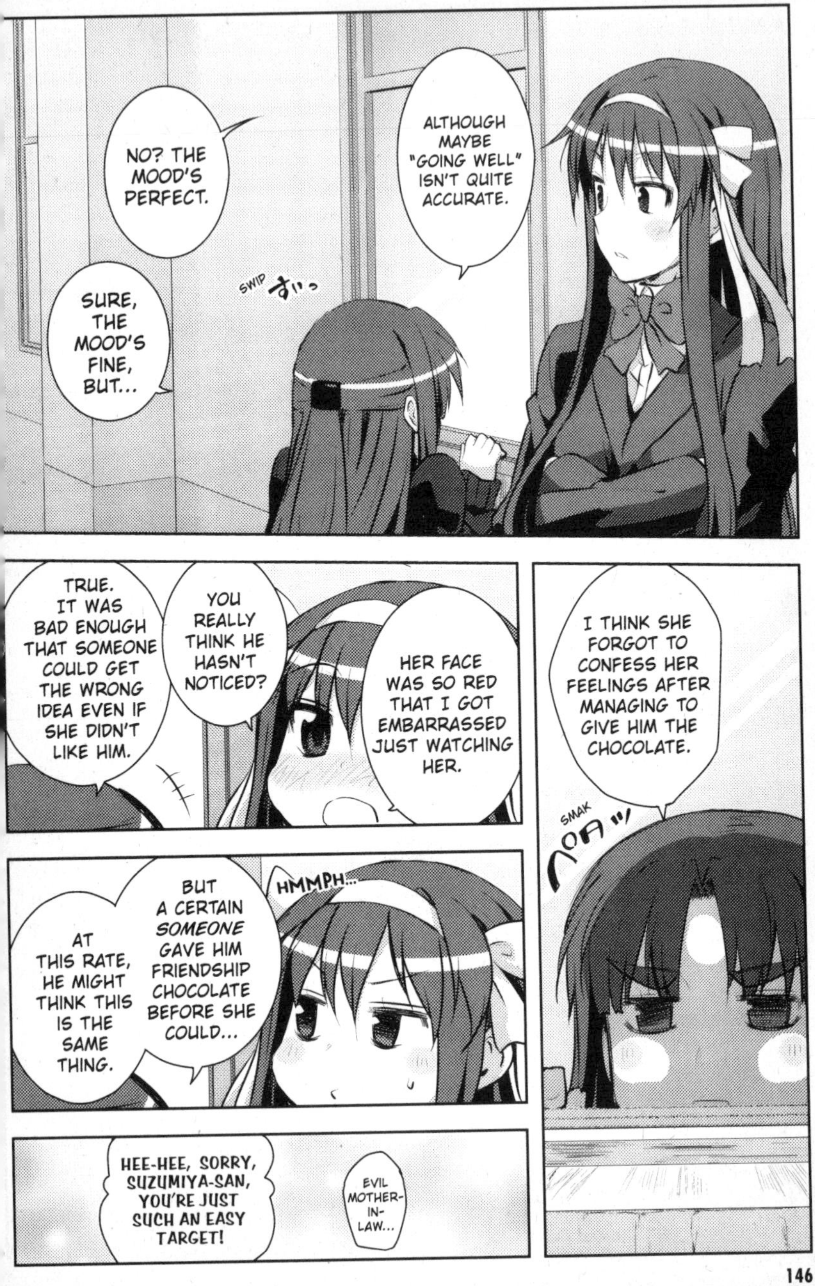
ALTHOUGH MAYBE "GOING WELL" ISN'T QUITE ACCURATE.
NO? THE MOOD'S PERFECT.
SWIP すいっ
SURE, THE MOOD'S FINE, BUT...
I THINK SHE FORGOT TO CONFESS HER FEELINGS AFTER MANAGING TO GIVE HIM THE CHOCOLATE.
SMAK ペロッ
HER FACE WAS SO RED THAT I GOT EMBARRASSED JUST WATCHING HER.
YOU REALLY THINK HE HASN'T NOTICED?
TRUE. IT WAS BAD ENOUGH THAT SOMEONE COULD GET THE WRONG IDEA EVEN IF SHE DIDN'T LIKE HIM.
HMMPH...
BUT A CERTAIN *SOMEONE* GAVE HIM FRIENDSHIP CHOCOLATE BEFORE SHE COULD...
AT THIS RATE, HE MIGHT THINK THIS IS THE SAME THING.
EVIL MOTHER-IN-LAW...
HEE-HEE, SORRY, SUZUMIYA-SAN, YOU'RE JUST SUCH AN EASY TARGET!

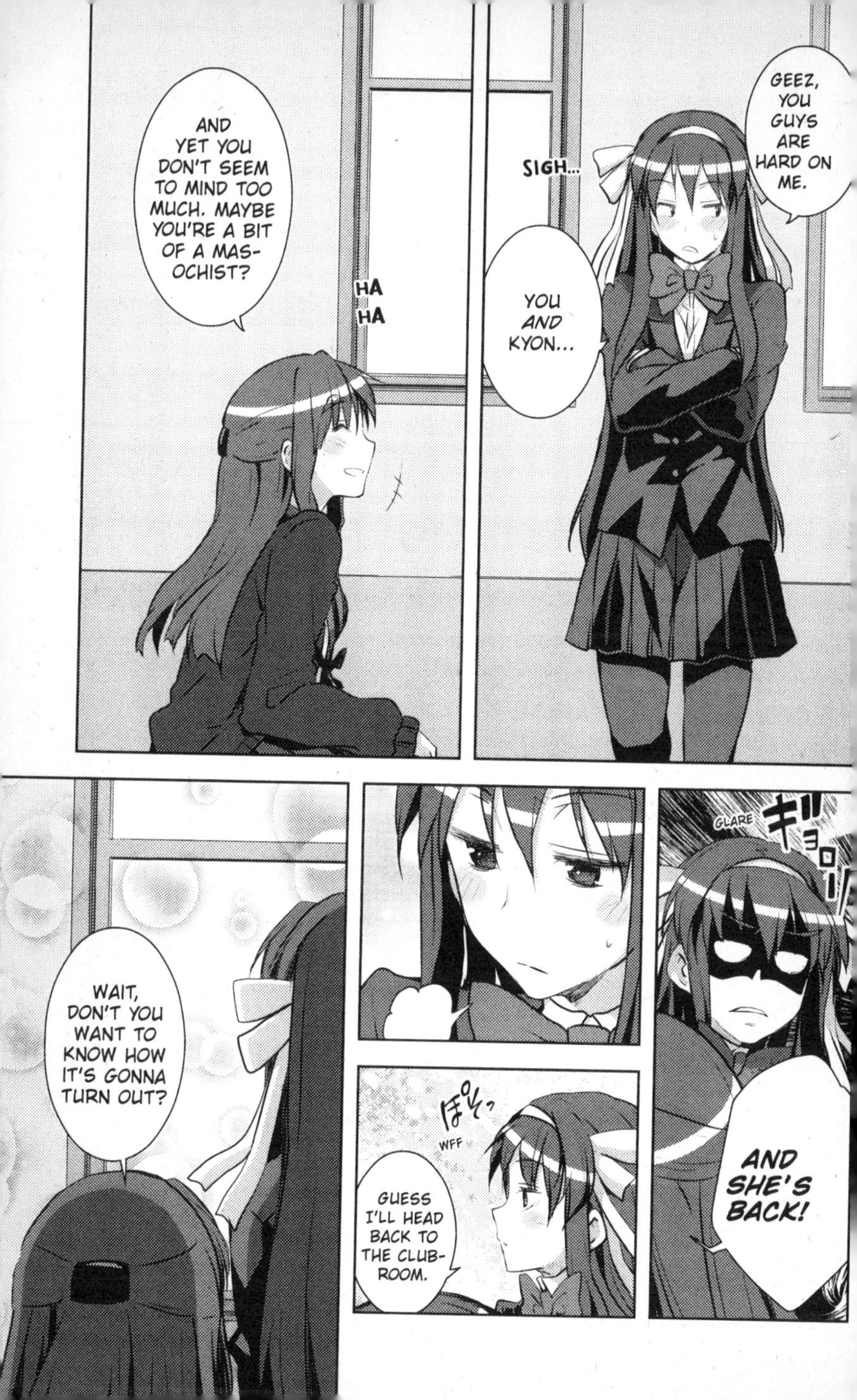
GEEZ, YOU GUYS ARE HARD ON ME.
SIGH...
YOU AND KYON...
HA HA
AND YET YOU DON'T SEEM TO MIND TOO MUCH. MAYBE YOU'RE A BIT OF A MAS-OCHIST?
GLARE
ギョロ
AND SHE'S BACK!
ぽそっ
WFF
GUESS I'LL HEAD BACK TO THE CLUB-ROOM.
WAIT, DON'T YOU WANT TO KNOW HOW IT'S GONNA TURN OUT?

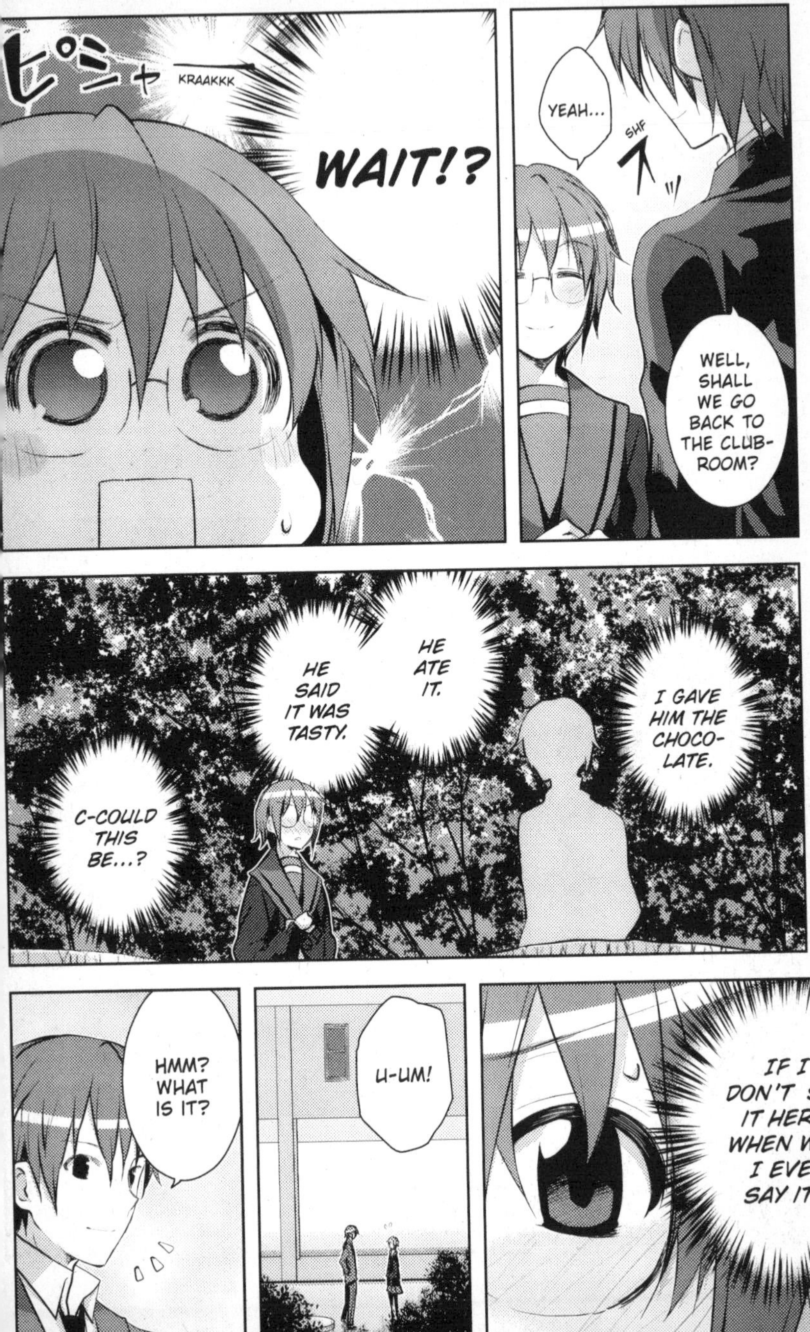
YEAH...
SHF
WELL, SHALL WE GO BACK TO THE CLUB-ROOM?
KRAAKKK
WAIT!?
I GAVE HIM THE CHOCOLATE.
HE ATE IT.
HE SAID IT WAS TASTY.
C-COULD THIS BE...?
IF I DON'T SAY IT HERE, WHEN WILL I EVER SAY IT!?
U-UM!
HMM? WHAT IS IT?

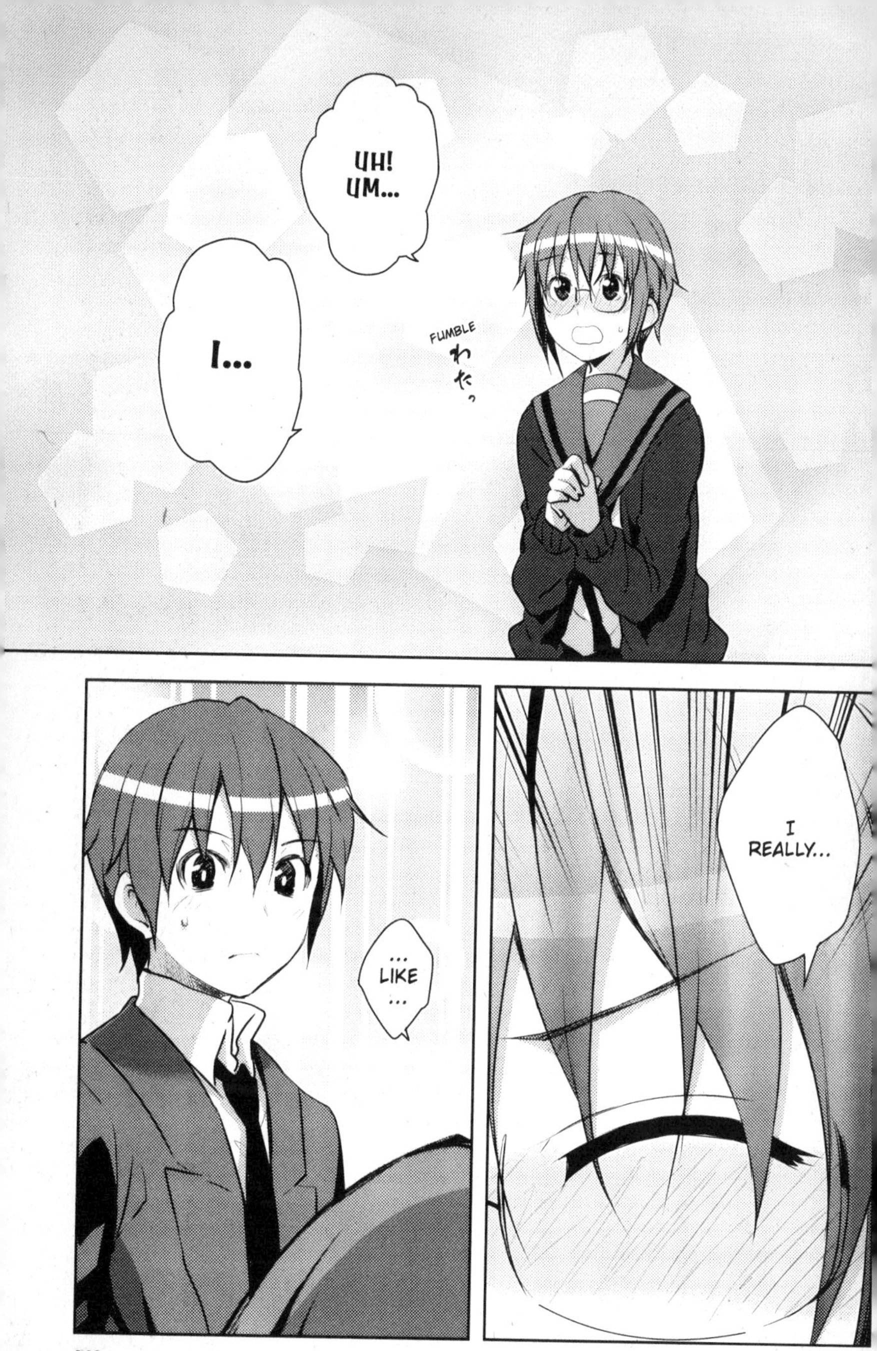
UH! UM...
FUMBLE
わたっ
I...
I REALLY...
...LIKE...

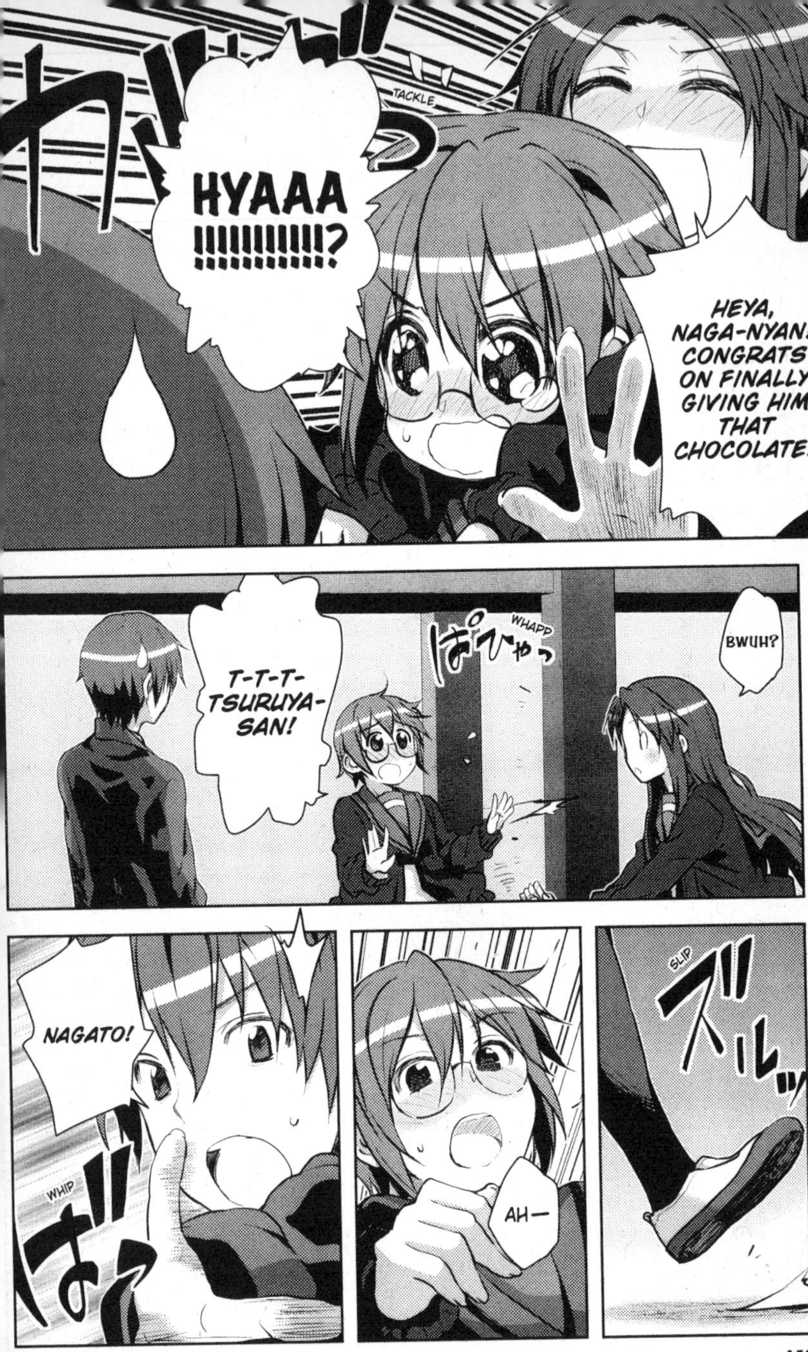
TACKLE
HEYA, NAGA-NYAN! CONGRATS ON FINALLY GIVING HIM THAT CHOCOLATE!
HYAAA !!!!!!!!!!!?
BWUH?
WHAPP
T-T-T-TSURUYA-SAN!
SLIP
AH—
NAGATO!
WHIP

AH...

BA-THUMP

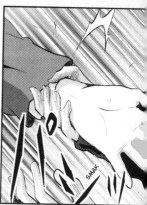

SMAK

TWIST

AH, NOT THE LEFT—

SHUDDER

EHHH!?

THUNK

WHA—!? NAGATO-SAN!?

WHUMP

AUGH!

151

UHH...
ケホ
KOFF
ケホ
KOFF
OWW...
パチ
BLINK
I FEEL...
HEAV...
!?
UGH...
...Y?

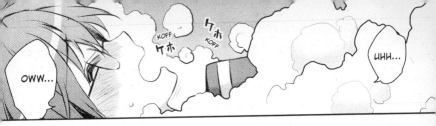

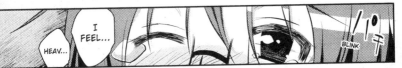

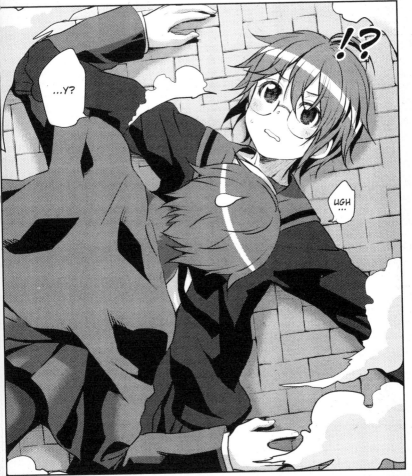

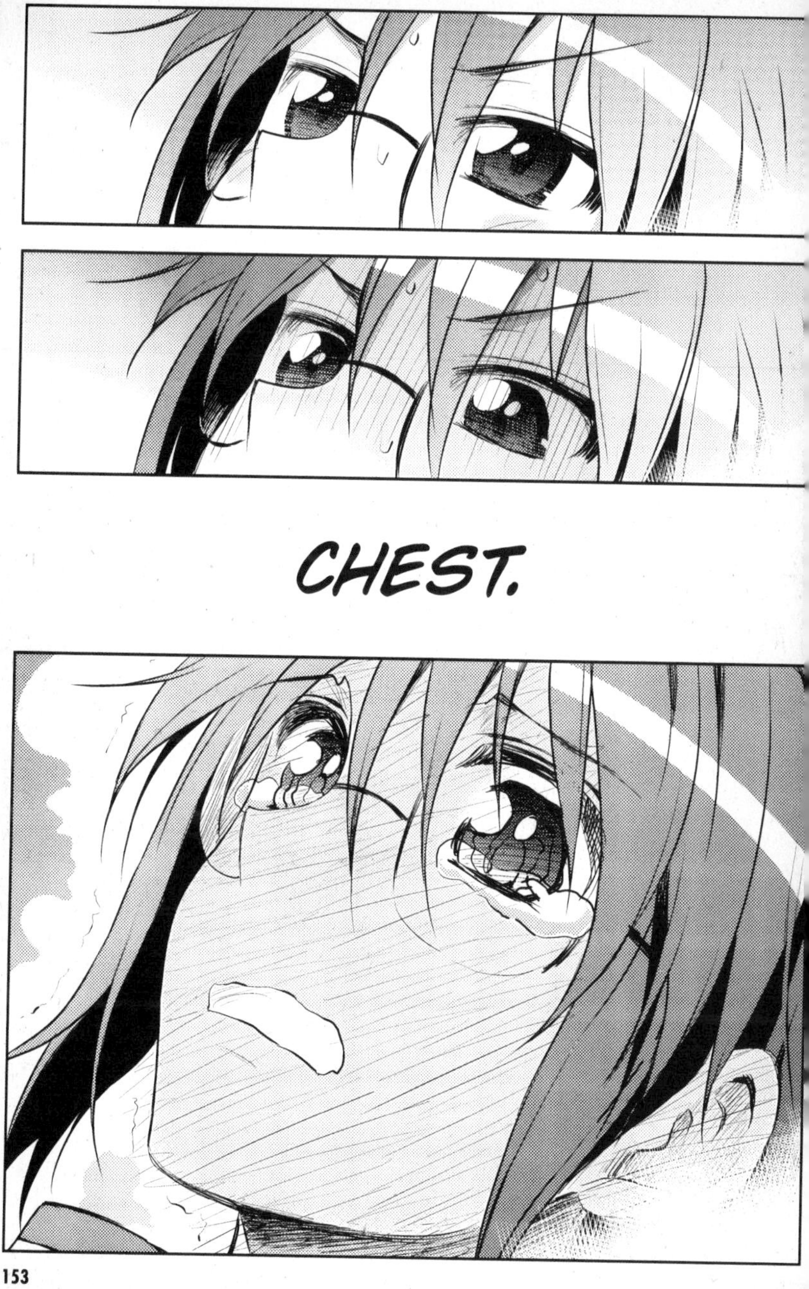
CHEST.

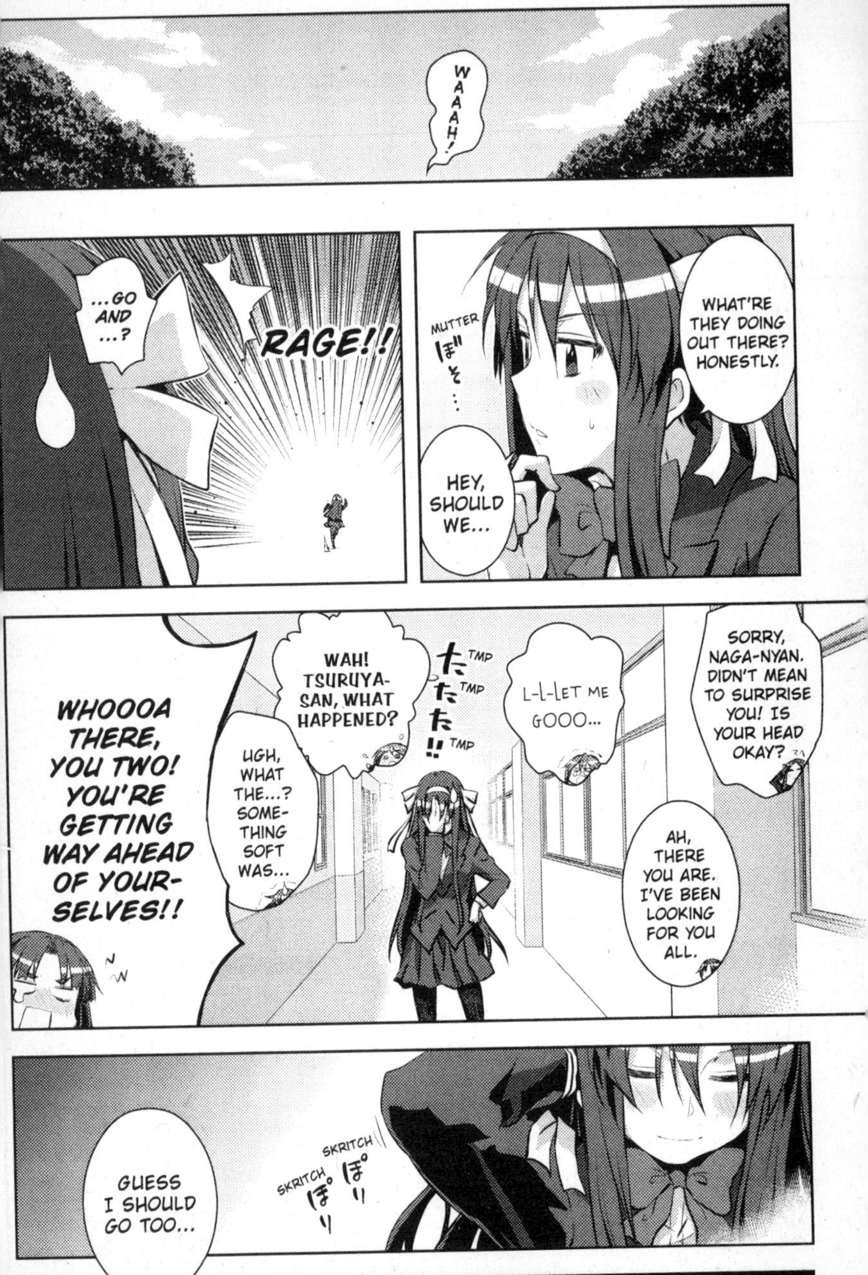
WAAAH!
MUTTER
ぼそ…
WHAT'RE THEY DOING OUT THERE? HONESTLY.
HEY, SHOULD WE...
...GO AND ...?
RAGE!!
SORRY, NAGA-NYAN. DIDN'T MEAN TO SURPRISE YOU! IS YOUR HEAD OKAY?
AH, THERE YOU ARE. I'VE BEEN LOOKING FOR YOU ALL.
L-L-LET ME GOOO...
TMP TMP TMP
たたた!!
WAH! TSURUYA-SAN, WHAT HAPPENED?
UGH, WHAT THE...? SOME-THING SOFT WAS...
WHOOOA THERE, YOU TWO! YOU'RE GETTING WAY AHEAD OF YOUR-SELVES!!
NN
SKRITCH SKRITCH
ぽり ぽり
GUESS I SHOULD GO TOO...

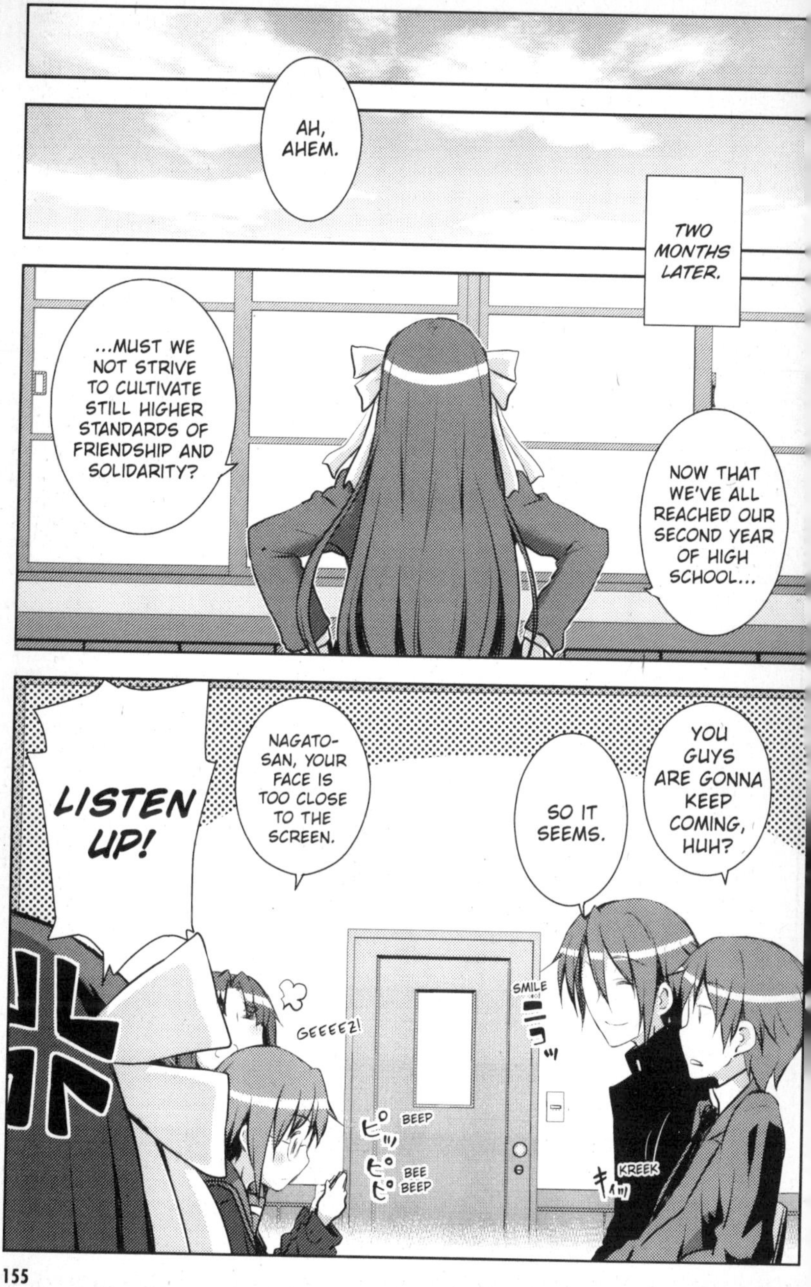
AH, AHEM.
TWO MONTHS LATER.
NOW THAT WE'VE ALL REACHED OUR SECOND YEAR OF HIGH SCHOOL...
...MUST WE NOT STRIVE TO CULTIVATE STILL HIGHER STANDARDS OF FRIENDSHIP AND SOLIDARITY?
YOU GUYS ARE GONNA KEEP COMING, HUH?
SO IT SEEMS.
SMILE
KREEK
NAGATO-SAN, YOUR FACE IS TOO CLOSE TO THE SCREEN.
GEEEEZ!
BEEP
BEE BEEP
LISTEN UP!

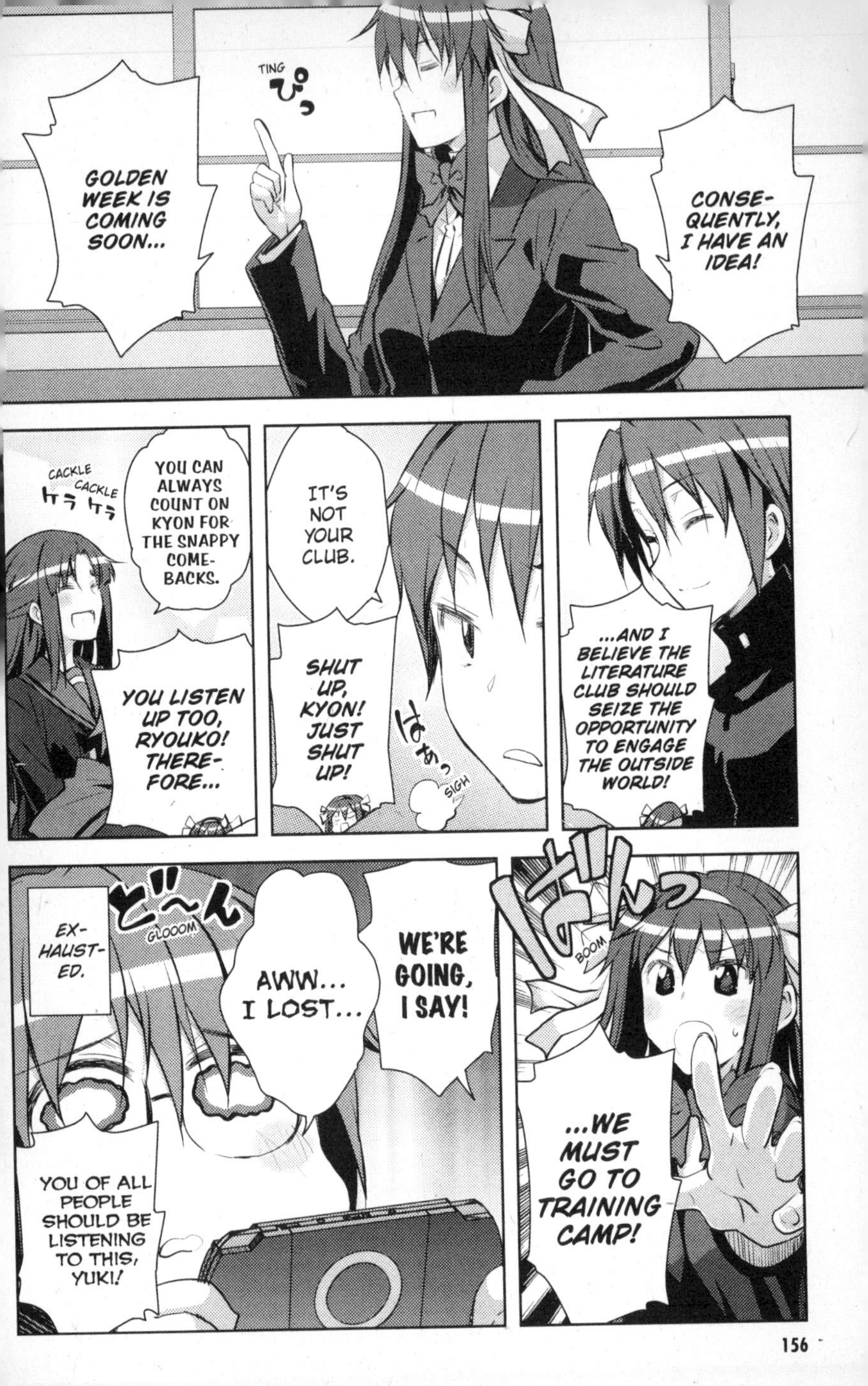

TING
ぴっ
GOLDEN WEEK IS COMING SOON...
CONSE-QUENTLY, I HAVE AN IDEA!
...AND I BELIEVE THE LITERATURE CLUB SHOULD SEIZE THE OPPORTUNITY TO ENGAGE THE OUTSIDE WORLD!
IT'S NOT YOUR CLUB.
SHUT UP, KYON! JUST SHUT UP!
はあっ
SIGH
YOU CAN ALWAYS COUNT ON KYON FOR THE SNAPPY COME-BACKS.
CACKLE CACKLE
ケラ ケラ
YOU LISTEN UP TOO, RYOUKO! THERE-FORE...
ばんっ
BOOM
...WE MUST GO TO TRAINING CAMP!
WE'RE GOING, I SAY!
AWW... I LOST...
ど〜ん
GLOOOM
EX-HAUST-ED.
YOU OF ALL PEOPLE SHOULD BE LISTENING TO THIS, YUKI!

COMICS
FROM
SNEAKER
MAGAZINE!

The Disappearance of Nagato Yuki-chan **BONUS MATERIAL**

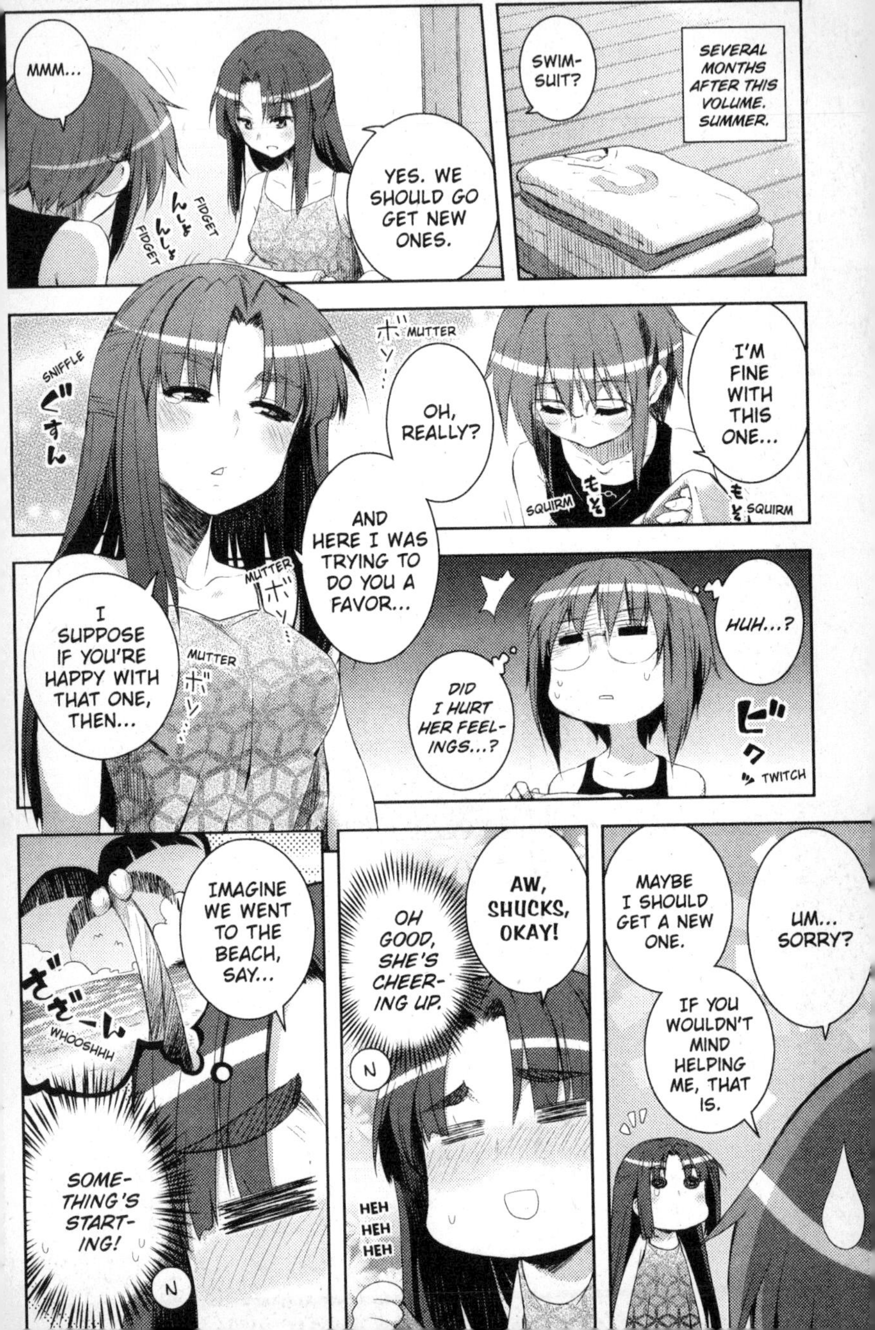
SEVERAL MONTHS AFTER THIS VOLUME. SUMMER.
SWIM-SUIT?
YES. WE SHOULD GO GET NEW ONES.
MMM...
んしょ んしょ FIDGET FIDGET
I'M FINE WITH THIS ONE...
もぞ SQUIRM もぞ SQUIRM
OH, REALLY?
ボソ MUTTER
ぐすん SNIFFLE
HUH...?
ビクッ TWITCH
DID I HURT HER FEEL-INGS...?
AND HERE I WAS TRYING TO DO YOU A FAVOR...
ボソ MUTTER
I SUPPOSE IF YOU'RE HAPPY WITH THAT ONE, THEN...
ボソ MUTTER
UM... SORRY?
MAYBE I SHOULD GET A NEW ONE.
IF YOU WOULDN'T MIND HELPING ME, THAT IS.
AW, SHUCKS, OKAY!
OH GOOD, SHE'S CHEER-ING UP.
N
HEH HEH HEH
IMAGINE WE WENT TO THE BEACH, SAY...
ざざーん WHOOSHHH
SOME-THING'S START-ING!
N

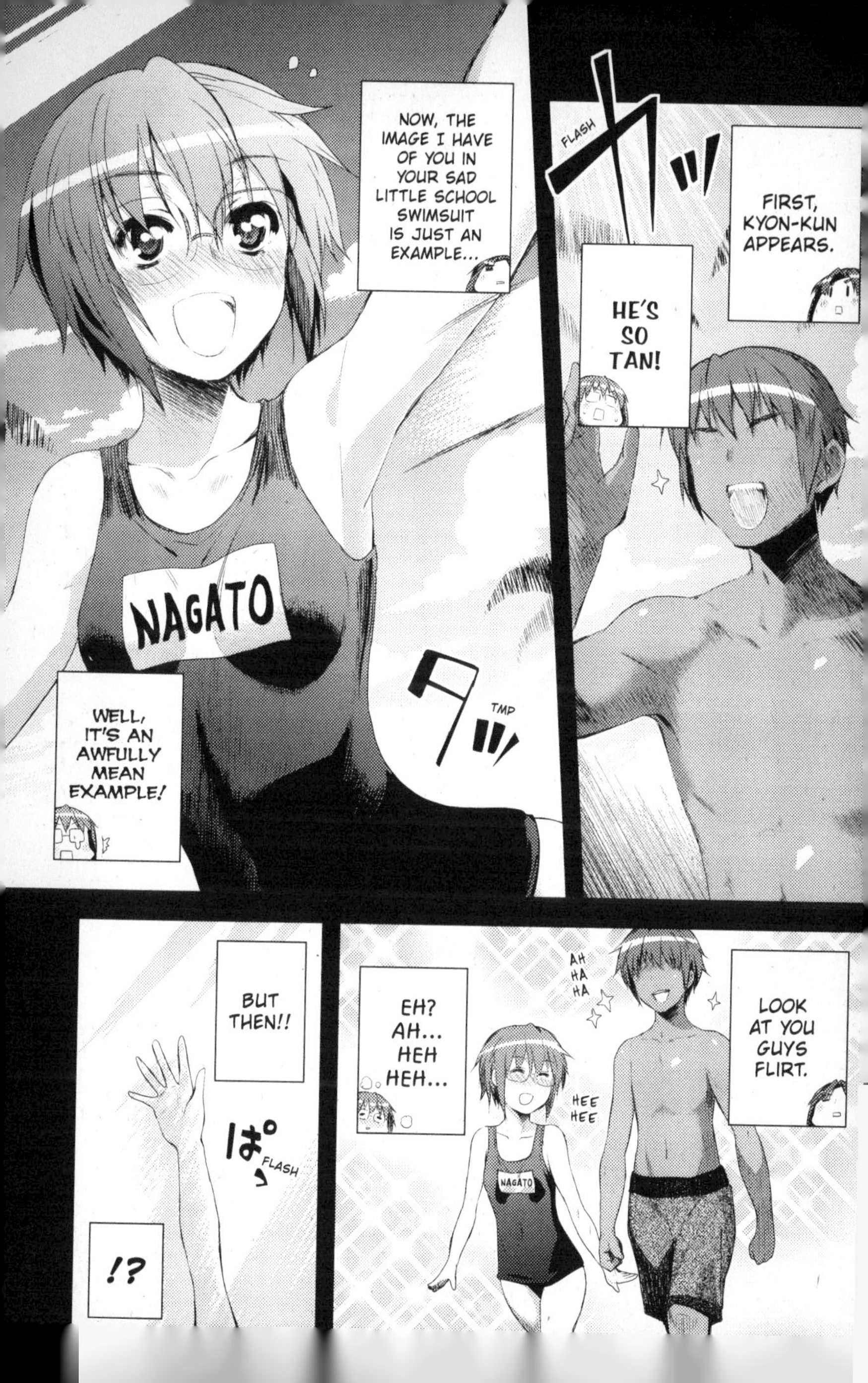
FLASH
FIRST, KYON-KUN APPEARS.
HE'S SO TAN!
NOW, THE IMAGE I HAVE OF YOU IN YOUR SAD LITTLE SCHOOL SWIMSUIT IS JUST AN EXAMPLE...
NAGATO
TMP
WELL, IT'S AN AWFULLY MEAN EXAMPLE!
LOOK AT YOU GUYS FLIRT.
AH HA HA
HEE HEE
EH? AH... HEH HEH...
NAGATO
BUT THEN!!
ぱっ
FLASH
!?

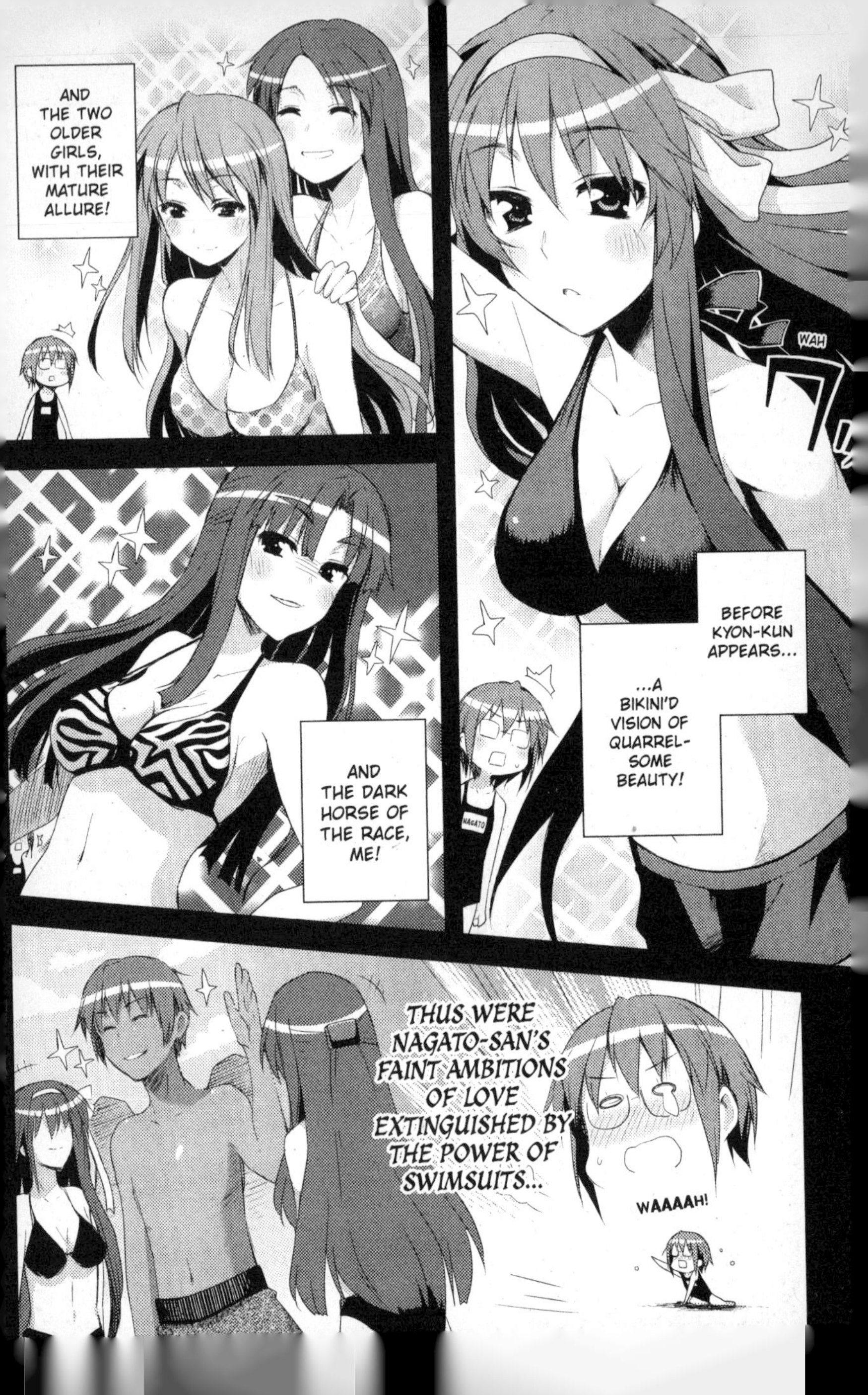
WAH
BEFORE KYON-KUN APPEARS...
...A BIKINI'D VISION OF QUARREL-SOME BEAUTY!
NAGATO
AND THE TWO OLDER GIRLS, WITH THEIR MATURE ALLURE!
AND THE DARK HORSE OF THE RACE, ME!
THUS WERE NAGATO-SAN'S FAINT AMBITIONS OF LOVE EXTINGUISHED BY THE POWER OF SWIMSUITS...
WAAAAH!

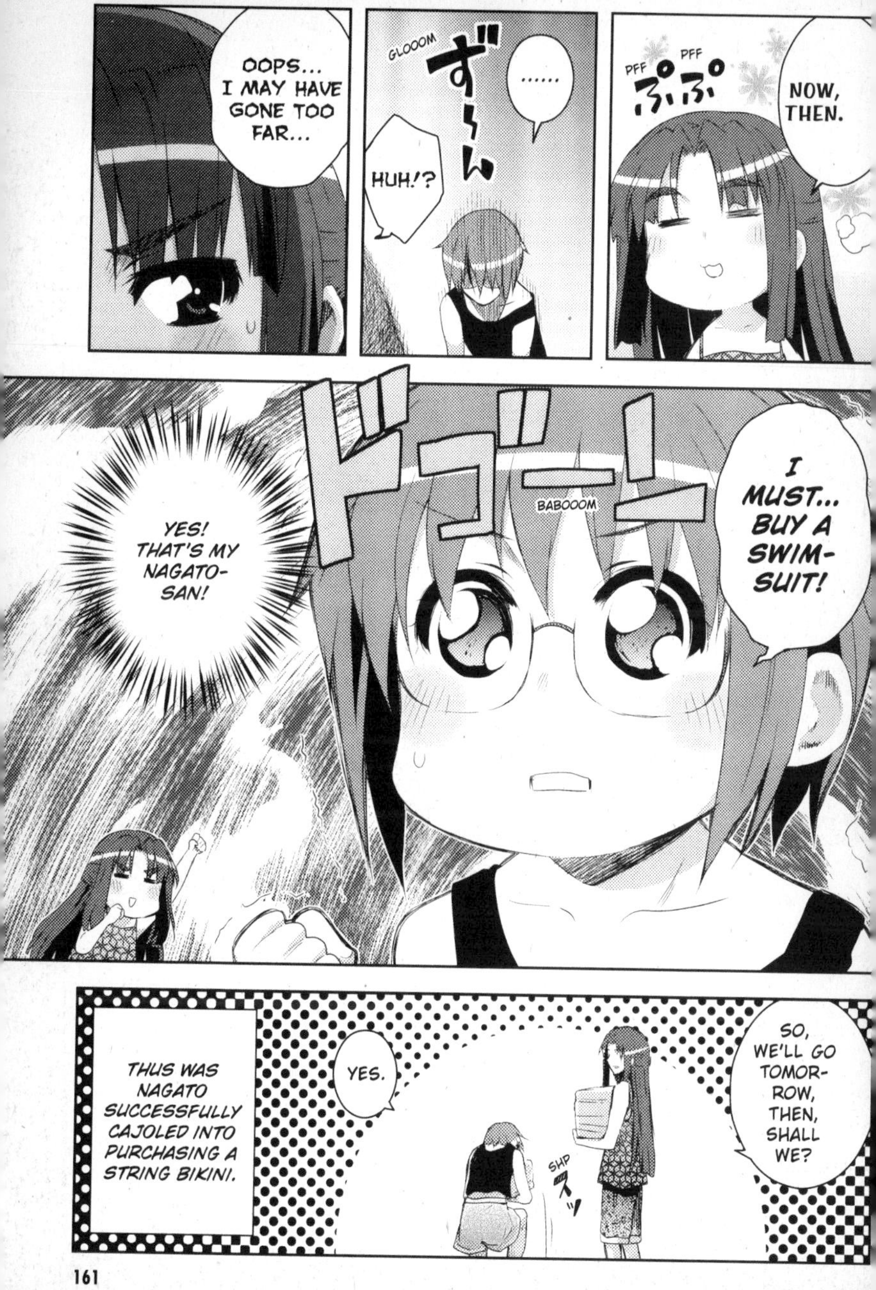
PFF PFF
ぷぷ
NOW, THEN.
GLOOOM
ず～ん
......
HUH!?
OOPS... I MAY HAVE GONE TOO FAR...
I MUST... BUY A SWIM-SUIT!
ドゴーン
BABOOOM
YES! THAT'S MY NAGATO-SAN!
SO, WE'LL GO TOMOR-ROW, THEN, SHALL WE?
YES.
SHP
THUS WAS NAGATO SUCCESSFULLY CAJOLED INTO PURCHASING A STRING BIKINI.

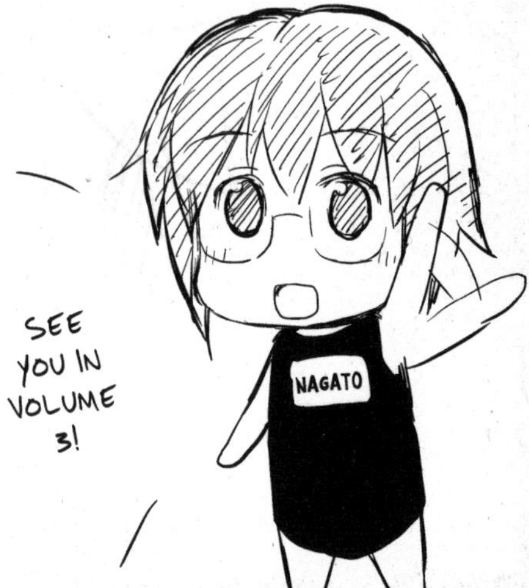
SEE YOU IN VOLUME 3!
NAGATO

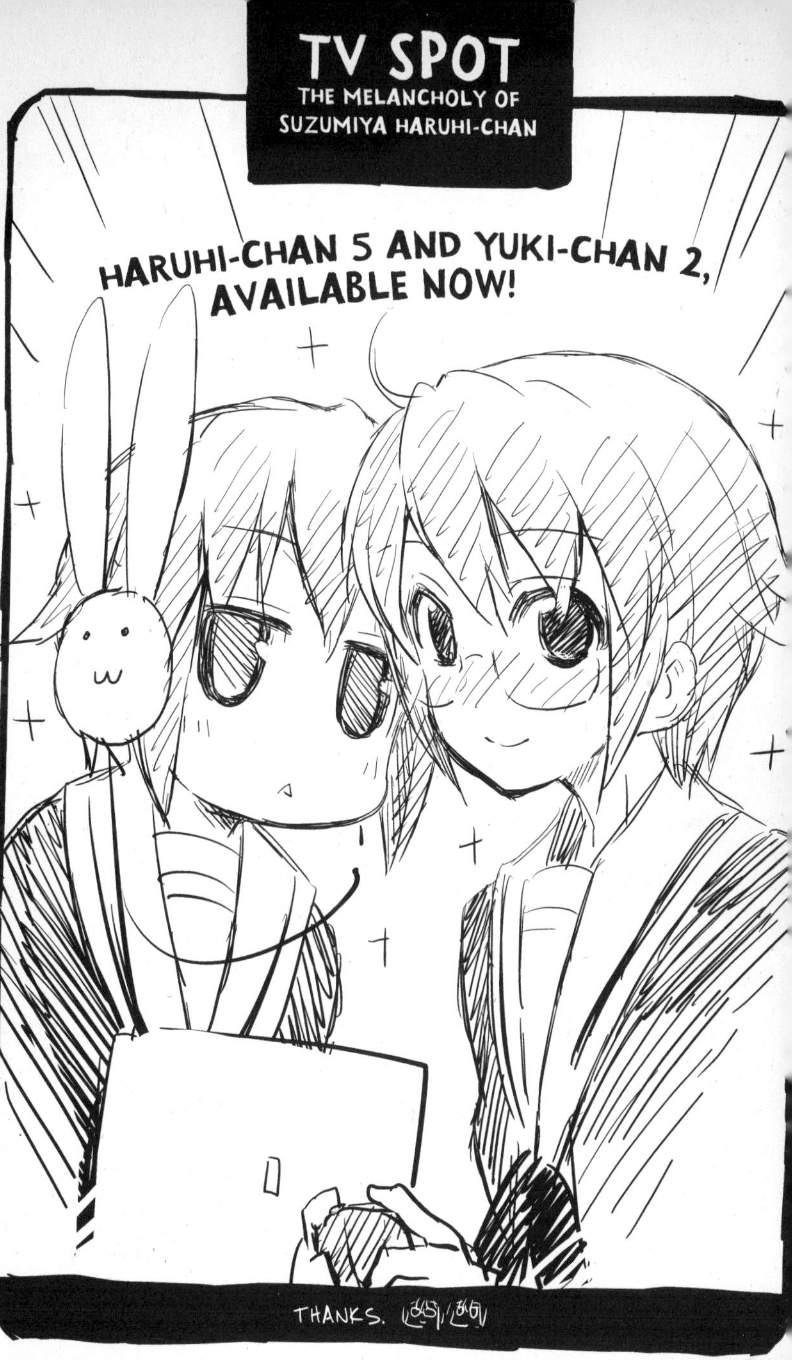
TV SPOT
THE MELANCHOLY OF
SUZUMIYA HARUHI-CHAN
HARUHI-CHAN 5 AND YUKI-CHAN 2,
AVAILABLE NOW!
THANKS.

THE DISAPPEARANCE OF NAGATO
YUKI-CHAN
❷

Original Story: Nagaru Tanigawa
Manga: PUYO
Character Design: Noizi Ito

Translation: Paul Starr
Lettering: Jennifer Skarupa

This book is a work of fiction. Names, characters, places, and incidents are the product of the author's imagination or are used fictitiously. Any resemblance to actual events, locales, or persons, living or dead, is coincidental.

NAGATO YUKI CHAN NO SHOSHITSU Volume 2 © Nagaru TANIGAWA • Noizi ITO 2010 © PUYO 2010. First published in Japan in 2010 by KADOKAWA SHOTEN Co., Ltd., Tokyo. English translation rights arranged with KADOKAWA SHOTEN Co., Ltd., Tokyo through TUTTLE-MORI AGENCY, INC., Tokyo.

English translation © 2012 by Hachette Book Group, Inc.

All rights reserved. In accordance with the U.S. Copyright Act of 1976, the scanning, uploading, and electronic sharing of any part of this book without the permission of the publisher is unlawful piracy and theft of the author's intellectual property. If you would like to use material from the book (other than for review purposes), prior written permission must be obtained by contacting the publisher at permissions@hbgusa.com. Thank you for your support of the author's rights.

Yen Press
Hachette Book Group
237 Park Avenue, New York, NY 10017

www.HachetteBookGroup.com
www.YenPress.com

Yen Press is an imprint of Hachette Book Group, Inc.
The Yen Press name and logo are trademarks of Hachette Book Group, Inc.

First Yen Press Edition: October 2012

ISBN: 978-0-316-21713-2

10 9 8 7 6 5 4 3 2 1

BVG

Printed in the United States of America